THE ENIGMA OF PIERO

· VERSO ·

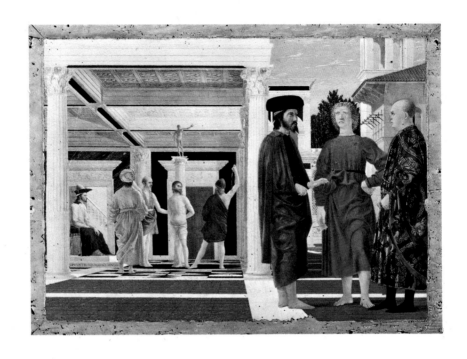

PIERO DELLA FRANCESCA, *Flagellation of Christ*.

CARLO GINZBURG

THE ENIGMA OF PIERO

Piero della Francesca

·

The Baptism
The Arezzo Cycle
The Flagellation

·

With an introduction by Peter Burke
Translated by Martin Ryle and Kate Soper

· VERSO ·

**British Library Cataloguing
in Publication Data**

Ginzburg, Carlo
    The enigma of Piero: Piero della Francesca:
    The baptism, The Arezzo cycle, The Flagellation.
    1. Piero, *della Francesca*
    I. Title
    759.5   ND623.F78

Indagini Su Piero was first published
by Giulio Einaudi editore s.p.a., Turin, 1981
© Giulio Einaudi editore

This edition first published 1985
© Verso, 1985

Verso is the imprint of New Left Books

Verso
15 Greek Street London W1V 5LF

Typeset in Bembo by
Leaper & Gard Ltd
Redfield, Bristol

Printed in Great Britain by
The Thetford Press Ltd
Thetford, Norfolk

ISBN 0 86091 116 0

Contents

FOR GABRIELE

List of Plates

Front. Piero della Francesca, *Flagellation of Christ.* Urbino, Galleria Nazionale delle Marche. (Alinari, Florence.)

27. Piero della Francesca, *Solomon Receiving the Queen of Sheba* (detail). Arezzo, Church of San Francesco. (Alinari, Florence.)
28. Casket, once the property of Cardinal Bessarion. Venice, Accademia Gallery. (Photograph courtesy of the Instituto centrale per il catalogo e la documentazione, Rome.)
29. Bessarion's Casket (closed). Venice, Accademia Gallery. (Böhm, Venice.)
30. Bessarion's Casket (open).
31. Pisanello, Medal of John VIII Palaeologus. Florence, Bargello. (Alinari, Florence.)
32. Anthem-book given by Bessarion, no. 2 in series (detail). Cesena, Biblioteca Malatestiana.
33. Medal of Constantine (face). Vienna, Kunsthistorisches Museum.
34. Medal of Heraclius (reverse side). Vienna, Kunsthistorisches Museum.
35. Piero della Francesca, *Queen of Sheba and her Retinue* (detail). Arezzo, Church of San Francesco. (Alinari, Florence.)
36. Giovanni di Piamonte, *Madonna Enthroned and Saints.* Città di Castello, Santa Maria delle Grazie. (Alinari, Florence.)
37. Pietro Lorenzetti, *Flagellation of Christ.* Assisi, Chiesa Inferiore di San Francesco. (Alinari, Florence.)
38. Maestro dell'Osservanza, *Flagellation of Christ.* Rome, Vatican Gallery.
39. Alejo Fernandez (?), *Flagellation of Christ.* Madrid, Prado.
40. Piero della Francesca, *Flagellation of Christ* (detail). Urbino, Galleria Nazionale delle Marche. (Alinari, Florence.)
41. Piero della Francesca, *Flagellation of Christ* (detail). Urbino, Galleria Nazionale delle Marche. (Alinari, Florence.)
42. Piero della Francesca, *Madonna of the Misericordia* (detail). San Sepolcro, Museum. (Anderson, Florence.)
43. Piero della Francesca, *Madonna of the Misericordia* (detail). San Sepolcro, Museum. (Anderson, Florence.)
44. Piero della Francesca, *Flagellation of Christ* (detail). Urbino, Galleria Nazionale delle Marche. (Alinari, Florence.)
45. Piero della Francesca, *Defeat of Chosroes* (detail). Arezzo, Church of San Francesco. (Anderson, Florence.)
46. Piero della Francesca, *Solomon Receiving the Queen of Sheba* (detail). Arezzo, San Francesco. (Anderson, Florence.)
47. Piero della Francesca, *Defeat of Chosroes* (detail). Arezzo, San Francesco. (Alinari, Florence.)
48. Piero della Francesca, *Defeat of Chosroes* (detail). Arezzo, San Francesco. (Alinari, Florence.)
49. Benozzo Gozzoli, *St Francis Stripping Himself of his Possessions.* Montefalco, Museo di San Francesco. (Alinari, Florence.)
50. Giotto, *Dream of Innocent III.* Assisi, Chiesa Superiore di San Francesco. (Alinari, Florence.)
51. Benozzo Gozzoli, *Dream of Innocent III.* Montefalco, Museo di San Francesco. (Anderson, Florence.)
52. Lorenzo Lotto, *Brother Gregorio Belo of Vicenza.* New York, Metropolitan Museum.
53. Taddeo di Bartolo (?), *Flagellation of Christ* (from *Articles of the Credo*). Siena, Museo dell'Opera del Duomo. (Photograph courtesy of the Soprintendenza alle Gallerie, Siena.)
54. Beato Angelico, *Flagellation of Christ.* Florence, Museo di San Marco. (Alinari, Florence.)
55. Filippino Lippi, *Triumph of St Thomas* (detail). Rome, Santa Maria sopra Minerva.
56. Marten van Heemskerk, *View of the Lateran.* Berlin, Kupferstichkabinett.
57. Giovanni Marcanova, *Antiquitates*: view of the Lateran. Modena, Biblioteca Estense. (Roncaglia, Modena.)
58. Head of Constantine. Rome, Musei Capitolini. (B. Malter, Rome).
59. Hand of Constantine. Rome, Musei Capitolini. (B. Malter, Rome.)
60. Sphere, formerly part of the statue of Constantine. Rome, Musei Capitolini. (B. Malter, Rome.)
61. Plan of the Lateran (from Severano's *Memorie Sacre*). Bologna, Biblioteca Communale.

Introduction

Carlo Ginzburg, Detective

The purpose of this brief note is not to introduce Carlo Ginzburg to the English-speaking world — a task fortunately made superfluous by the translation of his *Night Battles* and *The Cheese and the Worms* — but to comment on this particular book.[1] Why is the discoverer of the *benandanti* and Menocchio the miller writing about the paintings of Piero della Francesa? What has a 'plain' or 'general' historian to do with art history?

We should beware of type-casting Ginzburg too easily. If he is best known as a historian of popular culture, it does not follow that he lacks other interests. In 1966, for example, two years after a brief visit to the Warburg Institute in London (to which he later returned for a year), Ginzburg published a perceptive essay on the art historians associated with that institute, notably Aby Warburg (after whom 'the Warburg' is named), Fritz Saxl and Sir Ernst Gombrich. The problem he discussed was how — and how not — to use works of art as historical sources, noting in particular the danger of circularity involved in reading paintings as evidence of the painter's state of mind.[2]

In 1979 Ginzburg published two more essays with the visual arts as a major or minor theme. The first, written in collaboration with the art historian Enrico Castelnuovo, was a discussion of 'Centre and Periphery' in the history of Italian art, in other words the problem of the cultural lag between the works produced in a centre of artistic innovation, such as Florence, and the works produced in the provinces. The authors argue that the relation between centre and periphery is both a complex and a variable one. They deny the assumption that all lags are peripheral or that all peripheries lag. They also suggest that provincial imitations of the products of the centre express the 'symbolic dominance' of particular cities. This suggestive essay deserves to be better known outside Italy.[3]

Art is also a central theme in one of Ginzburg's most wide-ranging and controversial pieces, an article with the intriguing title, 'Clues'. Its purpose is to discuss what the author calls a *paradigma indiziario*, a phrase almost impossible to translate because *indiziario* refers not only to the phrase *prova indiziaria*, 'circumstantial evidence', but also to the various meanings of *indizio*, 'sign' no less than 'indicator' or 'clue'. The implication, which the article itself teases out, is that there is a sort of art of suspicion, an art which utilises small pieces of indirect evidence rather than direct or massive proof. Ginzburg begins with a striking comparison between the achievements of three masters of this art at the end of the nineteenth century; Sherlock Holmes, Sigmund Freud and the art historian Giovanni Morelli. All three investigators based important conclusions on apparently trivial pieces of evidence. Holmes attended to the barking of a dog and to other details overlooked by Watson; Freud based diagnoses on apparently trivial slips of the tongue, lapses of memory and so on; while Morelli worked out a system for attributing pictures to particular painters on the basis of such minor details as the shape of the painted ears. As Aby Warburg used to say. "God is in the details" (*Der liebe Gott steckt im Detail*). Ginzburg goes on to trace the history of this paradigm, which takes him back to the diagnoses of hippocratic medicine, practices of divination and finally to the prehistoric hunter who 'read' the tracks of the animal he was pursuing. He has particularly interesting points to make about the seventeenth-century art collector Giulio Mancini. Mancini, himself a physician famous for his diagnoses, told his readers to study the 'character' of a painting as they would that of a piece of handwriting, in order to infer its author's identity. This brilliant essay is at once a plea for and an example of historical clue-hunting or divination.[4]

Problems of historical method have long interested Carlo Ginzburg, as they interested his teacher Delio Cantimori (1904-66), a scholar who was particularly concerned with the history of heresy in Italy, but who also published important essays on the cultural historians Jacob Burckhardt, Johan Huizinga and Lucien Febvre.[5] Cantimori's two interests came together when he investigated the 'Nicodemites', those heretics who conformed to orthodoxy in their outward behaviour (they were named after Nicodemus in the gospels, who came to Christ by night). To track down men like these one needs a historical detective who is exceptionally conscious of problems of method.

Ginzburg too has published a study of 'Nicodemism' and the problems of religious simulation and dissimulation in the sixteenth century.[6] His books on the *benandanti* and on the cosmology of Menocchio the miller, hero of *The Cheese and the Worms*, also reveal his acute awareness of the awkward problems of method involved in the study of popular culture through sources produced by the learned; oral culture through written texts; and the views of the unorthodox via the investigations of the inquisitors who were trying to suppress them.

Problems of method are also raised by Ginzburg's investigation of Piero della Francesca. Piero's major paintings have been the subject of a long debate, particularly since the great Italian art historian Roberto Longhi published his essay on them in 1927. It is not the authorship which is in doubt this time but the dating of the paintings and also their meaning. The specific problems of interpreting the *Flagellation* and other paintings by Piero raise the burning question of the validity of the so-called 'iconographical' or 'iconological' approach. This approach was worked out from the 1920s onwards by a group of German art historians, notably two members of Aby Warburg's circle, Erwin Panofsky and Edgar Wind.

Panofsky defined iconography as "that branch of the history of art which concerns itself with the subject-matter or meaning of works of art, as opposed to their form".[7] He distinguished between two levels, iconography in the strict sense, which involves identifying a painted figure of a woman, say, as 'Venus', 'Judith' or 'Clio', and iconology, a less precise term. It might be rendered as the art of grasping the meaning of the whole, whether that whole is an individual picture; the 'programme' or unifying theme of a pictorial cycle; the oeuvre of a particular artist; or the distinctive quality of the art of a given period. Iconography proper depends very largely on the evidence of texts, but iconology, as Panofsky admitted, requires intuition or — as Ginzburg might say — the art of divination.

Since the publication in 1939 of Panofsky's famous book on the subject, there has been a great wave of studies of this kind. Among the most famous — and controversial — examples are those of Edgar Wind and E. de Jongh. Wind claimed to find references to pagan mystery religions in paintings of the Italian Renaissance, while de Jongh has argued that many seventeenth-century Dutch genre paintings, on the surface depictions of everyday reality, were intended to have a symbolic or emblematic meaning.[8] Botticelli's so-called *Primavera* and Giorgione's so-called *Tempestà* have given rise to a particularly rich literature of interpretation.[9] The iconographical approach, once unduly neglected, has become something of a fashion and there has inevitably been a backlash against it.

The critique of the iconographical approach to works of art rests on two main arguments. In the first place, it has been suggested that the programme or 'deeper meaning' of the work of art did not matter to most patrons (if indeed it mattered to the artists themselves).[10] There is also the argument that even if the artist or his humanist adviser once formulated a programme, and the patron understood this, the art historian may still have little hope of discovering what that programme was. Iconology can rarely meet strict standards of proof.[11] The divergence between the scholars who have written about the meaning of Botticelli's *Primavera*, for example, is so great as to remind one of the fable about the wise men and the elephant.

It is in this context that we should read Carlo Ginzburg's investigations into Piero. Like his friend Salvatore Settis, a classical archaeologist who has offered one of the most persuasive readings of Giorgione's *Tempestà*, Ginzburg wants to replace iconographic laxity with a more rigorous method. They both believe in the possibility of successful detective work in this field, provided that the detective follows strict rules. "The first rule", writes Settis, "is that all the pieces should fit together without leaving blank spaces between them. The second is that the whole should make sense".[12] Ginzburg adds a third rule — we might call it 'Ginzburg's razor' — to the effect that "other things being equal, the interpretation requiring fewest hypotheses should generally be taken as the most probable".

All the pieces should fit together. As a 'plain' historian, Ginzburg's advantage over his art-historian colleagues is that he has more pieces to play with. He has put the problem of Piero into a wider context, notably that of the theological and political conflicts of the time. The major political conflict was of course the one between the Byzantine Empire and the Ottoman Empire which was about to swallow it up. The Byzantines could see what was coming. That was why the emperor John VIII approached Pope Eugenius IV with a plan for a general council which would put an end to the theological disputes between eastern and western Christendom. The council was held at Ferrara and Florence in 1438-9, and the union was signed. However, western aid was ineffective; John VIII came to regret his approach to the pope; and, five years after his death in 1448, Constantinople fell to the Turks.[13] Ginzburg is not the first scholar to have noticed the references in Piero's paintings to John VIII's distinctive hat, any more than he is the first to have noticed the relation between Piero and Bessarion, the Greek archbishop who became a Roman cardinal. All the same, the link between art and politics is central to his study of Piero as it is not in those of his predecessors.

Christopher Hill once wrote of the need to take the history of law away from the lawyers and the history of theology away from the theologians. Ginzburg's essay shows the advantage of taking art history away from the specialist art historians (or to be fairer and more exact, of sharing it with them). For the plain historian has a good deal to say about art patronage. According to Salvatore Settis, for example, Giorgione's *Tempestà* cannot be understood without studying the intellectual interests of the man who — in all probability — commissioned it, the Venetian patrician Gabriele Vendramin. The meaning of the painting depends upon its context. In a similar way, Ginzburg argues below that it is important to study the humanistic interests of Giovanni Bacci, who was one of the patrons of Piero della Francesca, in order to discover the meaning of the Arezzo frescoes and other works by Piero. Art historians have been aware of Bacci's existence for some time, but it was Ginzburg who identified him with the minor humanist whose letters are preserved in the Archivio di Stato in Florence.

Politics and patronage have taken us a considerable distance away from Giovanni Morelli and his clues, but when Ginzburg attempts to identify the mysterious figures in the foreground of Piero's *Flagellation*, he offers us an analysis which Morelli would have appreciated. In the case of one figure, for example, he focusses on "the very unusual ear, sharply pointed and indented at the top, fleshy at the lobe", and in a second case he concentrates on a nose, "slightly humped, and rounded towards the end". Elsewhere he writes about beards, and about the meaning of certain hand gestures. One of this book's most remarkable features is the range of the sources which it exploits without regard to the frontiers between disciplines and what Aby Warburg used to call the 'watchmen' who guard them.

Like earlier essays on Piero della Francesca, Ginzburg's has already provoked considerable controversy.[14] Such a severe critic of the speculations of others and their excesses of "interpretative zeal", as he puts it, could hardly have expected his own hypotheses to have escaped criticism. Like Freud and Sherlock Holmes, Ginzburg has an urge to speculate and on occasion he presents these speculations as 'fact'. Indeed, in one passage he even tells us with great confidence what one figure in the foreground to the *Flagellation* must be saying to the other two. To be fair, he refers, elsewhere in the essay, to his own "chain of conjectures", and to the dangers of circular arguments in a case with so many unknown factors, a jigsaw puzzle in which so many pieces have been lost. His own hypotheses are at once ingenious, economical, and plausible. Whether or not readers will agree with the substantive conclusions, it will be hard for them to resist admiring the exemplary way in which the problems have been set out. But it is high time to let Carlo Ginzburg tell his own story.

PETER BURKE

Notes

1. C. Ginzburg, *The Night Battles* (1966; translated by A. and J. Tedeschi, London 1983); *The Cheese and the Worms* (1975; translated by A. and J. Tedeschi, London 1980).

2. C. Ginzburg, 'Da Warburg a Gombrich', *Studi Medievali* 7 (1966), 1015-65.

3. E. Castelnuovo and C. Ginzburg, 'Centro e Peripheria', *Storia dell'arte italiana* 1 (Turin, 1979), 285-352.

4. C. Ginzburg, 'Clues', in *The Sign of Three: Dupin, Holmes, Pierce*, ed. U. Eco and T.A. Sebeok (Bloomington, 1983), 81-118.

5. D. Cantimori, *Storici e storia* (Turin, 1971).

6. C. Ginzburg, *Il nicodemismo: simulazione e dissimulazione religiosa nell'Europa del '500* (Turin, 1970).

7. E. Panofsky, *Studies in Iconology* (New York, 1939), introduction.

8. E. Wind, *Pagan Mysteries in the Renaissance* (Oxford, 1958). E. de Jongh, 'Erotica in vogelperspectief', *Simiolus* 3 (1968), 22-72.

9. On the *Primavera*, Wind, ch. 6; E.H. Gombrich, *Symbolic Images* (London, 1972), pp. 37f; C. Dempsey, 'Mercurius Ver', *Journal of the Warburg and Courtauld Institutes* 31 (1968), 251-73. On the *Tempestà*, E. Wind, *Giorgione's Tempestà* (London, 1969); S. Settis, *La "Tempestà" interpretata* (Turin, 1978).

10. C. Hope, 'Artists, Patrons and Advisers in the Italian Renaissance', in *Patronage in the Renaissance*, ed. G.F. Lytle and S. Orgel (Princeton, 1981), 293-343.

11. E.H. Gombrich, 'Aims and Limits of Iconology' in his *Symbolic Images*, introduction.

12. Settis, p. 73.

13. A good brief account in S. Runciman, *The Fall of Constantinople* (Cambridge, 1965), ch. 1.

14. A. Pinelli, 'In margine a "Indagini su Piero"', *Quaderni Storici* 50 (1982) 692-701, followed by Ginzburg's reply.

Preface

In the following pages I offer an analysis of some of the major works of Piero della Francesca: the *Baptism of Christ*, the *Flagellation* and the Arezzo fresco cycle. My perspective is twofold: I am concerned with their commissioning, and with their iconography. I say nothing of the strictly formal aspects of the paintings, for, being a historian rather than an art historian, I lack the qualifications to do so. This is a serious limitation; it will be asked whether an investigation whose scope is thus confined can arrive at relevant conclusions. I believe that it can, both for reasons pertaining specifically to the nature of the research into Piero's work, and for reasons of a more general kind.

All in all, we have little certain knowledge of Piero's life; very few of his works can be dated.[1] In such conditions, the researcher is in the position of a climber confronted by a particularly severe rock face, smooth and without anything to which a rope-holding peg might be attached. The pegs of fact are few and far between: Piero was in Florence in 1439, among Domenico Veneziano's retinue; in 1445 he received a commission for the Misericordia altarpiece at San Sepolcro; the Rimini fresco, depicting Sigismondo Malatesta, dates from 1451; the record of payments made to him by the Vatican tells us that he was working in Rome in 1458-9. For the rest, we have nothing but conjectures, unreliable or second-hand testimony, and in the best cases *post quem* and *ante quem* dates that leave the intervening decades blank.

In his great book on Piero (first published in 1927 and subsequently enriched, over a period of thirty-five years, by the author's additions and revisions[2]), Roberto Longhi has shown how an in-depth examination of the paintings themselves may allow us to circumvent the paucity of external evidence. Today, we still have to come to terms with this fundamental reconstruction of Piero's artistic biography. Inevitably, however, given the more than fifty years which have passed since it was first set out, Longhi's treatment now seems doubtful in some respects.

Let us take one example: the dating of the Urbino *Flagellation*.[3] Longhi used to hold that this famous picture was painted in or about 1445. He derived this incredibly early date from a particular interpretation of the picture's subject — or rather, of the scene in the foreground. According to this interpretation, which had been developed and gradually modified during the eighteenth and nineteenth centuries in the local tradition of Urbino, and by students of the town's history, the blond youth with bare feet represented Oddantonio da Montefeltro, who was assassinated by conspirators in 1444, standing between two wicked counsellors. Thus Piero's picture was seen as homage to the memory of the Count, who had recently died a tragic death.

Though there is evidence of the young man's mistaken identification as Oddant-onio as early as the late sixteenth century (which is already, however, more than a hundred years after the picture was painted), the entire interpretation is certainly quite groundless. While it went unchallenged, Longhi accepted it as the "most probable" account, and held that the dating that followed from it was confirmed by the work's formal qualities: "The style, too, takes us back to a period before the Arezzo frescoes...".[4] To the quite justified objections put to him by Toesca, who rejected (even if on the basis of a not entirely satisfactory argument) both the iconographic interpretation and the early relative dating, Longhi replied in 1942. He reiterated his own acceptance of what was then the orthodox thesis: "and since the work was intended for Urbino, so also may well have been its mysterious modern theme [the figures in the foreground]; which in turn lends credence to the local tradition concerning its interpretation – an interpretation quite in keeping with the style of a painting which is connected with the more primitive works, and which is clearly a prevision, rather than a consequence, of the Arezzo frescoes".

Longhi, of course, would never have dreamed of uncritically accepting the attribu-tion of a work to any artist on the basis of a local tradition a hundred, or indeed three hundred, years later than the work in question. In questions of iconography, however, he was altogether less meticulous. Expert though he was, Longhi's eyes were misled, in the case of the *Flagellation*, by pseudo-evidence of an extra-stylistic kind; the result was dis-tortion of a crucial phase in Piero's development as a painter. However, Longhi did even-tually modify his view, writing in 1962 that he was now "inclined to date the work a few years later". The theory that the picture commemorated Oddantonio's death was on the point of collapsing, and the question of its iconography was thus opened once again. Longhi continued at all events to maintain that the painting belonged to "a phase earlier than the Arezzo frescoes".[5]

I shall have more to say later about the dating of the Arezzo cycle and of the *Flagel-lation* itself. For the moment, I wish simply to make some general comments on the problems raised by Longhi's argument and by his subsequent change of mind.

It is well known that Longhi regarded the dating of a work as a crucially important element in its analysis. His uncanny insight as a connoisseur should not, however, lead us into the mistaken supposition that datings such as "Cremona, 1530"[6] always or only had a stylistic basis. They actually depended upon the interplay and cross-comparison of a range of documentary evidence, concerning style, biography, even the picture's framing – and perhaps, though more rarely, its iconography and other features. Now it is clear that any suggested dating depends on a convergence of stylistic and extra-stylistic infer-ences: but this convergence, this "agreement" (as Longhi terms it), is a point of arrival, not a point of departure. Which series of dates, when we are actually carrying out a piece of research, will weigh most heavily with us, and thus form the basis of any agreement? The answer will, of course, vary from one case to the next. In the present instance, there can be no doubt that most weight was given to extra-stylistic factors, and particularly to data concerning iconography.

It is significant that Longhi, until his change of mind in 1962, always began his discussions of the painting's date by identifying what it represented. And indeed, if one accepted the view that it commemorated Oddantonio's death, then this did provide a fairly exact indication of its date, which could not have been more than a couple of years later than 1444. (Federigo da Montefeltro, the painting's likely patron if we accept the theory in question, would surely not have delayed long before honouring his murdered brother's memory.) Longhi's own arguments, meanwhile, always make it clear that stylistic evidence could not offer anything approaching such chronological precision: "earlier than the Arezzo frescoes", "clearly a prevision, rather than a consequence, of the Arezzo frescoes". Complementary to this *terminus ante quem*, which Longhi placed in 1452, was the implicit *terminus post quem* provided by the oldest parts of the San Sepolcro Misericordia altarpiece, commissioned in 1445 and probably painted in that year or soon afterwards. This means that Longhi, in assigning a date to the *Flagellation*, faced the choice between a margin of error of two or three years at most (if he went on the basis of iconography), and a margin more than twice as wide (about seven years). For a scholar seeking to establish the date with the smallest possible approximation, the problem was to establish whether the first dating was compatible with the second — compatible, rather than coincident, for we have seen that there was no question of coincidence. Longhi's remark that the interpretation of the picture as representing Oddantonio can be accepted as valid "simply because it is consistent with the formal character of the painting"[7] might encourage the mistaken view that iconographic and stylistic factors were accorded equal weight. On the contrary: in this case, the former were clearly given predominance (where the iconography is markedly stereotypic, the reverse sometimes happens). "Formal" criteria enjoyed a kind of right of veto, should the iconographic hypothesis prove incompatible with stylistic analysis; but only on the basis of its iconography could the painting be precisely dated.

We have seen that it took thirty-five years for the veto derived from stylistic inferences to be lifted, leading Longhi to abandon without comment both the absurd iconographic interpretation linked with Oddantonio, and the dating which this implied. We may legitimately see in this long delay evidence of a disposition widespread among connoisseurs (even of Longhi's stature) towards an acceptance of the precise dating offered by a painting's iconography when it apparently refers to an external historical event. In general (though not in the present case), the caution implicit in this tendency is justified. To say this is not, of course, to belittle the considerable success achieved by stylistic or cultural dating techniques in the domain of art history, and in the historical study of peoples without written culture or with only scanty or indecipherable written remains.[8] Even so, it must be remembered that datings based solely on stylistic evidence allow us only to say that x happened before y and after z — to establish, in other words, a relative chronological sequence. Only when datings derived from external evidence can be coupled with the stylistic analysis is it possible to turn this "before" and this "after" into absolute chronological landmarks — and sometimes even into precise *ad annum* dates. Thus when Longhi, in his essay on a youthful *Crucifixion* of Benozzo Gozzoli's, concludes, in a delightful trick of rhetoric, that he "can refrain only with difficulty from adding that it dates 'from Montefalco, in 1450'",[9] he is relying on the date of Benozzo's Montefalco frescoes — a date that is not conjectural but established. If, on the other hand, the historian refers to other works which have themselves been dated on stylistic grounds, there is a serious danger of falling into a vicious circle, from which yet more erroneous datings will be inferred.

Longhi's final change of mind about the dating of the *Flagellation* offers a case in point. Having tacitly rejected the false precision of a date based on a mistaken icono-graphic interpretation, Longhi simply continued to repeat that the painting predated the beginning of Piero's work on the Arezzo cycle. But in what year did Piero commence work on the Arezzo frescoes? The safest answer is: after 1452, the year in which Bicci di Lorenzo, who had begun the task of decorating the chapel of San Francesco, died (though some scholars argue that Piero may have taken Bicci's place a few years earlier, Bicci being already ill). Now Longhi turns this *terminus post quem* into an absolute date, basing his argument on the stylistic similarities between the oldest parts of the Arezzo cycle and the Rimini fresco, depicting Sigismondo Malatesta, which dates — one of our "pegs" — from 1451.[10] But this absolute date is clearly arrived at in an arbitrary fashion, since we do not know how fast Piero's style was evolving during these years. Turning again to the date of the *Flagellation*, we can see that the *terminus ante quem* invoked here — "earlier than the Arezzo cycle" — refers in its turn to a *terminus post quem* (later than 1452). I shall try later on to show that this date, fragile in itself, has to be corrected both on the plane of relative chronology and on that of absolute or calendar chronology.

All this shows how difficult it is, even for so exceptional an expert as Longhi, to date a work on the basis of style alone in the more or less complete absence of external docu-mentation. Few of Piero's works escape this difficulty (which makes his a case of great methodological significance, quite apart from his artistic excellence). The suggested datings of the *Flagellation* fall anywhere within a margin of fully thirty years; the *Baptism of Christ*, which some scholars regard as a mature work, has been assigned by others to the painter's earliest youth; and so on.[11] The datings involved are in many cases absurd; and yet it has been possible to put them forward — possible, that is, without their proposers losing scholarly credibility. On the other hand, anyone who denied that Piero was working in Rimini in 1451, or in Rome in 1458-9, these dates being established respectively by a dated fresco and by the Vatican records, would thereby place them-selves beyond the pale of scholarship — unless, as would of course be theoretically possible, they proved that the date was falsified or the records inaccurate. But in that case, the onus of proof would lie with whoever wished to argue for such falsification or inaccuracy.

In the matter of dating, the rope of stylistic interpretation is in fact always tied, with more or less convincing results, to the pegs of available documentary evidence. (This seems to me to imply a tacit acceptance that stylistic data are less trustworthy in the establishment of a precise date.) What is indispensably necessary, in the case of Piero, is a greater number of pegs: that is, to abandon the metaphor, an amplification of the scanty documentary evidence — evidence, in the first place, about the commissioning of his work.

In fact, documentary research into the commissioning of Piero's works came to a halt in the first decades of this century: the last substantial contribution was made by G. Zippel in his essay proving that Piero had worked at Rome in the service of Pius II.[12] Studies such as those of M. Salmi, who had been working a few years earlier on the commissioning of the Arezzo cycle, were never taken any further — not even by scholars such as C. Gilbert, who (as we shall see) was in a position to develop them.[13] As for the biographical summary that is perhaps the most useful part of E. Battisti's lengthy monograph, while this does supply fresh information on the time Piero spent in Borgo San Sepolcro, it adds nothing about the dating of his works (apart from a request concerning the Misericordia altarpiece[14]).

In their reconstructions of the commissioning of Piero's work, scholars have often chosen, not to go on the basis of documents in libraries or archives, but to decode the evidence of the works themselves — in particular, of their iconography. Indeed, recent years have seen a large number of iconographic or (to use a term now current) iconological[15] studies of Piero: of these, some have been excellent, others unconvincing or downright bad. This is inevitable — even if, to an outside observer, the minimum requirements of intellectual rigour seem sometimes to have been disturbingly ignored. To see how, in Battisti's work, one gratuitous iconological hypothesis is followed at random by another, which may well contradict what has gone before, is to wonder whether, in a domain where verification is so hard to come by, any odd conjecture may be permissible.[16]

The difficulties of verification are readily stated. When, in their study of Piero's works, the iconologists reveal what are often very complex allusions, they are postulating the existence of specific instructions, conveyed to the artist by the painting's patron or by some intermediary. Of instructions, however, not a trace remains, perhaps because they were given orally rather than in writing. So far, there is nothing extraordinary about this, for there are in fact very few surviving examples of detailed iconographic instructions dating from before the middle of the sixteenth century. However, there is a very serious risk of constructing circular chains of interpretation, based entirely on conjecture. The chain relies on the reciprocal reinforcement of its various links, and the whole construction is suspended in a vacuum (there is an obvious analogy with the risks involved in dating works on exclusively stylistic grounds). The work itself ends up, as we see in numerous pieces of iconological research, by becoming the pretext for a series of free associations, generally based on some presumed symbolic interpretation.

Similar problems are encountered in other fields of research — for example, in the study of pre-industrial peasant culture, which was largely oral.[17] They cannot be resolved by tacitly doing away with the requirements of documentary verification, but only by developing adequate means of verification. This (let it be clear) does not mean that the interpreter's task is limited to the identification of the explicit meanings attributed to the work by the painter, or the patron. But the interpreter who does not observe these initial precautions risks presenting what are no more than private musings in the guise of a broadening or deepening of Piero's — or, say, Titian's — works. There are plenty of examples, nowadays, of such ridiculous presumption.[18] This underlines the wisdom of Gombrich's suggestion that we should begin by analysing institutions or genres, rather than symbols; then, we might avoid the pitfalls that lie in wait for what we might call "uncontrolled" iconology.[19] But there is one other element of verification that allows us to restrict the range of possible interpretations: research into commissioning. To be sure, if we seek to identify a work's patron on the basis of an iconological interpretation, then we land ourselves in yet another vicious circle. The only course is to carry out research simultaneously into commissioning and into iconography, and to bring together the data derived from both sets of investigations. That is what I have tried to do in this book.

In order to demonstrate the limits of a purely stylistic reading of Piero's paintings (and, by extension, of works of art in general), we began with the problem of dating. This, doubtless, can be put down to the habitual vice of the professional historian, whose immediate response to any piece of evidence (pictures included) is to ask, "When?" (and, straight after, "Where?"). Dating, however, is no more than the first step towards a historical reading of a work of art. The body of extra-stylistic data concerning commissioning and iconography, which we propose to examine in order to fill out the results of stylistic research, poses forcibly the question (trite, but terribly real) of the relation between the work of art and the social context in which it was born.

We have chosen to raise the question only now, and in what might be called an indirect way — coming to it, that is, only by way of an elementary but inescapable need (the need to date the work), which is felt by anyone whose relationship with works of art goes beyond a purely aesthetic appreciation. Our reason is this. The relations between a work of art and its context have too often been stated in brutally reductive terms — as, for example, in the recent claim that behind the paintings of Piero della Francesca we can reveal "agricultural and patriarchal Umbria".[20] Those scholars who are less interested in the social history of artistic expression, or who would even oppose its study on ideological grounds, obviously have no difficulty in dismissing that kind of sterile playing with the metaphor (itself an unfortunate one) of "structure" and "superstructure".

What is much harder for the prejudiced to reject (but also much harder and more laborious to achieve) is an analytical reconstruction of the intricate web of minute relations that underlies the production of any work of art, however simple.[21] Even the preliminary historical task of dating often necessitates, as we have seen, a simultaneous examination of stylistic choices, iconographic forms and relations with patrons. It is only by way of an ever more assiduous analysis of this type that we shall attain the infinitely more ambitious goal of writing a social history of artistic expression; we shall never get there by drawing precipitate or far-fetched parallels between the sequence of artistic phenomena and the sequence of socio-economic phenomena.

The most determined steps towards our goal were taken by Aby Warburg, whose essays[22] testify to a breadth of vision and a wealth of analytic techniques only in part accountable to the decoding of symbols traditionally regarded as the defining characteristic of the "Warburg method". Nor is it to be overlooked, here, that it was Warburg's attention to the specific social and cultural context that preserved him from the interpretative excesses to which even so great a scholar as Panofsky (not to speak of some of his successors) occasionally succumbed. Rather closer in spirit to Warburg's researches is a work such as M. Baxandall's study of fifteenth-century Italian painting, where the examination of style in relation to concrete social situations and experiences produces highly original results.[23]

It is some time now since historians ceased to feel obliged to work only with written evidence. Lucien Febvre has already invited us to take account of weeds, field formations, eclipses of the moon: why not paintings, then — for example, Piero's paintings? After all, they, too, are documents of political or religious history. There has been too much talk, to be sure, of interdisciplinary research (which has not, in most cases, led to much practical result): nonetheless, there is obviously every reason why historians and art historians should collaborate, each deploying their own techniques and their own expertise, in order to arrive together at a deeper understanding of the evidence given by figurative works.[24] Nor should anyone object if a scholar working in an overtly historical perspective decides not to venture into the field of stylistic analysis.

The present work, however, has, it seems to me, means and ends that are different, and perhaps more ambitious. I have been obliged to take account of the limits of my training, which have prevented me from fully coming to terms with the scholarly work on Piero's paintings; and I have tried neither to hold the disciplines apart, nor to run them into one. I have conducted myself rather like someone making a foray into what is certainly foreign, though by no means definitely hostile, territory. Had I referred to Piero's paintings as evidence of fifteenth-century religious life, or had I contented myself with rediscovering the network of Arezzo patrons, I could no doubt have established peaceful relations with the learned body of art historians. But they will probably take it amiss that I have outlined an image of Piero that differs from the familiar one, and have even disputed the chronology of some of his major works. It will be surprising indeed if nobody advises me to stick to the trade I know best.

As a matter of principle, I believe that forays such as this should become more and more frequent. Because people are unhappy about what are held to be artificial separations between disciplines, there has been a tendency to juxtapose the conclusions of different disciplines (though this, as we have said, has been more in the wish than the deed). Summit meetings of this kind are not much use, and leave everything unchanged; far better to engage with concrete problems — such as the problem dealt with here, concerning the dating and interpretation of individual works. Only in this way will it be possible to reopen real questions about the techniques, the scope and the language of the individual disciplines. Beginning, of course, with historical research.

Notes

I must express grateful thanks to Augusto Campana, whose comments I sought at an early stage in my research; to don Agnoletti, my guide to the Archives of the Curia at San Sepolcro; to Giorgio E. Ferrari, Micaela Guarino Buzzoni, Marité Hirschkoff Grendi, Piero Lucchi, Cristina Mundici, Agostino Paravicini Bagliani, Vittorio Peti and Odile Redon, who helped find the illustrations; and to those students at Bologna with whom I enjoyed useful discussion of the present work, then in course of development, in a seminar of 1979–80. Among friends whom I asked to read my typescript I must mention with especial gratitude Enrico Castelnuovo, Gianni Romano and Salvatore Settis, who drew my attention to mistakes and inexactitudes. Bologna, March 1981.

This translation has been made from the third Italian edition, but it incorporates a number of alterations made subsequent to that edition by the author. Chapter Four in particular has been extensively revised.

1. Schlosser's words in this connection are worth recalling: "It is already a matter of exceptional significance for this type of artist – one of the purest, in our opinion – that empirical biography is of no importance." (J. von Schlosser, *Xenia*: p. 50 of the Italian translation, subtitled *Saggi sulla storia dello stile e del linguaggio nell'arte figurativa*, Bari 1938).

2. R. Longhi, *Piero della Francesca*, Florence 1963 (vol. 3 of *Opera Complete*).

3. For the present author's views on this, see ch. 3.

4. Longhi, *Piero*, p. 209; and also p. 25: "Dating to the same period – probably shortly after 1544, the year which saw the death of Oddantonio da Montefeltro, to whose wretched fate it most likely alludes – is the small painting entitled the *Flagellation of Christ* …". In both cases, as can be seen, the iconographic interpretation (described as "likely" or "most probable") is not just the preface to but the grounds for the proposed dating.

5. Ibid., pp. 196–7 (for the reply to Toesca; for the latter's objections, see below, ch. 3). For Longhi's revised opinion of 1962, see ibid., p. 201.

6. G. Contini, "Sul metodo di Roberto Longhi", in *Altri Esercizi*, Turin 1972, p. 103. On the "divinatory" implications of the connoisseur's activity, see the present author's "Spie. Radici di un paradigma indiziario", in A. Gargani (ed.), *Crisi della Ragione*, Turin 1979, pp. 57–106.

7. Longhi, *Piero*, p. 148.

8. G. Kubler, *The Shape of Time. Remarks on the History of Things*, New Haven and London 1973, p. 14.

9. R. Longhi, "Fatti di Masolino e di Masaccio e altri studi sul Quattrocento", Florence 1975 (*Opere Complete*, VIII/I), p. 127.

10. Longhi, *Piero*, p. 100: "We can assume in all probability that Piero replaced Bicci di Lorenzo almost immediately upon his death in 1452. At that point, the vault of the Chapel of San Francesco di Arezzo, which the Bacci family intended to decorate completely with paintings, was nearly finished. Intuitively one must incline to this view, for had there been any serious break in the work, some other painter of Bicci di Lorenzo's calibre would surely have been found to complete the small unfinished portions of the vault and the entrance arch, and to see to whatever else required attention; whereas in fact Piero himself made good even these tiny omissions. And the same date seems explicitly vouched for by the Rimini fresco which is already, in 1451, on a par with the Arezzo frescoes in breadth, coherence and maturity."

11. C. Gilbert has rightly emphasized that this is an unsatisfactory state of affairs: see his *Change in Piero della Francesca*, Locust Valley, New York 1968.

12. G. Zippel, "Piero della Francesca a Roma", in *Rassegna d'Arte*, XIX (1919), pp. 81–94.

13. M. Salmi, "I Bacci di Arezzo nel sec. XV e la loro capella nella chiesa di San Franceso", in *Rivista d'Arte*, IX (1916), pp. 224–37. On the line of enquiry which Gilbert opens up, but does not follow, see below, ch. 2.

14. E. Battisti, *Piero della Francesca*, 2 vols, Milan 1971. The documentary register, compiled by E. Settesoldi, is in the 2nd vol., pp. 213-46. For the request from the *Compagnia della Misericordia*, see vol. 2, p. 221 (but the date of the document, and its interpretation, must be corrected in the light of J. Beck's remarks: see "Una data per Piero della Francesca", in *Prospettiva*, 15 [1978], p. 53).

15. On the way in which Panofsky himself came progressively to identify iconology and iconographic analysis, see G. Previtali's introduction to the Italian translation of E. Panofsky, *Studi di iconologia. I temi umanistici nell'arte del Rinascimento*, Turin 1975.

16. See the comments of S. Settis on "indulgent iconologists" in *La 'Tempesta' interpretata. Giorgione, i committenti, il soggetto*, Turin 1978, pp. 15-16. Settis and myself are described by Battisti as "pathetic victims of a recurrence of neo-Warburgian rigourism" (cf. E. Mucci and P.L. Tazzi (eds.), *Teoria e pratiche della critica d'arte, Atti del convengno di Montecatini maggio 1978*, Milan 1979, p. 241).

17. Cf. P. Burke, *Popular Culture in Early Modern Europe*, London 1978, pp. 77ff, and the preface, pp. ix-xi.

18. The prize must go (for the time being) to M. Calvesi, "Sistema degli equivalenti ed equivalenza del Sistema in Piero della Francesca", in *Storia dell'arte*, 24-5 (1975), pp. 83-110. For the distinction between explicit and implicit meanings, see G. Previtali's preface to Panofsky, especially pp. xxiv ff. (commenting on Panofsky's discussion with Pächt).

19. See E.H. Gombrich, "Aims and Limits of Iconology", in *Symbolic Images. Studies in the Art of the Renaissance*, London 1972, pp. 1-25.

20. G. Previtali, "La periodizzazione della storia dell'arte italiana", in *Storia dell'arte italiana*, Turin 1979, vol. 1, p. 46. Calvesi, for his part, discovers by contrast a correspondence between "the call to centralism to be heard in Piero's work" and "the first moves towards an organized system of exchange (with the advent of the bourgeoisie and the emergence of capitalism)" ("Sistema degli equivalenti", p. 84).

21. E. Castelnuovo does not share this positive view of the opportunities offered by this kind of analytical investigation: see his important essay "Per una storia sociale dell'arte" (*Paragone*, 313 [1976], pp. 3-30, 323 [1977], pp. 3-34).

22. A. Warburg, *Die Erneuerung der heidnischen Antike*, 2 vols, Leipzig-Berlin 1932. G. Bing is the editor of the Italian volume, *La rinascita del paganesimo antico. Contributi alla storia della cultura* (Florence 1966): this is a much fuller selection, and includes the first full Italian version of a lecture referring to Piero: see below, ch. 2, n. 60.

23. M. Baxandall, *Painting and Experience in Fifteenth Century Italy*, Oxford 1972.

24. On the question of figurative documents as historical sources, the present author has already commented, in a different context (see "Da A. Warburg a E.H. Gombrich", in *Studi medievali*, s. 3a, VII [1966], pp. 1015-66).

Abbreviations

ACAU   Archivio della Curia Arcivescovile, Urbino
ACS   Archivio Comunale, San Sepolcro
ASC   Archivio di Stato, Cesena
ASF   Archivio di Stato, Firenze
ASG   Archivio di Stato, Gubbio
ASR   Archivio di Stato, Roma
BCCF   Biblioteca Comunale, Castiglion Fiorentino
BNCF   Biblioteca Nazionale Centrale, Firenze
BUU   Biblioteca Universitaria, Urbino

On 15 February 1439, John VIII Palaeologus, the Eastern Emperor, made his entry into Florence. The previous year he had disembarked in Italy, together with his retinue, to take part in the Council debating the union of the Eastern and Western Christian Churches. The Council had recently removed from Ferrara to Florence. A contemporary chronicle tells us that the following citizens assembled to do homage to the Emperor: "the Signori, the Colleges, the Captains of the Parties, ten of the Balia, eight of the Officers of the *Monte*, six of the *Mercatanzia*, and the seven greater Guilds, and many other citizens with the banner, and then seven Cardinals with the whole court, and all the barons, and other Greeks of the said Emperor, who were already in Florence. It was a fine and a large company." The Emperor "wore a white gown with over it a mantle of red stuff and a white hat coming to a point in front in which he had a ruby bigger than a pigeon's egg and many other precious stones". Men and women thronged the streets to watch the procession: but "then it began to rain very heavily, so that it spoiled the festivity ...".[1]

Among the spectators scattered by the downpour may perhaps have been the young Piero della Francesca. We know for certain that on 7 September of the same year he was working, with Domenico Veneziano, on the (now vanished) frescoes of the S. Egidio chapel.[2] And when, some twenty years later, he was required to portray the face of John VIII Palaeologus on the walls of the church of San Francesco at Arezzo, he placed upon the figure's head the unmistakable "white hat coming to a point in front" by which the anonymous Florentine chronicler — like Pisanello and Filarete — had been so struck.[3]

His stay in Florence in 1439 does indeed mark the start of Piero's history as an artist: but not only (as has hitherto been held) because he then met Domenico Veneziano. The dense network of connections that bound him to the world of the Council was also destined to leave upon his painting its own unforeseeable and ineradicable mark.

Notes

1. *Istorie di Firenze dall'anno 1406 fino al 1438*, in L.A. Muratori, *Rerum Italicarum Scriptores*, Mediolani 1731, XIX, col. 182; and see also the account in J. Gill, *The Council of Florence*, Cambridge 1959, whose translation of the contemporary chronicle is here partly reproduced (see pp. 183-4).

2. Longhi, *Piero*, p. 97.

3. The Constantine of *Triumph of Constantine* was identified as a portrait of Palaeologus by E. Müntz (1883) in a contribution that went unregarded (cf. Battisti, *Piero*, vol. 1, p. 492, n. 282). A. Venturi and A. Warburg (1911 and 1912) later arrived at the same conclusions independently: cf. A. Warburg, "Piero della Francescas Constantinschlacht in der Aquarellkopie des Johann Anton Ramboux", in *Die Erneurung*, vol. 1, pp. 253-4 (and see the editors' note on p. 390). Kenneth Clark (*Piero della Francesca*, London 1969, p. 78) maintains that in painting the portrait of Palaeologus, Piero drew upon his direct experience of seeing him at Florence, rather than upon Pisanello's medallion, as is supposed by the other scholars we have mentioned; but see below, ch. 2. The sleeping Constantine of the *Dream* has also been identified as Palaeologus; cf. C. Marinesco, in *Comptes-Rendus de l'Académie des Inscriptions et Belles-Lettres*, 1957, p. 32, and, independently, M. Vickers, "Some Preparatory Drawings for Pisanello's Medallion of John VIII Palaeologus", in *The Art Bulletin*, LX (1978), p. 423. This second identification has been rightly called into question by Battisti; I, p. 492, n. 283.

I

The *Baptism of Christ*

Most scholars (though not all) hold the *Baptism of Christ* — now in the National Gallery, London — to be among the earliest of Piero's surviving works. The painting's subject is readily identifiable. De Tolnay, however, noted a departure from the traditional iconography of the Baptism: the three angels are not holding up Christ's robes as he immerses himself in the Jordan. Here, the angel on the left is watching the scene, while the one on the right has one arm over the shoulder of the central angel, whose right hand he also holds. This grouping was compared by De Tolnay to the attitude of the three Graces shown on a contemporary medal designed by Niccolò Fiorentino, which bears the legend "Concordia": he interpreted it as an allusion to the Graces as symbols of Harmony.[1] M. Tanner has recently developed this interpretation in greater detail, seeing the gesture made by the two angels in the sight of the third as a reference, modelled on the Roman iconographic depiction of Concord, to the religious concord between the Western and Eastern Churches ratified by the Council of Florence of 1439.[2] Tanner's entire interpretation hinges on her reading of the precise significance of this gesture. The figures in the background are identified as Byzantine priests by their oriental clothes and headgear (which will appear again in the Arezzo frescoes). The three angels, and also the colours of their robes — red, blue and white — are an allusion to the Trinity, in accordance with the symbolism proposed by Innocent III on the founding of the Order of the Holy Trinity; and they evoke the theological debates conducted over a period of two years, first at Ferrara and then at Florence, between the theologians of the two Churches on the doctrine of the Trinity. In clasping hands, the two angels not only symbolize the end of the schism and the restoration of harmony between the two Churches; they also represent the most theologically important of the conclusions upon which the Council had agreed: the addition to the Credo of the so-called "Filioque" clause, which decreed (after prolonged resistance from the Eastern Church) that the Holy Spirit proceeded both from the Father and from the Son.[3] And the tondo that originally hung above the *Baptism* (and which is now lost) likewise emphasized the trinitarian implications of the ceremony that took place on the banks of the Jordan.

The suggestion that the painting dates from 1440 or soon afterwards follows from all this. Any date much later would be incompatible with the fact that the harmony between the Churches was soon broken, thanks to the renewed strength of the faction in Constantinople hostile to unity with the Church of Rome. It is worth noting that this dating, based exclusively on iconographic features, is substantially the same as that proposed by Longhi on exclusively stylistic grounds (1440-5).[4]

As we have seen, Tanner's interpretation draws together the elements of the

Baptism into a single, compact and coherent design, which then provides a convincing explanation for the iconographic anomalies. However, Battisti, taking as his starting-point precisely the most striking of these anomalies (the gesture of concord to which De Tolnay drew attention), had suggested, a little earlier, an altogether different interpretation.

Before its final removal from San Sepolcro, Piero's *Baptism* formed part of a polyptych kept in the cathedral church of St John the Evangelist. On the side panels and the predella (now in the San Sepolcro museum) are depicted, respectively, saints and doctors of the Church, and scenes from the life of St John the Baptist. Neither is by Piero, and both are undoubtedly later than the *Baptism*. They are hesitantly attributed to Matteo di Giovanni, and dated betwen 1455 and 1465.[5] The predella bears the family tree of the Graziani family, one of the most prominent families in San Sepolcro, and it was unquestionably a Graziani who commissioned the predella and the side panels of the polyptych. Battisti suggests that the same person also commissioned the central panel and the tondo that hung above it, painted by Piero. From De Tolnay's reading of the work, he (unlike Tanner) singles out the comparison between the angels and the three Graces, paying no attention to the theme of Concord. He offers an explanation of the presence of the angels in the attitude of the Graces on the basis of a passage from Leon Battista Alberti's *Trattata della pittura* (*Treatise on Painting*), which explains that this disposition of the Graces, when clad as opposed to naked, signifies one who at once bestows and receives a gift. The iconography of Piero's *Baptism* implies a combination between this passage in Alberti and another, in St Thomas Aquinas's *Summa*, where Christ is presented as the supreme example of generosity. The painting, then, may have been commissioned (so the argument runs) by a rich merchant — probably, one of the Graziani — who wished to expiate, by a generous act, his own sins of usury. Piero, having originally been commissioned by this merchant to paint the entire polyptych, completed the *Baptism* and the lost tondo depicting God the Father before he began to slacken in his work. This obliged the patron to enter into a second contract with Matteo di Giovanni. It follows, suggests Battisti, that the *Baptism* should be dated around 1460, which is almost twenty years later than the traditional dating. In confirmation of all this, Battisti cites a stylistic feature of the painting, the echoes of classical sculpture perceptible in the figures of the angels — echoes that oblige us, he claims, to date the painting after Piero's journey to Rome in 1458-9.[6]

Here, then, are two interpretations, both beginning from the same detail (the handclasp of the two angels), which nonetheless arrive at completely different conclusions about both the work's iconographic implications and its dating. I should say at the outset that I find Tanner's interpretation very convincing, and Battisti's altogether implausible. However, both are conjectural. To treat them on a par — which in effect would be to place them both in abeyance pending the arrival of external documentary proof that may never be forthcoming — is hardly a reasonable course. What we need, then, is a clarification of what is meant, in this context, by terms like "convincing" and "implausible"; of our grounds for preferring one given interpretation to another; and, more generally, of the way we conceive the problem of how written materials can help in the verification of iconographic research.

We have already seen that the picture is hard to interpret because it does not altogether fit into pre-existing iconographical tradition (the tradition, in this case, of "the Baptism of Christ"). There may be only the slightest anomaly (the attitude of the two angels); but this may sometimes be enough — as in the famous instance of Giorgione's *Tempest* — to permeate the whole work and to set us the most tantalizing iconographic puzzles. Settis, discussing the various interpretations of Giorgione's picture, has formulated two rules: a) every piece of the puzzle must fit into place; b) the pieces must form a coherent composition.[7] I would add a third: c) other things being equal, the interpretation requiring fewest hypotheses should generally be taken as the most probable (though we must not forget that the truth is sometimes improbable).

By these three criteria (comprehensiveness, coherence, economy), Tanner's suggestion is manifestly preferable. For Battisti introduces hypotheses that give rise to further hypotheses, as when the three Graces, to which the angels are said to allude, are made in their turn to symbolize Christian generosity. He can link these two hypotheses together only by surmising a cross-contamination of two texts, connected only by accidental associations that could be indefinitely extended[8]. Finally, since his own interpretation centres on the notion of usury, a feature such as the Eastern priests in the background becomes frankly heterogeneous, and can be integrated only through a quite gratuitous postulate that there are several simultaneous layers of meaning[9]. Tanner's reading, by contrast, seems harmoniously to unite the picture's multitude of iconographic elements around the theme of the Trinity debated at the Council of Florence. Even in this case, however, we cannot rule out the possibility that this coherence has been unwittingly introduced by the interpreter[10]. First of all, the selection of pieces of the puzzle (that is, of features regarded as iconographically significant) is itself a factor in the interpretation — as we can see from the fact that no scholar before De Tolnay had paused to remark on the attitude of the two angels. Hence the danger of picking out features without iconographic relevance, and then building up from them an interpretation that may be coherent, but which is remote indeed from the painter's intentions. Second, every iconograhic feature is polyvalent, and can thus open the way to divergent series of significations. We can follow De Tolnay's suggested comparison between the angels of Piero's *Baptism* and the medal designed by Niccolò Fiorentino in either of two directions: three angels — three Graces (Battisti), or three angels — concord (Tanner). To entertain such an alternative is legitimate, it may be objected, so long as the research is at an early stage: as work proceeds, the initial conjecture is bound to be strengthened or destroyed as internal confirmation is, or is not, forthcoming. The danger, however, is that the polyvalence or plasticity of the images will be more or less consciously exploited to yield apparent confirmation of the favoured hypotheses. How are we to know, in any given picture, if a lamb stands for Christ, or for meekness — or if it is just a lamb? Sometimes the context may determine this: all interpretation (of literary passages, pictures, or whatever) undoubtedly presupposes a reciprocal interchange between the whole and the parts. In some cases, however, this healthy circularity of hermeneutic interpretation easily becomes a vicious circle[11]. It is thus appropriate to introduce into the process of iconographic decoding elements of an external kind, such as commissioning, which allow for verification — and which broaden the notion of context to include the social context. To be sure, research into commissioning does not always yield unambiguous iconographic clues. In cases such as the one we are discussing, however, where there is a partial or total iconographic anomaly, to identify the patron does at least help to cut down drastically the number of iconographic hypotheses under consideration. And in the event of a convergence between the results of the two branches of research (into iconography and into commissioning), the possibility of error is reduced practically to nothing.

In Tanner's reconstruction, the missing piece is, precisely, the unsolved problem of the picture's patron. The subtle theological allusions that she deciphers tend to rule out the possibility that any member of the Graziani family could have commissioned the *Baptism*. The question can now be approached on the basis of the factual data and new hypotheses put forward in E. Agnoletti's recent researches into the painting's peregrinations.

It was known already that the *Baptism*, transferred in 1807 (when the Priory was closed down) from the high altar of the Priory of St John the Baptist in San Sepolcro to the Cathedral of St John the Evangelist, was then put up for sale as an antiquity in 1859. Agnoletti has now succeeded in finding evidence about the picture that predates what was previously known, and he has at the same time proposed a new hypothesis about its commissioning. The *Baptism*, it is suggested, was painted for the altar of the confraternity of St John the Baptist, founded in 1406 by Diosa di Romaldo di Mazarino de Mazetti, widow of Giovanni di Fidanza. She had endowed a chapel situated "in the *Badia del Borgo*" — that is, the Abbey of San Sepolcro — "near the main gate upon the right-hand side and supported by the first column, and which is known by the title of St John the Baptist", with the stipulation that mass was to be celebrated there each day for her soul and for her husband's. The *Baptism* may have remained in the abbey, which by this time had become a cathedral, until 1563, when the altar was dedicated in perpetuity to St Egidius and St Arcanus. What then became of the picture, or rather of the polyptych, we do not know. Agnoletti suggests that it was removed to the priory of St John the Baptist in 1583, in which year the building's frescoed walls, fallen into disrepair, were whitewashed on the instructions of the Papal emissary, Monsignor Peruzzi. The polyptych was certainly in the priory in 1629, for the records of that year's pastoral visitation mention an "iconam depictam in tabula cum imagine S. Iohannis Baptistæ et aliorum sanctorum cum ornamento ligneo deaurato". This, the earliest evidence we possess for the presence of the picture in a particular place, is later confirmed in the records of subsequent pastoral visitations (1639, 1649) and in the inventories of 1673, 1760 and 1787. In 1807 the polyptych returned, as we have said, to the Cathedral of St John the Evangelist, where, according to Agnoletti's reconstruction, it had originally been. This last hypothesis is further supported by the lack of any mention of the polyptych among the property of the Priory at the time of its suppression[12].

This chain — made up in part of documents, in part of hypotheses bringing them into a whole — contains one weak link: its first. The patron of the *Baptism* cannot be identified as the Confraternity of St John the Baptist, for the excellent reason that no confraternity of that name has ever existed in San Sepolcro. We can trace it, supposedly, in just one piece of evidence, the will of its presumed founder, the Lady Diosa. However, if we examine the original document, rather than the sixteenth-century recension tracked down by Agnoletti, no doubt on the point is possible. The will forms part of the record of the acts and dealings of the Confraternity of San Bartolomeo (the richest and most important in San Sepolcro), because this was the confraternity "instituted" by, or in other words made guarantor for, the last will of one of its members, the testatrix Diosa di Ranaldo (not Romaldo) di Mazarino de Mazzetti. She it was who, on 10 March 1406, "instituted the fraternity" (*'instituì la fraternita'*) and "endowed its chapel in the Abbey of the town near the main gate which is of St John the Baptist and is supported by the first column, with the properties undermentioned, to wit: first, with a plot of arable land", and so forth (there follows a full inventory of the properties comprised in the bequest). "For which gift," the will continues, "she desires that the abbot of Borgo San Sepolcro (*l'abbate del Borgo*) be required in perpetuity to see to the officiating of the said chapel" and that masses be celebrated there "for the soul of the present testatrix and of the said Giovanni her husband and for the worship of God and of the glorious Virgin Mary and of St John the Baptist." In the celebration of these masses, use was to be made of the "gilded silver chalice" and of the "missal made therefor" which Diosa had previously given. The bequest was also to cover the expenses of Diosa's funeral, as agreed with Bartolomeo, the Abbot of the *badia del Borgo* (the Abbey of San Sepolcro). In default of this, the bequest was to be transferred "from the said monastery and abbey ... to the said fratern-ity" of San Bartolomeo[13].

The bequest, then, was made to the Camaldolite Abbey (later the Cathedral) of Borgo San Sepolcro. Diosa's will proves that there already existed, in 1406, an altar in the abbey dedicated to St John the Baptist. It is for this altar, according to Agnoletti's shrewd reconstruction, that Piero must have painted his *Baptism*. The hypothesis could be definitively confirmed only by the hitherto untraceable record of the painting's commis-sioning. It is nonetheless extremely probable. Once we stop imagining the patron to have been the non-existent Confraternity of St John the Baptist, and put in its place the Camaldolite Abbey, then the accuracy of Tanner's iconographic interpretation does indeed seem scarcely open to doubt. For it was in 1439 that Ambrogio Traversari, Abbot-General of the Camaldolites, distinguished humanist and determined advocate of reconciliation with the Greek Church, died at Camaldoli. He had been one of the parti-cipants in the recently concluded Council of Ferrara and Florence (besides acting as second interpreter, thanks to his having taught himself Greek). He was entrusted, among other tasks, with that of translating into Greek the decree *Laetantur coeli* (6 July 1439), which officially ratified the ending of the Schism[14]. This explains perfectly how the *Baptism* came to adorn the Abbey of St John, for it is a picture dense with allusions to the religious concord achieved at the Council. To the eyes of a selected group of spectators, able to follow its implications, the iconography of the *Baptism* yielded its meaning as an act of homage to Traversari's recently completed labours, and thus as an exaltation of the glories of the Camaldolite Order.

However, the implicit homage to Traversari also touched on local politics and local pride. The abbey of St John the Evangelist, consecrated in 1340, was the symbol of the religious and political power which, since the end of the twelfth century, the Camaldolite monks had exercised over the Borgo (despite its enfeoffment to various feudal lords). The bishops of Città di Castello had on several occasions tried, without success, to displace the monks and to incorporate Borgo San Sepolcro into their own diocese. Traversari had recently played an important part in this often bitter history of antagonism. On assuming the post of Abbot-General, he had at once set out on a series of journeys, described in detail in his *Hodoeporicon*, which took him to the various abbeys of the Camaldolite Order. In the autumn of 1432 he stayed in San Sepolcro, where Pascasio, the Abbot, gave him details of the struggle with the Bishop of Città di Castello. When he returned home after this journey, Traversari wrote to inform Pascasio that Ugolino, the former Abbot of Faenze, had been sent to Rome to pursue the matter further. The Bishop's claims on the monastery were sure to be rejected, declared Traversari; the "ancient privileges" were certain to remain "inviolate". A year later, Traversari made direct representation to Pope Eugenius IV, asking him to reaffirm, against all machinations from other quarters, the rights of the abbots over the Borgo[15].

Following an unsuccessful invasion by the Bishop of Città di Castello, who was driven out by an uprising of the townspeople, Eugenius IV granted Borgo San Sepolcro to Florence (1441), in payment for the costs of the Council. The period of Florentine rule was inaugurated by a frenzy of building: an anonymous Camaldolite monk wrote to Nicholas V that the town walls had been rebuilt, the churches embellished, and the dwelling-houses renovated[16]. The commission for Piero's *Baptism* may perhaps date from this same period, and may have come from the Camaldolite Abbot, who at this time was Pascasio — about whom, however, we know almost nothing[17]. The painting's iconography was an indirect tribute to Traversari: not only because the angels' attitude of concord and harmony, and their trinitarian symbolism, invoke his vital contribution to the Council's successful outcome, but perhaps also because we should see, in the image of Borgo San Sepolcro in the background[18], an allusion to his defence of the rights of the Camaldolite Abbey at a difficult period in its history.

Notes

1. C. de Tolnay, "Conceptions religieuses dans la peinture de Piero della Francesca", in *Arte antica e moderna*, VI (1963), p. 214. Salvatore Settis has pointed out to me that the gesture of the angel on the left (the palm of the hand turned down, with the fingers extended) denotes the peacemaker in classical art.

2. J. Gill, *The Council of Florence*, Cambridge 1959.

3. M. Tanner, "Concordia in Piero della Francesca's 'Baptism of Christ'", in *The Art Quarterly*, XXXV (1972), pp. 1-20. Though Tanner does not mention it, it had already been suggested by C. Marinesco ("Échos byzantins dans l'oeuvre de Piero della Francesca", in *Bulletin de la Société Nationale des Antiquaires de France*, 1958, p. 192) that the figures in the background of the *Baptism* should be identified as dignitaries who had come to Italy in the retinue of John VIII Palaeologus. M. Aronberg Lavin's comprehensive study of the *Baptism*, (*Piero della Francesca's Baptism of Christ*, New Haven and London 1981) had not yet appeared when the present chapter was written.

4. Tanner ("Concordia", p. 20, n. 84) lists various other proposed datings, all of them rather later and thus difficult to reconcile with the iconographic allusions to the Council.

5. Ibid., p. 2.

6. Battisti, I, p. 117 (the surprising hermeneutic use that he makes, on pp. 117-18, of Pasolini's *Gospel According to St Matthew* would require separate discussion). Battisti suggests the second half of 1459 or 1460 as the date when work began on the painting (p. 113), and 1460-62 as the date of completion (II, p. 19). Both dates are obviously conjectural.

7. Settis, La 'Tempesta', p. 73.

8. The chain running from Leon Battista Alberti to St Thomas Aquinas is pursued further by Calvesi, who introduces passages from Gregory of Nazianzus and Marsilio Ficino on the basis of the allusion (of Calvesi's own discerning) of the three Graces to divine Grace. Thus he describes an emerging "free-trade metaphor whereby the three Graces represent the circulation of goods redounding to the benefit of its instigators ... The Christ-Sun, or Christ-Gold, numinous and numismatic, becomes a model of 'liberality', or even a prefiguring of liberalism; the entire logic of the capitalist economy, from 'interest' ... to consumerism ... is here already delineated in a strikingly coherent manner" (Calvesi, "Sistema", pp. 106 ff., esp. p. 108).

9. See the objections to this notion of "simultaneous layers of meaning" put by Gombrich in *Symbolic Images*, pp. 15-20.

10. On this point, see also C. Ginzburg and A. Prosperi, *Giochi di pazienza. Un seminario sul "Beneficio di Cristo"*, Turin 1975, p. 84.

11. See C. Ginzburg, "Da A. Warburg a E.H. Gombrich", art. esp. pp. 1054-6 (discussing an interpretation suggested by E. Wind).

12. E. Agnoletti, *La Madonna della Misericordia e il Battesimo di Cristo di Piero della Francesca*, Sansepolcro 1977, pp. 33-40. Don Agnoletti kindly drew my attention to this last point in a conversation.

13. ACS, s. XXXII, n. 182, cc. 33r-v (it is will no. 182). The will's content is repeated in brief in c. 129v, as well as in a loose sheet inserted in s. XXXII, n. 179. Certain codicils added on 1 November 1411 did not affect the bequest to the Abbey (cf. s. XXXII, n. 179, unnumbered papers). For a summary account of the documents deriving from the archive of the Confraternity of San Bartolomeo, see G. Degli Azzi, "Sansepolcro", in *Gli archivi della storia dell'Italia*, Rocca San Casciano 1915, s. II, vol. 4, pp. 139 ff. (there is a reference to Diosa's bequest on p. 148). On the confraternity, see I. Ricci, *La fraternita di S. Bartolomeo*, Sansepolcro 1936 (see pp. 22-3 for two extracts, imperfectly transcribed, from Diosa's will).

14. For Traversari, see especially the eighteenth-century edition of his correspondence (*Ambrosii Traversarii generalis Camaldulensium aliorumque ad ipsum, et ad alios de eodem Ambrosio latinae epistolae*, 2 vols, Florentiae, 1759; anastatic reprint, Bologna 1968). On the merits and demerits of this edition see the seminal researches of G. Mercati, *Ultimi contributi alla storia degli umanisti*, I, *Traversariana*, Vatican City 1939, with copious

unpublished documentation. On the part played by Traversari in the Council of Florence, see Gill, *The Council*, p. 287, and *passim*.

15. There is an eighteenth-century edition of the *Hodoeporicon* (Florentiae, n. d.), reprinted as an appendix to A. Dini Traversari, *Ambrogio Traversari e i suoi tempi*, Florence 1912; on his stays in Borgo San Sepolcro, three in all, see pp. 46, 53, 125 ff (of the appendix). A detailed account of Traversari's abbot-Generalship is given, on the basis of the correspondence and the *Hodoeporicon*, by G.B. Mitarelli and A. Costadoni, *Annales Camaldulenses*, VII, Ventiis 1762. On his interventions in the struggle with the Bishop of Città di Castello, cf. *Epistolae*, XVII, 5; V, 13; I, 4; II, 3; II, 24. For a brief chronicle of events, see E. Agnoletti, *Sansepolcro nel periodo degli abati (1012-1521)*, Sansepolcro 1976.

16. Mitarelli and Costadoni, *Annales Camaldulenses*, p. 203; "... instauratus antemuralis terrae nostrae per gyrum omnino totus, et propugnacula circum repatrata, et etiam denuo constructa; delubra Sanctorum intra muros miro ordine pulchificata; arces, aedesque publicae roburatae, instauratae, novatae, constructae ..."

17. Traversari sent him two letters, in 1431 and 1432, about the quarrels between the Abbey and the Bishop of Città di Castello: cf. *Epistolae*, l. XVIII, 5 and 6. The "Pascasius Burgensis" who contributed two epigrams to Piero di Nicolò da Filicaia's mathematical *Giuochi* is unfortunately a Minorite, not a Camaldolite (cf. BNCF, ms Magl. XI, 15, to which P.O. Kristeller draws attention in *Iter italicum*, Leiden-London 1965, I, p. 118). If Salmi ("*Piero della Francesca e Giuliano Amedei*", *L'arte*, XXIV [1942], pp. 26-44) is right in his suggestion that the Camaldolite abbot Giuliano Amedei collaborated in the Misericordia polyptych, this would testify to the persistence of the links between Piero and the Camaldolite order. On Amedei, see also J. Ruysschaert, "Miniaturistes 'romains' sous Pie II" in *Enea Silvio Piccolomini – papa Pio II* (Conference Proceedings), D. Maffei (ed.), Siena 1968, pp. 257 ff.

18. On the identification of the fortress in the background as Borgo San Sepolcro, see Longhi, *Piero*, p. 19. He is followed by Tanner, "Concordia", pp. 1 and 14, who sees (perhaps in an excess of interpretative zeal) in the Tiber flowing past Borgo an allusion to the supremacy of Rome.

II

The Arezzo Cycle

It has been suggested that while Piero was in Florence as a follower of Domenico Veneziano, he met Traversari[1]. To prove that meetings of this kind took place is hardly ever possible. There is evidence that Piero was in Florence in September 1439; in the summer of that year, the Council's deliberations being over, Traversari left the city to seek repose at the monastery of Camaldoli. On 19 October he died, unexpectedly, at Camaldoli[2]. Chronological difficulties apart, however, the Abbot-General of the Camaldolite Order, his time taken up with the business of the Council, would in any case hardly have come within the social ambit of a painter taking the first steps in his career. Nonetheless, Piero did come into contact with Traversari's circle, and this contact did not express itself only in the *Baptism*. For among that circle was a member of the Bacci family who were the patrons of Piero's greatest work — the Arezzo cycle of frescoes.

The Bacci in question was Giovanni, eldest son of Francesco and grandson of Baccio. The latter, an extremely wealthy spice merchant, made the original bequest for the decoration of the family chapel in the church of San Francesco; it was Francesco who decided to set the project in motion, selling a vineyard in 1447 to pay the painter originally entrusted with it, Bicci di Lorenzo[3]. Giovanni is a rather different figure. It was Creighton Gilbert who first drew attention to him. Gilbert, drawing upon the materials collected by the seventeenth-century scholar Gamurrini in his *Istoria genealogica delle famiglie nobili toscane et umbre*, noted that Giovanni, whose father and grandfather were merchants, graduated at Siena in 1439, and pursued a career in the Papal administration, becoming a clerk to the Camera Apostolica. This is the basis for suggesting that he played a decisive role (perhaps even putting forward theological ideas) in endowing the iconographic scheme of the Arezzo cycle with the innovations that distinguish it from traditional depictions of the Legend of the True Cross[4].

This trail — a very promising one, as we shall see — was almost immediately abandoned by Gilbert. However, further research into Giovanni Bacci yields additional, and invaluable, clues. The starting point for this further research is an allusion in a letter published by Gamurrini and remarked on by Gilbert. In this letter, written in 1449, Giovanni Bacci addresses himself to Cosimo de Medici, and refers to Giovanni Tortelli, a confidential attendant of the Pope, as "his relative"[5]. Following the path pointed out by Gilbert, and taking note also of M. Regoliosi's almost contemporaneous researches into Tortelli, who was a celebrated humanist, and into Bacci himself, we can at least sketch a portrait of the man whose impact on Piero was certainly decisive.

In the first evidence we have about him, Giovanni Bacci's name is closely linked with that of Traversari. It was Traversari, in fact, who in 1432 mentioned a young man whom he calls "Giovanni Aretino" (that is, Giovanni of Arezzo) in a letter to his brother Girolamo, newly appointed Provost of the Lemmo hospital at Florence. Traversari recommends this young man to his brother, mentioning that he has been on the closest terms with him at Rome. Regoliosi rightly suggests that this "Giovanni Aretino" (who at the time cannot have been much older than twenty) is Giovanni Bacci, rather than the much better-known Giovanni Tortelli, who also came from Arezzo[6]. This would seem to be the same Giovanni Aretino whom Traversari, while at Ferrara in 1439 for the Council, again recommended, this time to Daniele Scotto, Bishop of Concordia and Governor of Bologna. In this latter case, we can be sure Bacci is meant, for in the course of praising his character and his passion for learning Traversari says that he is a clerk to the Camera Apostolica. Bacci was probably appointed to this post during the preceding year; he certainly owed the appointment to the support of the Medici, with whom he was closely connected all his life[7]. The position was important, and well-paid: in 1438, Pope Eugenius IV had determined that there should be seven clerks to the Camera Apostolica, explicitly justifying this limited number on the grounds that each clerk would have the prospect of a reasonable income[8].

By this time, Giovanni Bacci was already well established in humanist circles. Writing from Bologna in 1437, Lapo da Castiglionchio the Younger recommends him in glowing terms to the Bishop of Arezzo, Roberto degli Asini[9]. A year later, the Aretine humanist Carlo Marsuppini writes to congratulate him on his recent appointment as a clerk to the Camera, promising (in response, clearly, to his specific request) to send him a codex of Plato's *Symposium* which had formerly belonged to Niccolò Niccoli, and which had been transcribed by a collaborator of Traversari, the monk Michael[10]. It was at this period that Giovanni was joined at Bologna by Tortelli. We do not know quite how these two were related: both families, the Tortelli and the Bacci, certainly came from Capolona, a village not far from Arezzo[11]. Tortelli had just returned from a long voyage in Greece and the Orient, where he had been transcribing codices and epigraphs, collecting material later used in his most important work, the great treatise on Latin orthography, presented in the form of a dictionary (*De Orthographia*), which was to achieve notable success[12]. At Constantinople he had become acquainted with important figures such as Isidore of Kiev (the future Ruthenian Cardinal) who favoured religious union with Rome; he had then returned to Rome with the Greek delegation sent to the Council of Basel to discuss the reconciliation of the two Churches.

In 1439, Tortelli left Bologna for Florence. The Council — in which his patron, Cardinal Cesarini, was playing a prominent role — moved there at the same time. Bacci, who took his degree in law at Siena this same year,[13] may have followed him. We know that Giovanni Bacci was in Florence in October 1439, for he is mentioned in a letter to Leonardo Bruni from Girolamo Aliotti, a native of Arezzo and the Prior of the Benedictine monastery of St. Fiora and St. Lucilla (Bacci's devotion to Bruni is emphasized in this letter). Shortly afterwards, this same Aliotti wrote to Bacci from France, where he had been sent as Papal legate, asking for news of the relatives he had left in Arezzo and sending greetings to their common friends at Florence. These friends were Poggio Bracciolini, Carlo Aretino (this is Marsuppini, whom we have already come across, and who had succeeded Leonardo Bruni a few years earlier in the office of Chancellor to the

Florentine *Signoria*), and Leon Battista Alberti. In connection with Alberti, Aliotti recalls "this matter regarding Ambrogio", about which, he says, he has written to Bacci *ad nauseam*.[14] This is a reference to the project, very dear to Aliotti, of compiling a life of Traversari. After having spoken of it to Marsuppini, he referred the idea to Alberti, declaring that the theme offered great possibilities and was fully worthy of his high talents.[15] However, neither Marsuppini nor Alberti wrote a life of Traversari: this, perhaps, was one reason why Aliotti, when he came to write his dialogue *De erudiendis monachis* (completed in 1442), gave a very prominent place among the interlocutors to "Ambrogio the Camaldolite, that incomparable phoenix of our age", as he wrote in the book's dedication to Pope Eugenius IV.[16]

The greatest weight must be given to this documentary proof that Giovanni Bacci, who was to commission work from Piero at Arezzo, was friendly with some of the most illustrious figures of Tuscan humanism (and Bruni's name, as we have said, must be added to those just mentioned).[17] Hitherto, our only certain evidence of any link between Piero and this milieu was the known fact that he stayed at the same time as Alberti in the court of Rimini in 1451, and again in the court of Pius II Piccolomini in 1458-9. It is now possible to reconstruct more fully and more concretely how Piero, through Bacci and his circle, may have assimilated, and developed along new and original lines, certain elements of humanistic culture.

Bacci figures as one of a veritable clan of Aretine humanists. Besides Bacci himself, there were Tortelli, Aliotti and Marsuppini; and less central, because they belonged to a different generation, were such weighty persons as Leonardo Bruni and Poggio (who was not from Arezzo, but from the nearby Valdarno region). In this context, it is also noteworthy that the Alberti family (related, how we do not know, to the Bacci) came from Catenaia, in the Valdarno.[18] We glimpse, here, a solidarity that was geographical as well as generational and cultural. This operated, and reinforced itself, in a dense network of mutual favours and reciprocal recommendations (which are notoriously frequent in the correspondence of the humanists). Bonds of practical help and support often derived from bonds of kinship, whether of the flesh (Bacci was a relative of Tortelli) or of the spirit (Tortelli was Marsuppini's godfather).[19]

These links were further strengthened by common cultural and religious interests. On the one hand, there was the passion for the classical world, and more especially for ancient Greece, which found expression in Tortelli's voyage or in Marsuppini's translations of the *Iliad* and of *The Battle of the Frogs and the Mice*; on the other, a desire to bind together again the cords severed in the schism with the Eastern Churches. These themes were harmoniously fused in the character of Traversari, with whom the Arezzo group were all linked, directly or indirectly.

But they are also the themes of Piero's work.[20] His iconographic and stylistic choices continued, right into his maturity, to draw upon a double image of Greece, classical and modern. The uncorrupted forms of a classicism which (to our eyes anyway) appears much more Greek than Roman gave him, more than once, the means to express a political and religious call for the reconquest of Greece and of the once Christian Orient. By tracing the links between these iconographic and stylistic choices and the social network[21] in which they took form, we shall avoid both unverifiable iconological interpretations and ahistorical invocations of "those visual springs which flow forever underground".[22]

We last heard of Tortelli in Florence, together, probably, with Bacci. At this point, their lives took different courses. In 1445, Aliotti recommended Tortelli to the humanist Guarino Veronese.[23] The recommendation evidently bore fruit, for we hear soon afterwards, in a letter from Aliotti to someone identified only as Michelangelo di Borgo San Sepolcro, that Tortelli is likely to obtain a post in the Curia.[24] When Niccolò Parentucelli (Nicholas V), a great protector of the humanists, became pope, Tortelli's career in the Curia began: he was appointed a privy servant and made one of the custodians of the Vatican library, then in process of being formed.[25] We possess no certain record, on the other hand, of Bacci's movements during these years.[26] We know only that at some point he fell into disgrace and was dismissed from the Camera Apostolica. On 6 June 1447, he wrote to Giovanni di Cosimo de Medici, from Arezzo. His letter is full of lamentations and pleas for help: "All my hope is set on your noble father and on you, his son ... My Giovanni, consult with master Alesso as to how you may remove me from here and give me employment in some place where I may be of some good to you. I beg you, come what may, to answer me at once, for things could not be worse with me here and I do not know how I shall stay here any longer. To tell you further how things are, I must say that I have not a very good understanding with my father, for he did not wish me to have worked always against the Patriarch, by whose doing I am now unjustly dismissed".[27] This Patriarch, who had brought Bacci's career in the Curia to an abrupt halt, was Ludovico Trevisano, the Patriarch of Aquileia, subsequently Archbishop of Florence and (from 1440) *condottiere* of the Papal army and Cardinal of S. Lorenzo in Damaso. As Cardinal Camerlingo (Treasurer of the Papal court), he was Bacci's immediate superior — and thus well placed to hound him out.[28] Political differences may have contributed to the antagonism between the two men. In 1440, Cardinal Ludovico, together with the troops of the Medici and Francesco Sforza's men, had defeated the Florentine exiles and Niccolò Piccinino at Anghiari. Two years later, these alliances were reversed: in an (unsuccessful) attempt to conquer the Marca, Cardinal Ludovico found himself fighting alongside Piccinino, who had been appointed standard-bearer to the Papal States, against Sforza, now allied with the Medici.[29] Perhaps Giovanni Bacci's devotion to the cause of the Medici helped draw down the wrath of the extremely powerful Cardinal Camerlingo. The clash between the two men must in any case have been memorable. Some years later, in 1449, Marsuppini implored Tortelli to use all his authority with the Pope in Bacci's favour, exclaiming: "If he has gone astray in the tumult of his anger and passion, as can happen even to the wisest amongst us, it is not right that he should on that account pass his whole life in humiliation — especially now that we may hope he has mended his ways[30]."

4 Moreover, if Bacci was quick to anger, Cardinal Ludovico was no mouse either, to judge from Mantegna's portrait of him.

Thanks to Marsuppini's insistence and to the prestige that Tortelli enjoyed with the Pope, Giovanni Bacci managed to obtain a pardon. On 28 September 1449, he wrote from Arezzo the letter cited above to Cosimo de Medici, telling him that he had gone to

Fabriano, where the Papal court had removed to escape the plague at Rome. Through Cardinal Colonna's good offices, he had met with Cardinal Ludovico, and had put right the "scandals" of the past. He at once repaid the favours he had received, recommending Marsuppini ("an intimate of mine") to Cosimo on behalf of Tortelli ("a relative of mine"). He then turned to the latest political news: at Fabriano, he had read a letter in which Sigismondo Malatesta showed himself unduly keen to justify the recent capture of Cremona by the Venetians. "Knowing signor Malatesta as I do," he remarks at this point:[31] and this evidence of Bacci's closeness to Malatesta at that time (1449) has, in the context, an obvious importance. For two years later, Piero was to paint the portrait of Malatesta for the Tempio Malatestiano. It is more than probable that none other than Giovanni Bacci introduced Piero to the court of Rimini. During this period, Bacci (who may have resumed a lay status) had begun a career, benefiting probably from the support of the Medici, in the courts of northern central Italy — a career much less brilliant than the one he had embarked on in the Curia, but which did at least allow him to get away from the detested Arezzo. His links with the Malatesta family continued for many years: in 1461, he obtained from Malatesta Novello the office of *podestà* at Cesena[32].

The hypothesis that Giovanni Bacci may have made use of his own personal connections to get patrons for Piero presupposes that the two men were already acquainted at this time. For the moment, we have no proof that this was so. Still, it is worth noting that Sigismondo Malatesta is not the only example of a connection of Giovanni Bacci's who can be shown to have commissioned work from Piero. Writing from Arezzo to Giovanni di Cosimo de Medici in 1461, Bacci declared: "Giovanni, it seems to me that nature has made two gentlemen who resemble one another in many respects: Duke Borso and the Signore Federico, who are in their manner of life wiser and more refined than any other gentlemen of Italy". The names of the same two men, here implicitly praised also for their Maecenas-like qualities as patrons of the arts ("refined in their manner of life": Bacci writes "artificiosissimi nel vivere"), reappear a decade later in a letter dated 1472 to Lorenzo de Medici, where they are mentioned alongside Battista Cannedoli, Malatesta Baglioni and Francesco Sforza: to all these people, declares Bacci, he is "very dear"[33]. Vasari tells us that Piero had first begun work at Ferrara while Borso ruled there, and although doubt was for long cast upon this claim, Gilbert has recently shown it to be well-founded[34]. As for Fedrico de Montefeltro, it is almost certain, as we shall see, that his connection with Piero did indeed begin through Giovanni Bacci.

All this also allows us to offer a plausible explanation of how Piero came to be entrusted with the painting of the frescoes in the Chapel of San Francesco in Arezzo. These, as we have said, were begun no later than 1447 by Bicci di Lorenzo, and it is certain that Bicci was commissioned by Francesco Bacci, who thus fulfilled the terms of his father Baccio's will. Bicci, old and unwell, managed to paint no more than the vault and part of the entrance arch, doing so in his habitual old-fashioned manner; in 1452, aged almost eighty, he died. Why the work's continuation should have been entrusted to a painter such as Piero, barely thirty at the time and a follower of the most modern pictorial style, it is hard to understand — unless Francesco employed Piero on the advice of his

5-14

eldest son, Giovanni, who had returned to Arezzo after two years in Milan, where he had held the office of "iudex maleficiorum" in the court of Francesco Sforza[35]. Then, the great difference between the vault and the walls of the chapel would be readily explained by the generational and cultural gap separating Bacci from his son Giovanni, who had received a humanistic education, and had enjoyed the protection of Traversari and the friendship of Leonardo Bruni and of Alberti.

When Piero obtained the commission for the Arezzo frescoes we do not know. The chronology of the Arezzo cycle, Piero's greatest work, poses problems still unresolved today. The only sure date is a *terminus ante quem*: in 1466, the cycle is referred to as completed[36]. The *terminus post quem*, on the other hand, is less certain: 1452 is the likely date, although we cannot rule out the possibility that Piero took over the work a little earlier from Bicci, who was seriously ill by then.

Fourteen years is a long time, even for a painter who habitually worked at a slow pace[37]. Repeated efforts have accordingly been made to narrow the span of Piero's activity at Arezzo. Given the usual plentiful lack of evidence, the preferred approach has been by way of internal, stylistic or (more rarely) iconological analysis: the results have been predictably varied. Let us consider some of the more widely debated theories.

Longhi's datings are based solely on stylistic criteria. He makes use of the Rimini fresco, whose date (1451) we know, as a kind of fossil guidebook for the reconstruction of the entire series. The clue that he follows is the initial presence, and progressive attenuation, of "graphisms" (*grafismi*) of Florentine origin of the kind met at Rimini. This is the foundation of his internal chronology, according to which the cycle begins with the

5, 14, two lunettes (the *Death of Adam* and the *Exaltation of the Cross*) and ends with the *Defeat of*
13 *Chosroes*. To be more precise, Longhi sees the left-hand part of the *Defeat* — one of the few parts of this fresco that is undoubtedly Piero's own work — as marking the end of his activity in the chapel of San Francesco. As we move downwards from the top, "evidence of linear borders of Florentine stamp" (as Longhi again stated in 1950) gives way to an ever more chromatic technique[38].

Longhi invoked this criterion of stylistic development in order to establish the chronological place of undated works such as the Monterchi *Madonna del Parto* (*Madonna in Childbirth*), the San Sepolcro *Resurrection*, and the *St Mary Magdalen* in the cathedral at Arezzo: the first two works he dates respectively to the beginning and to the culmination (or thereabouts) of the Arezzo cycle, the last to the period immediately after its comple-
15 tion[39]. The *St. Luke the Evangelist* at Santa Maria Maggiore, in Rome, poses a more complex problem. Longhi identifies it as the sole surviving work from Piero's activity at Rome, and suggests two alternative dates for it: either 1455, during a break in work on the Arezzo cycle, or else 1459. This uncertainty arises from Vasari's mentioning but one occasion when Piero was in Rome, during the Pontificate of Nicholas V — that is, between 1447 and 1455; whereas we have firm evidence only for his having stayed there in 1459, when Pius II was Pope[40]. This gives two possibilities: either Vasari confused Nicholas V and Pius II, as we might infer from his further claim that Piero left Rome to return to San Sepolcro "on the death of his mother", Romana, who died on 6 November 1459[41]; or else he is referring to a first stay, of which there is no documentary evidence (as there is of the second).

Now Longhi argues that Piero took over from Bicci immediately on the latter's death, in 1452; and that he had "substantially" completed the cycle *before* his stay in Rome of 1459. At the same time, he draws a stylistic parallel between the *St Luke* and the *early* phase of the Arezzo frescoes, and especially those of the second tier (*Solomon Receiving the Queen of Sheba* and the *Discovery and Proof of the Cross*).[42] All this ·7, 12 necessarily leads us to rule out the possibility that *St Luke the Evangelist* can have been painted in 1459 — unless, of course, we reconsider either its place in Piero's stylistic development, or the cycle's initial and final dates. However, Longhi does not commit himself unequivocally to the view that the *St Luke* was painted during Piero's hypothetical stay in Rome at the court of Nicholas V: these "chronological niceties", he says, are beside the point given the difficulty of establishing precise *ad annum* dates for the "development which took place during the Arezzo fresco cycle"[43]. In truth, though, this is a matter, not of "niceties", but of whether the various hypotheses advanced are or are not consistent with each other. It is significant that Longhi waits until this moment to warn us how hard it is to translate the relative chronology, so painstakingly reconstructed on stylistic grounds, into an absolute and, so to speak, calendar chronology — significant, that is, that he utters the warning when confronted with a work like the *St Luke* which, being situated in Rome rather than in Arezzo or its environs, provides more scope for research into validating documentary evidence of a more or less reliable kind. At this point, moreover, we are entitled to ask what basis there is for the absolute dates (1452 — *ante* 1459) between which Longhi believes Piero's activity at Arezzo must be confined. These are certainly not derived from the internal stylistic progression made out in the cycle. The Rimini fresco, dated 1451, does indeed give us an unquestioned *post quem*; but nobody can say how fast Piero's style was evolving during these years. Nor can we invoke any of the works identified by Longhi as contemporaneous with the Arezzo cycle, for none of them — not the *Madonna del Parto*, nor the *Resurrection*, nor any of the others — is dated.

Clark suggests an altogether different dating, both relative and absolute. Let us begin with the relative dating. According to Longhi's internal chronology, the two lunettes, and then the various tiers below them, are each to be seen as almost synchronous strata; which implies that Piero must have worked on a single scaffold, occupying the entire chapel. Clark, on the other hand, seems to hypothesize the existence of two scaffolds and two distinct phases of work, the first carried out by Piero himself and the second done largely by his assistants: this hypothesis is based on the fact that (as Longhi had already noted) the frescoes on the right-hand wall show almost no sign of the assistants' participation, which is clearly evident, by contrast, in almost all those on the left-hand wall[44]. It must certainly be rejected — first of all, because it seems unlikely that two scaffolds would have been built, since this would have been more expensive and less safe, and second because the greater participation of the assistants on the chapel's left-hand wall can be far more simply explained by the assumption that Piero himself was working at the same time, virtually unaided, on the right-hand wall. Thus while Piero was painting the *Death of Adam* and the right-hand prophet (both universally recognized as his ·5 own work), the assistants were completing a considerable part of the *Exaltation of the* ·14 *Cross* and the whole of the left-hand prophet; and so forth. (This does not, of course, imply that Piero had no hand in the frescoes on the left-hand side: in the *Defeat of Chosroes*, he himself clearly did a small part of the work, as he did a large part of it in the *Discovery and Proof of the Cross*. Piero's almost unaided completion of this latter painting is balanced by the fact that on this same tier, each of the small paintings that flank the window was entrusted to his assistants[45].) In addition to all this, we must take note of the stylistic points convincingly adumbrated by Longhi, which tend to rule out the chronological succession proposed by Clark.

13, 12

As we have said, this proposed succession implies a break in the work between the right-hand wall's completion and the commencement of the left-hand wall. According to Clark — and here we enter the domain of absolute or calendar chronology — this break corresponds with Piero's stay in Rome of 1458-9. Piero, Clark argues, having begun work in Arezzo straight after Bicci di Lorenzo died (in 1452), broke off to go to Rome on the completion of the *Triumph of Constantine*. In 1459, he recommenced his labours (entrusting to his assistants, however, most of the execution of the left-hand wall), and he completed them around 1466. The key-stone of this chronological edifice is the *Triumph of Constantine*, which Clark holds to have been painted in 1458 on account of its links with Paolo Uccello's *Battle of San Romano*, painted *circa* 1458[46]. This, plainly, is a very fragile prop; its dating is controversial; at the most, it may provide us with a *terminus post quem*, being insufficient for any *ad annum* dating. This is not to deny that the hypothesis prompts Clark to make some important iconographic observations, to which we return below.

10

Battisti endorses Longhi's reconstruction of the internal chronology, and explicitly argues, against Clark, that there was only one scaffold. But whereas Longhi held that the cycle was completed before Piero went to Rome, Battisti believes that it was begun only on his return, in about 1463. He offers various reasons for this shifting forward of the cycle's absolute chronology. Let us consider the most important (with one exception, to which we return below). When, in 1473 and in 1486, Piero claimed the payment owed him for the Arezzo cycle, his suit was against various members of the Bacci family, but not the heirs of Francesco. According to Battisti, this proves that neither Francesco's name nor those of his sons figured in the lost contract, and this in its turn is supposed to show that "in all probability" Francesco was at this time "either ill in some way or else absent" or dead; and, since he was buried on 28 March 1459, we are to deduce that the contract was signed only after Piero's return from Rome.[47] This train of conjectures is patently illogical; Piero, moreover, may have brought no suit against Francesco's heirs for the simple reason that they had already paid their appointed share of the costs of decorating the family chapel. Equally baseless is Battisti's attempt to deduce that Piero cannot have made a long stay in Arezzo in the years before 1458, because we have no record of his having empowered his brother Marco to act on his behalf as he did before going to Rome: Battisti himself is the first to acknowledge that "Arezzo is very close to San Sepolcro", which means that Piero would have been well able to manage his own affairs even while busy working on the San Francesco chapel. As Battisti recognizes, the other reasons that might persuade us to post-date the beginning of the cycle until after Piero's return from Rome are (in his own words) "largely hypothetical"; what is more, they are largely inconsistent, or entirely beside the point.

The only consideration that appears at first to have some weight is that the *Death of Adam* contains conspicuous classical echoes. However, even this need not presuppose that Piero had visited Rome. Copies of Scopa's *Pothos*, for example, echoed in the figure of the naked youth leaning on a stick, were equally to be found in Florence[48]. It is worth remarking here that Battisti bases his late dating of the *Baptism* (he puts it at around 1460, whereas it actually dates from some fifteen years earlier) on the same absurd grounds, namely the claim that Piero can have encountered classical sculpture only during his stay in Rome of 1458-9, and not by way of artefacts such as sarcophagi or jewellery, which would have been available, in copies or even in the original, elsewhere[49].

Gilbert, writing at almost the same time as Battisti, has put forward a different chronology, fusing Clark's relative dating and Longhi's absolute dating. In the former, Gilbert distinguishes three successive stylistic phases. 1) The lunettes (the *Death of Adam* and the *Exaltation of the Cross*); the two prophets flanking the window; and the *Burying of the Wood* (which, as we shall see, should properly be called the *Raising of the Wood*), on the right of the large window opposite the entrance. In these frescoes, the outlines are more marked, the gestures are more dramatic (as in the upper, and earliest, part of the Misericordia altarpiece at San Sepolcro), the figures are given greater physiognomical individuality (as in the profile of the aged and feeble Eve), and perspective is rarely employed. 2) The two middle tiers (the *Queen of Sheba and her Retinue* and *Solomon receiving the Queen of Sheba* on the left; on the right, the *Discovery and Proof of the Cross*) and the *Torture of the Jew* to the left of the window. Here apparent for the first time are the features later generally associated with Piero's painting: the impassive aspect of the figures, the solemnity of composition, the complex perspective enhanced by the presence of buildings. 3) The *Annunciation* and the *Dream of Constantine*, as well as the lower tier on either side (the *Triumph of Constantine* and the *Defeat of Chosroes*). Already manifest here, according to Gilbert, is a dominant interest — conceived under the influence of the Flemish school — in rendering the effects of light.

This reconstruction offers little that is new compared with Longhi's, although Gilbert does place more emphasis on the emergence of a distinct stylistic phase (the third) towards the cycle's end, and sees a wider divergence between the middle tiers and the preceding ones (that is, between the second and the first phase). Much more important is his proposal that this divergence is traceable to Piero's journey to Rome of 1458-9. According to Gilbert, the great prominence given to architectural forms in the *Solomon* and the *Discovery* is the fruit of Piero's encounter with Alberti, and with the whole circle of Pius II's court[50]. His stay in Rome would thus have divided his work at Arezzo into two periods, as already hypothesized by Clark; but Gilbert follows Longhi, and differs from Clark, in supposing there to have been a single scaffold, such as would have allowed Piero and his assistants to recommence their interrupted labours simultaneously on both sides of the chapel.

In arriving at a date for the beginning and end of the cycle of the True Cross, Gilbert has recourse, by contrast, to the altarpiece that Piero painted for the Augustinian friars at San Sepolcro during approximately the same period (between 1455, the date of the contract, and 1469, the date of the final payment). Here, once again, we cannot be certain when the work was actually carried out. But Gilbert does point out a likely *post quem* for the St Augustine polyptych: the spring of 1455. For the contract dates from October 1454, and in January 1455 Piero was away from San Sepolcro, as can be inferred from the fact that the Confraternity of the Misericordia of that town sent for him, requesting him to come and carry out some further work on the polyptych commissioned from him ten years earlier[51]. Now the *Saint* in the Frick collection — universally recognized, because of its style, as the earliest surviving panel of the St Augustine polyptych (the central panel is lost) — is supposed by Gilbert to date from the same time as the first phase of the Arezzo cycle (the lunettes). One would accordingly expect him to propose a later dating for these lunettes, taking 1455 as a *terminus post quem*. However, Gilbert rather inconsequentially follows Clark in supposing Piero to have begun work in Arezzo around 1452, finishing about fifteen years later[52].

We have seen that there is very general agreement with the internal chronology proposed by Longhi (Clark's being the most important of the few dissenting voices), whereas on the question of when the cycle was begun and completed in calandar terms there are the widest differences of scholarly opinion. The differences involve only a few years — seven, eight, at the most a decade — but they are decisive years. Depending on whether we suppose that Piero's major work was completed *before* his journey to Rome and his stay at Pius II's court (as does Longhi), *after* it (as does Battisti), or *both before and after* (as do Clark and Gilbert), we shall be led to offer widely

2   different reconstructions of Piero's development as a painter. We propose to examine the question afresh, following the path already taken with the *Baptism*, and combining an analysis of iconography with an analysis of commissioning.

We do not know when the iconographic scheme of the Arezzo cycle was worked out. That is, we do not know whether Bicci di Lorenzo had already contracted to take as his theme the Legend of the True Cross, which Piero thus took over together with his commission, or whether (but this is a far less likely hypothesis) the scheme was fixed only with the change of artist. Even Longhi, inclined as he was to ignore questions of iconography, came to attach "great weight" to the resolution of this question[53]. It does indeed seem at first sight something of a paradox that a modern painter such as Piero, imbued with humanistic culture, should have turned his hand to a fresco-cycle on a legendary theme, in part handed down in the apocrypha and later elaborated by Jacopo da Varazze in his *Golden Legend*.[54] To soften this paradox, Longhi remarked that if we accept the hypothesis that Piero found himself working on an already pre-determined theme, he undeniably reinterpreted it, transforming the sacred narrative into "an epic of lay, profane life": scenes of work and of court life, battles that resemble tournaments, landscapes by day and by night[55].

In assessing the likelihood that Piero (or his patrons) reinterpreted its iconography, we must first of all note that the Legend of the Holy Cross was a traditional theme, generally (though not exclusively) associated with the Franciscan order. This strengthens the hypothesis that it was the Franciscans of Arezzo themselves who suggested to the Bacci that the legend would make an appropriate subject for the walls of the principal chapel, at the time when Bicci was originally commissioned to do the work. Of the three

fresco cycles on the legend that predate (admittedly by some decades) the Arezzo frescoes, two had been painted for churches of the Franciscan order, Santa Croce at Florence
(by Agnolo Gaddi, 1388-93) and San Francesco at Volterra (by Cenni di Francesco, *circa*
1410). Agnolo Gaddi's frescoes, in particular (and their iconography was imitated by
Cenni at Volterra), were studied very closely by Piero[56]. Before comparing the two
cycles, however, it will be as well to outline the legend as retold by Jacopo da Varazze in
his *Legenda Aurea* — this being the version drawn upon both by Agnolo and, sixty years
later, by Piero.

Adam, at the point of death, recalls that the Archangel Michael had promised him
a miraculous oil which would save his life. His son, Seth, is sent to the gates of Paradise to
fetch the oil, but the angel gives him instead a branch, from which the oil of salvation
will flow — but only after five thousand five hundred years have elapsed. Seth returns to
his father, but finds him dead, whereupon he plants the branch on his grave. From it, a
tree springs up, which Solomon tries to use in the building of the Temple. But he is
unable to do so, for whenever the wood is cut it turns out to be either too large or too
small. The tree is then lifted out of the ground and thrown across the river Shiloh as a
bridge. The Queen of Sheba, on her way to visit Solomon, sees the wood and has a
premonition. Instead of walking across it, she kneels before it in veneration. From this
wood, she prophetically tells Solomon, will come the end of the reign of the Jews.
Solomon, to thwart this prophecy, has the wood submerged in a sheep-pond; but it
returns to the surface, and is used to build the Cross upon which Christ is crucified.
Three hundred years later, on the eve of his battle against Maxentius at the Milvian
Bridge, Constantine sees a vision: an angel appears to him and exhorts him to fight under
the sign of the Cross. Constantine does as he is bade, wins the victory, and becomes
Emperor of Rome. Converted to Christianity, he sends his mother, Helena, to Jerusalem in search of the wood of the True Cross. Only a Jew by the name of Judas knows its
whereabouts, and he refuses to speak. The Empress Helena thereupon has him thrown
into a well. When he is brought out seven days later, Judas reveals that the Cross is
buried beneath a temple dedicated to Venus. The temple is destroyed on Helena's orders,
and the three crosses of Calvary are brought to light. The True Cross is recognized when
a dead youth is restored to life by touching it. Helena brings the relic back to Jerusalem.

Three centuries later, the Cross is stolen by Chosroes, King of Persia, who places it
upon an altar decorated with idolatrous images and has himself worshipped as God.
Heraclius, the Eastern Emperor, makes war on Chosroes, defeats him, and has him
beheaded. He returns to Jerusalem with great pomp, but finds the city gates miraculously blocked against him. Only when he obeys the exhortations of an angel and decides
to imitate Christ's humble entry into Jerusalem do the gates open. Thus the relics of the
Cross are returned to the Holy Sepulchre.

Jacopo da Varazze arranges all this narrative under two headings, which correspond to two dates in the liturgical calendar: the discovery of the True Cross (3 May), and
the exaltation of the True Cross (14 September). Under the first, we find the part of the
legend that runs from the death of Adam to the Empress Helena's entry into Jerusalem
with the rediscovered relic. Under the second, the concluding part is given — the theft of
the Cross by Chosroes and its return to Jerusalem by Heraclius.

16-23   In the chapel of Santa Croce, Agnolo Gaddi had depicted eight stages of the legend, in six panels and two lunettes. The story begins with the lunette high up on the right (for a spectator facing away from the altar), and is to be followed downwards from there; it is taken up again in the left-hand lunette, at the top, and finishes with the lowest panel on the left. The following stages of the story are shown:

1)   the *Death of Adam*
2)   the *Queen of Sheba Kneeling before the Wood of the True Cross*
3)   the *Making of the Cross*
4)   the *Proof of the Three Crosses by the Empress Helena*
5)   the *Empress Helena taking the Cross to Jerusalem*
6)   *Chosroes Taking the Cross from Jerusalem*
7)   *Chosroes worshipped by his Subjects*. The *Dream of Heraclius*
8)   the *Beheading of Chosroes. Heraclius takes the True Cross back to Jerusalem.*

The Santa Croce cycle, which includes both the discovery and the exaltation of the Cross, follows the text of the *Legenda Aurea* faithfully in all respects but one: the angel appears not to Constantine but to Heraclius. Nor can there be any doubt that the figure in question is Heraclius[57], given the presence of Chosroes in the picture itself and in the one that follows.

       Let us now turn to the Arezzo cycle. Here, the Legend of the True Cross is depicted in ten paintings: more precisely, four large panels, four small ones, and two lunettes. There are also the figures of two unidentified prophets. The whole is laid out along the two side walls and on the two sections of the end wall that flank the chapel window. The following scenes are represented:

1)   the *Death of Adam*
2)   the *Raising of the Wood* (usually, and mistakenly, called the "Burying of the Wood")
3)   the *Queen of Sheba and her Retinue* (which shows the Queen kneeling before the wood) and *Solomon Receiving the Queen of Sheba*
4)   the *Annunciation*
5)   the *Dream of Constantine*
6)   the *Triumph of Constantine*
7)   the *Torture of the Jew*
8)   the *Discovery and Proof of the Cross*
9)   the *Defeat of Chosroes*

5-14   10) the *Exaltation of the Cross* (which depicts its return to Jerusalem by Heraclius).

       These scenes, listed here in their narrative order, are spatially arranged thus:

10	prophet		prophet	1
8	7		2	3
9	4		5	6

This means that (leaving out the figures of the two prophets) the story begins with the lunette high up on the right, and finishes with the one high up on the left. Along the side walls, the scenes follow each other from top down (on the right-hand wall) and from the bottom up (on the left-hand wall). Each larger panel is preceded by a smaller painting on the section of the wall that flanks the window; this is on the left in the case of the right-hand wall, on the right in the case of the left-hand wall. The beholder's eye is thus drawn along a double trajectory: from top to bottom and from left to right (on the right-hand wall), and from bottom to top and from right to left (on the left-hand wall).

The undeniable coherence of this ordering justifies us in regarding the so-called *Rimozione del ponte* (*Removal of the Bridge*: usually known in English by the equally mis-   6
leading titles of the *Burying of the Wood*, or the *Queen of Sheba's Prophecy*) as a depiction, rather, of the *Raising of the Wood of the Cross* and its carrying to the river Shiloh, which in the legend comes immediately before the arrival of the Queen of Sheba. None the less, there remain two striking anomalies, situated side-by-side, which visibly impair the narrative succession: the *Annunciation* and the *Defeat of Chosroes*. The reasons for this   8, 13
double alteration must lie (though we cannot clearly understand them) in Piero's gradual departure from the cycle's traditional iconography.[58]

If we consider the earliest part of Piero's work at Arezzo — the lunettes — we see that they do indeed depict the two scenes corresponding, though the spatial arrangement is different, to the beginning and the end of the legend as depicted in Agnolo Gaddi's Santa Croce frescoes: the *Death of Adam* and the *Exaltation of the Cross*. Leaving aside the   5, 14
obvious stylistic differences between the two cycles, which are not our present concern, we can make out in both cases one and the same iconographic scheme: the scheme, probably, which the Franciscans of Arezzo, with Francesco Bacci's agreement, suggested to Bicci di Lorenzo. Piero evidently began by following this scheme, though he would no doubt have kept the option of introducing minor variations. However, from the middle tier of the Arezzo cycle onwards we find iconographical novelties appearing, and these endow the entire cycle with implications quite different from those it originally pos- sessed. We do not refer here to the scenes of everyday life depicted in two of the smaller panels at the side of the window (the *Torture of the Jew* and the *Raising of the Wood*): these   11, 6
can be seen simply as digressions in the narrative. We have in mind the following features, which indicate a decisive alteration in the iconographic scheme:

1)   the scene of *Solomon Receiving the Queen of Sheba*   7
2)   the transformation of Agnolo Gaddi's *Dream of Heraclius* into the *Dream of Constan-*   22, 9
    tine — a transformation whose significance is enhanced by the evident analogy between the two compositions
3)   the scene showing the *Triumph of Constantine* over Maxentius   10
4)   the depiction, in the *Triumph*, of Constantine with the features of John VIII Palaeo-   1
    logus, the Eastern Emperor.

In all these cases — with the obvious exception of the last — the changes are justified by the text of the *Legenda Aurea*. However, we shall see that their insertion does not appear to derive from any wish of Piero's to abide by the story as told by Jacopo da Varazze.

The depiction of the meeting between Solomon and the Queen of Sheba is a quite

unexpected element in the pictorial narrative of the Legend of the True Cross. It was
often found on Tuscan marriage-chests of the time[59], and Piero would seem to have
echoed these in planning his composition, recasting their almost Gothic richness within
strictly defined volumetric and spatial dimensions[60]. L. Schneider[61], however, has identified a true iconographic forerunner of the Arezzo cycle in the panel on the same subject
sculpted by Ghiberti, in 1436 or 1437, for the east doorway of the Baptistry in Florence.
This has been interpreted by Krautheimer as alluding to the hope that unity could be
restored between the Christian Churches of the West (Solomon) and the East (Sheba): he
has suggested, convincingly, that the theme may have been proposed to Ghiberti by
Ambrogio Traversari, whose portrait appears among the bystanders[62]. The same interpretation, argues Schneider, holds good for Piero's fresco. We must note, however, that
the situation had been gradually changing during the two decades or so that had intervened. As a result, the allusions perceptible in the scene also changed. When the public
first saw Ghiberti's doorway, in 1452, the panel could be understood as a reinvocation of
the religious union achieved at the Council of Florence, which had then quickly dis-
solved. The meeting between Solomon and the Queen of Sheba bore a new meaning
when it figured on the walls of the Arezzo chapel, for Constantinople had fallen to the
Turks (in 1453), and the theme of religious union with the Eastern Church was henceforth linked inextricably with the theme of the Crusade against the infidel.

Let us now turn to Constantine. Whereas he does not appear in Agnolo's Santa
Croce cycle (unlike his mother, the Empress Helena), in the Arezzo cycle two pictures
are devoted to him: the *Dream* and the *Triumph*. The fact that he also painted this second
picture makes it clear that we cannot see the first simply as Piero's correction of Agnolo's
Dream of Heraclius on the basis of the text of the *Legenda Aurea*. Piero, moreover, fuses
together in his *Dream* two distinct passages, which describe respectively the appearance,
before the battle of the Danube, of an angel pointing to a Cross in the heavens, and the
appearance of Christ holding a Cross in his hand before the battle of the Milvian Bridge.
We see here not so much a desire to follow Jacopo da Varazze's text more faithfully as an
effort to give unusual prominence to the figure of Constantine. This is clear in the
Triumph, which Clark has interpreted as alluding to the theme of the Crusade.[63] Such an
allusion would be strengthened by the identification of Constantine with John VIII
Palaeologus — an identification that has often been pointed out, but never justified
except in general terms[64].

All these elements, then, suggest that from the second tier on we can perceive the
emergence of an iconographic scheme connected, in ways that will be made clear, with
a Crusade. We should recall, moreover, that Longhi had already remarked on the stylistic novelty of the frescoes in the second tier, in comparison with the lunettes that still
show a Florentine treatment of the outlines. Gilbert, for his part, had seen in the architectural forms of the *Solomon* and the *Discovery*, forms that reflect Alberti's influence, a
legacy of Peiro's Roman visit of 1458-59. If we accept this hypothesis, we see that the
stylistic and iconographic break coincides with a change of patron: Francesco Bacci died
on 28 March 1459, and his son Giovanni then took over the responsibility for the

decoration of the family chapel[65].

It is certainly plausible that Giovanni may have suggested the insertion of the scene showing *Solomon Receiving the Queen of Sheba*. His personal ties with Traversari, and more generally with the group favouring unity between the two Churches, readily explain why he might have turned to Ghiberti's panel, a product of that same milieu. It is worth noting that the gesture of concord, emotional fulcrum both of Ghiberti's bas-relief and of the Arezzo fresco, had already appeared, bearing the same symbolic and allusive references to Church union, in the picture painted by Piero for the Camaldolites of Borgo San Sepolcro in indirect homage to Traversari's memory: the *Baptism of Christ*.

But what we know of Giovanni Bacci's life and personality does not explain how John VIII Palaeologus came to appear in the Arezzo cycle under the guise of Constantine. This detail, crucially important in identifying the cycle's iconographic scheme (or, better, its ultimate implications), is to be explained by the intervention of another, much more famous figure: Cardinal Bessarion.

That there was a connection of some sort between Piero della Francesca and Bessarion has been suggested by other scholars, even if their arguments have been vague or (as we shall see) not entirely convincing[66]. However, the suggestion has never been thought relevant to the Arezzo frescoes. A series of factual data nonetheless exists, which makes it very probable that Bessarion did intervene in the reworking of the Arezzo cycle's iconographic scheme.

Among the Greek prelates who came to Italy for the Council in 1438, Bessarion, Metropolitan of Nicea, held a prominent place. Despite his youth (he was born in 1403), he was distinguished both by his erudition and by the personal ties that for some time had bound him to the Emperor John VIII Palaeologus. As the Council's deliberations proceeded, he drew gradually nearer to the positions of the Western theologians, eventually becoming one of the most committed advocates of union with the Roman Church[67]. It was Bessarion who, together with Cardinal Cesarini, solemnly proclaimed the act of union in Santa Maria del Fiore on 6 July 1439. On his return to Constantinople, he heard news of his appointment as a Cardinal, as priest of the Basilica of the Holy Apostles. In Italy, where he was to return the following year and where he settled permanently, he came to enjoy unquestioned prestige — religious, cultural and political. In 1449, he became Cardinal Bishop first of Sabina and then of Tuscolo; from 1450 to 1455, he was legate *a latere* for Bologna, Romagna and the March of Ancona; in the 1455 Conclave, he was all but elected Pope. His house in the precincts of the Basilica of the Holy Apostles was the real centre of Roman humanism. Here, he gathered together and had transcribed a great number of Latin and above all Greek manuscripts. To bring about a better knowledge of Plato's thought, he had embarked on a volume entitled *In calumniatorem Platonis*, taking issue with George of Trebizond, which was published in Latin in 1469.

This is not the place to give a detailed account of Bessarion's life. We should, however, note that on 10 September 1458 he was appointed Protector of the Order of Greyfriars or Friars Minor[68]. This is one of the missing pieces of the mosaic we are reconstructing. His responsibilities as Protector would indeed have fully entitled Bessarion to intervene in the decoration (temporarily interrupted just at this period) of the Bacci chapel in the church of San Francesco. More than that: such an intervention would not only have been legitimate, but also understandable, given the relations that must have existed between Bessarion and Giovanni Bacci — relations owing less to the latter's past position in the Papal administration than to his kinship, discussed above, with the humanist Giovanni Tortelli, the former Vatican librarian. By this time, Tortelli's career in the Curia was over, but until a few years earlier he had had the closest links with Bessarion, especially through the latter's secretary, Niccolò Perotti[69].

All this makes it likely that there was a direct relationship between Bessarion and Giovanni Bacci. There is one additional circumstance that makes it well-nigh certain.

28-30   In August 1451, a few years before Piero began work on the Arezzo cycle, a relic of the True Cross, enclosed in a casket adorned with images, arrived in Italy from the Orient. It was brought by Gregory Melissenus, known as Mammas, Patriarch of Constantinople, who was seeking the protection of Rome against the hostility of the faction opposed to the union of the Churches, who had not forgiven him the role he had played some ten years previously at the Council of Florence[70]. Following the fall of Constantinople (1453), the casket containing the relic remained in Italy. Shortly before his death (in 1459), Gregory left it to Bessarion, who had fought so hard for the union of the Churches. In 1472, Bessarion, by this time an elderly and sick man, travelled on an embassy to France; on the eve of his departure, he left the relic, which was very precious to him (and which had already been the object, in 1463, of a donation "*inter vivos*"), to the Scuola Grande della Carità at Venice — today the site of the Accademia gallery, where the relic is still to be found[71]. Previously, this relic had belonged to the Palaeologus family. The casket containing it bears a Greek inscription attributed to a certain Princess Irene Palaeologa, "daughter of a brother of the Emperor". This Irene was traditionally identified as the daughter of the Emperor Michael IX, crowned Empress in 1335; nowadays, scholars prefer the view that she was a niece of the Emperor John VIII, which brings the date of the reliquary down to the early fifteenth century[72]. Certainly it was John VIII who gave it to the Patriarch Gregory, his confessor, who left it, as we have seen, to Bessarion. In the document accompanying it on its donation to the Scuola Grande della Carità, Bessarion gives a detailed account of how the precious relic had come into his hands[73].

Of all the relics of the True Cross that had appeared in Italy by this time (including the one preserved at Cortona, not far from Arezzo[74]), only this one justifies the inclusion in Piero's cycle of the portrait of John VIII Palaeologus. This portrait gives the cycle commissioned by the Bacci an extra dimension, as a glorification of the Palaeologus dynasty and in particular of the Emperor with whom Bessarion had been linked in his youth. More indirectly, the depiction of Constantine, the Emperor who had moved the capital from Rome to the Orient, with the features of John VIII Palaeologus, his remote descendant, was a proclamation of the ideal for which Bessarion had fought, the union of the Churches, and of that for which he was now fighting: the Crusade against the Turks.

All this is not to deny that the walls at Arezzo indeed display Longhi's "epic of lay, profane life"; but it is to enrich that epic's meaning with religious and political themes of a quite different order.

At this point, we can sum up the series of circumstances underlying the stylistic and iconographic break dividing the beginning of the Arezzo cycle, the lunettes, from the frescoes that followed. On 10 September 1458, Bessarion was appointed protector of the Franciscan order; in the autumn of 1458, Piero travelled to Rome; on 28 March 1459, Giovanni Bacci's father, Francesco, was buried; in 1459 (before 20 April), Gregory Mammas died[75], leaving to Bessarion the casket containing the relic of the True Cross that had formerly belonged to the Palaeologi.

This closely linked sequence of documented events perhaps allows us to suggest approximately the limits between which we must date one further, and decisive, happening, for which documentary evidence does not exist (and perhaps never will): the meeting during which Bessarion suggested to Giovanni Bacci that he should insert into the decoration of his family chapel a portrait of the last Eastern Emperor but one.

Between 1458 and the early months of 1459, Bessarion remained the whole time in Rome. He then left for Mantua, to join the council called by Pius II in response to the Turkish threat. We do not know the date of his departure, but at all events — and contrary to some accounts[76] — he did not follow Pius II in the leisurely journey towards the north which the latter began on 22 January. It is probable that he left Rome towards the beginning of April; on 27 May 1459, he was certainly among the Cardinals who took part in Pius II's solemn entry into Mantua. Now in the account that accompanied Bessarion's gift to the Scuola Grande della Carità, he wrote that he had been left the casket during his stay in Mantua for the Papal council[77]. This can mean only that it was while he was at Mantua that Bessarion heard the news of the Patriarch Gregory's death. We know, in fact, that on 20 April 1459 — the day Isidore of Kiev, the Ruthenian Cardinal, was made Patriarch of Constantinople — his predecessor had been dead only for a short time ("nuper"). However, Gregory had received Pius II's permission to make a will on 20 September of the previous year[78]. The will itself, now lost, must have been drawn up soon afterwards. Gregory, an old man now at the point of death, would no doubt have told Bessarion, who was preparing to leave for a long journey, of his plan to leave him the precious relic. It is Bessarion himself who tells us that Gregory loved him like a son[79].

It follows from all this that Bessarion's decision to celebrate in fitting style the acquisition of the relic was made either shortly before he left for Mantua, or while he was actually there for the council. To choose between these two alternatives, we would need to know Giovanni Bacci's movements during this same period. Of these, however, we are ignorant except that it is reasonable to suppose that he was called back to Arezzo (if not there already) when his father died towards the end of March 1459.

There is, however, reason to think that Bessarion, as well as suggesting the inclusion of John VIII's portrait, may actually have played an active part in its composition. The profile of Constantine in the *Triumph* is derived, we know, from Pisanello's famous medal, struck during the Council either at Ferrara or at Florence and generally regarded

1, 31

as the first modern medal[80]. Surviving examples have on their upper side a representation of John VIII Palaeologus, wearing on his head the "white hat coming to a point in
front" that we met earlier; on the reverse side, Palaeologus is shown on horseback,
followed by an equerry. There seems also to have existed a variant, of which no example
survives, described by Giovio (who owned one) as bearing on the reverse side "the Cross
of Christ, upheld by two hands, representing the Latin and Greek Churches". Only
recently have scholars recognized this last image as Bessarion's personal symbol.
However, they have also raised doubts as to whether such a medal existed: but Giovio's
description[81] is too precise, as well as historically too probable, to be set down as a
mistake. It is more plausible that Pisanello's medal did indeed exist in the two versions,
and that it was from one of these (the one now lost) that Bessarion, on his return from
Constantinople to Rome in 1440, drew inspiration in his choice of a personal symbol as
Cardinal.

    An examplar of this lost version must have been given or lent to Giovanni Bacci by
Bessarion, to be used as a model for the portrait of Palaeologus inserted in the Arezzo
cycle. Under the circumstances, we can also legitimately suppose that Bessarion showed
Bacci, and perhaps Piero, two other medals, struck in gold, which were the immediate
historical forerunners of Pisanello's. Could we show that this was the case, it would
establish that the meeting with Bacci took place in Rome, between late 1458 and the first
months of 1459; for it is unthinkable that Bessarion would have taken his collection of
medals along with him on his journey to Mantua. We shall return to this hypothesis in
our analysis of the *Flagellation*.

    The two medals, showing Constantine and Heraclius, are first mentioned early in
the fifteenth century in the inventory of the Duc de Berry's collections. The Duc de
Berry most likely bought them as antiquities (they were at any rate regarded as such in
the sixteenth century). Schlosser gives a full account of them in connection with Pisanello's first medal (the one of John VIII), supposing them to form part of a series, probably of Flemish origin, based on the Legend of the True Cross[82]. He later attributed them
to either Pol de Limbourg or one of his brothers[83]. The connection between them and
the Constantine of the *Triumph* has never been pointed out: but Piero would seem to
have combined the two medals, giving to Constantine — who is mounted, and seen in
profile — the gesture with which Heraclius grasps the Cross in his outstretched arm.
Moreover, the Black coachman who is turning aside, in the Heraclius medallion, because
he has seen that the gates of Jerusalem are miraculously blocked, strongly recalls the
Black servant whom Piero painted among the retinue of the Queen of Sheba: it is
enough to look at their snub-nosed profiles and their characteristic conical caps. All this
seems to indicate that Piero was familiar with the medals. It is also worth noting that the
latter are accompanied by writings in Greek that display a minute knowledge of Byzantine bureaucratic terminology. These (so Weiss has argued) were drawn up by some
official of the imperial chancellory, probably during the visit to Paris of Manuel II Palaeologus, which ended in 1402 — the year the Duc de Berry acquired the Constantine
medallion from a Florentine merchant[84]. This circumstance makes it all the more
probable that Bessarion may have owned the two medals, and may have shown them to
Bacci, given their connection with the theme of the Arezzo cycle — the Legend of the

True Cross — as well as with the relic that had belonged to the Palaeologi. This would explain why Piero made use of the Heraclius medallion only in the middle and lower tiers of frescoes, executed after his return from Rome, rather than in the lunette showing Heraclius carrying the Cross back to Jerusalem (the *Exaltation of the Cross*), where its use would have been more obviously appropriate.

14

The hypothesis that Bessarion intervened to modify the overall iconographic scheme of the Arezzo cycle depends on a series of very precise factual coincidences; the hypothesis that he met Giovanni Bacci at Rome, upon a chain of conjectures. The meeting, in other words, may perhaps have been at Mantua, some months later. However, this uncertainty does not affect the core of the argument, based as it is upon a convergence between biographical, stylistic and iconographic data, and data concerning the commissioning (direct and indirect) of the cycle.

This convergence confirms with fresh arguments Gilbert's hypothesis that the major part of the cycle (excluding only the lunettes) was painted after Piero's return from Rome in the autumn of 1459. This dating is not contradicted by the one solid argument that Battisti advances: the argument based on the Città di Castello altarpiece, prominently dated 1456 and signed by the same Giovanni di Piamonte whom Longhi identifies as Piero's collaborator in the two scenes flanking the windows, the *Raising of the Wood* and the *Torture of the Jew*[85]. As Battisti rightly remarks, the altarpiece shows a knowledge of Piero's work, but not of the Arezzo frescoes[86]: this, however, provides a *terminus post quem* for the start of Giovanni di Piamonte's collaboration, not for the beginning of the cycle as a whole.

36

6, 11

When the cycle was begun, we do not know[87]. What is certain, on the other hand, is that the year spent at Rome was of crucial importance for Piero's development, and not only for his stylistic development. The platonic and mathematical inspiration of his mature works, as well as the religious and political implications that we have deciphered in the Legend of the True Cross, were fostered by his meetings in Rome with Alberti and with the humanists of Pius II's court — perhaps with Bessarion himself. To this moment we must ascribe the *Flagellation of Christ*, a painting lying precisely on the frontier that (chronologically as in other senses) divides the two phases of the Arezzo cycle.

front.

Notes

1. M. Salmi, *La pittura di Piero della Francesca*, Novara 1979, p. 165.

2. It was Scarmagli who established this precise date, on the basis of a letter from Aliotti to Alberti (G. Aliotti, *Epistolae et opuscula*, Arretii 1769, I, p. 33, n. e).

3. Salmi, "I Bacci di Arezzo" p. 229.

4. Gilbert, *Change*, pp. 85-6. It is from Gilbert that Battisti draws (unless I am mistaken) the one and only reference to Giovanni Bacci in his monograph (p. 482, n. 181: this reference does not appear in the name index).

5. E. Gamurrini, *Istoria genealogica*, Florence 1673, III, pp. 334-5. G.G. Goretti Miniati reprinted this letter, in a very poor text, and stating it to be hitherto unpublished, in an article "Alcuni ricordi della famiglia Bacci", in *Atti e Memorie della R. Accademia Petrarca di lettere, arti e scienze*, n.s., VIII (1930), pp. 96-7. It is here wrongly attributed to a different Giovanni Bacci, from a collateral branch of the family – Giovanni di Donato di Angelo di Magio. Gamurrini's *Istoria* (pp. 328, 334-5), as well as the discussion that follows, makes it quite clear, however, that the Giovanni in question is indeed Giovanni di Francesco di Baccio, of the branch that commissioned the Arezzo frescoes. For the Bacci family tree, see ibid., pp. 324-35, and Salmi, "*I Bacci di Arezzo*", art., which has later information. Research into the *Spogli Gamurrini* (ASF, mss 296-313: this is the documentation Gamurrini worked from) has failed to bring to light any fresh data on Giovanni Bacci's biography.

6. On Tortelli, see G. Mancini, "Giovanni Tortelli cooperatore di Niccolò V nel fondare la Biblioteca Vaticana", in *Archivio Storico Italiano*, LXXVIII (1920), pp. 161-282; R.P. Oliver, "Giovanni Tortelli", in *Studies presented to David Moore Robinson*, II, St. Louis 1953, pp. 1257-71; O. Besomi, "Dai 'Gesta Ferdinandi regis Aragonum' del Valla al 'De Orthographia' del Tortelli", in *Italia medioevale e umanistica*, 9 (1966), pp. 75-112; M. Regoliosi, "Nuove ricerche intorno a Giovanni Tortelli," ibid., pp. 123-89, and 12 (1969), pp. 129-96 (on Giovanni Bacci, cf. pp. 149-57); O. Besomi, "Un nuovo autografo di Giovanni Tortelli: uno schedario di umanista", ibid., 13 (1970), pp. 95-137; M. Cortesi, "Il 'vocabolarium' greco di Giovanni Tortelli", ibid., 22 (1979), pp. 449-83. Traversari's letter to his brother is discussed by Regoliosi ("Nuove ricerche", 2nd part, p. 152). We do not know the date of Giovanni's birth, only that his parents were already married in 1416 (see the family tree reconstructed by Salmi). That he was the first born is suggested both by one of the provisions of his grandfather Baccio's will and by the fact that his name precedes those of his brothers in a document of 1458 (Salmi, "I Bacci di Arezzo", p. 236). In giving a large sum to the hospital of Spirito Santo "for the poor Germans" ("*per li poveri Alemanni*"), Baccio expressed the wish that his grandson Giovanni should be its first rector (J. Burali, *Vite de'vescovi aretini ... dall'anno CCCXXXVI fino all'anno MDCXXXVIII*, Arezzo 1638, pp. 91-2; the bequest and the provision relating to it are not in the extract from the will given in Salmi, "I Bacci di Arezzo", pp. 233-5). It is out of the question that Giovanni was then (in 1417) of an age to assume the duties of hospital rector, given that in 1432 Traversari was speaking of him as "young". The provision in the will must therefore have referred to the future. In any case, 1417 can be taken as a *terminus ante quem* for Giovanni's birth, which we should probably date around 1410-15.

7. Regoliosi, "Nuove ricerche", p. 151. Mancini ("Giovanni Tortelli", pp. 180-81) mistakenly identifies Tortelli as the "Giovanni Aretino" whom Traversari recommended. It is this mistaken identification that explains why Mancini (p. 180) uses the expression "back from the Orient", which actually does not occur in Traversari's letter (*Epistolae*, l. II, ep. XXV).

8. The Bull dated from Ferrara, 11 July 1438, in *Bullarium Romanum*, vol. 5, Augustae Taurinorum, 1860, pp. 32-3; this was reaffirmed on 8 July 1444 (ibid., pp. 76-80).

9. F.P. Luiso, "Studi su l'epistolario e le traduzioni di Lapo da Castiglionchio juniore", in *Studi italiani di filologia classica*, VII (1899), pp. 254-5 (and Regoliosi, "Nuove ricerche", p. 152).

10. Ibid., pp. 153-4.

11. On the Tortelli family's origins in Capolona, see Mancini, "Giovanni Tortelli", p. 162; for those of the Bacci, see Gamurrini, *Istoria*, p. 314. The Bacci enjoyed the patronage of numerous church places in Capolona: ibid., pp. 316-17 (and Salmi, "I Bacci di Arezzo", p. 233).

12. The volume, probably completed in the summer of 1453, and dedicated to Nicholas V, was first published in 1471, and went through several later printings.

13. Gamurrini, *Istoria*, p. 318 (it is clear from the context that the Giovanni Bacci who graduated at Siena was a different person from his namesake Giovanni di Donato Bacci).

14. Aliotti, *Epistolae*, I, pp. 27-33.

15. Ibid., pp. 33-4 (see also G. Mancini, *Vita di Leon Battista Alberti*, Florence 1882, pp. 179-80).

16. Aliotti, *Epistolae*, II, p. 182. On the relations between Aliotti and Traversari, see ibid., I, p. XIV.

17. Ibid., pp. 27-8.

18. Gamurrini, *Istoria*, III, p. 327.

19. The kinship of the Bacci to the Tortelli is discussed above. As for Marsuppini, a letter from him to Giovanni Tortelli, whom he addresses as "dearest godfather" (*"conpatri carissimo"*), is given in R. Sabbadini, "Briciole umanistiche", I, in *Giornale storico della letteratura italiana*, XVII (1891), pp. 212-13 (Sabbadini made use of a copy; the original is in the Vatican, Vat. lat. 3908, c. 53*r*).

20. In 1979 Salmi put forward (though only in general terms) the hypothesis that Traversari may have influenced Piero in his *La pittura di Piero*, p. 165.

21. Our term "network" (Italian *reticolo*: trans.) is here employed metaphorically, rather than in the rigorous sense in which it is now extensively used in sociological and anthropological literature.

22. It would be worth citing the entire passage in which Longhi (*Piero*, p. 16) writes of these "visual springs which flow forever underground, coming at crucial moments to the assistance of those whose invention is flagging, and leading them back to the mainstream of the figurative tradition". The suggestion of a "return to order" occasionally hinted at in the monograph of 1927 is here particularly audible. It should nonetheless be emphasized that the ahistorical tone of this passage is belied by all Longhi's concrete studies, beginning with those on Piero.

23. Aliotti, *Epistolae*, I, p. 143.

24. Ibid., pp. 161-2.

25. Mancini, "Giovanni Tortelli", pp. 208 ff.

26. Bacci's name has not hitherto emerged in the course of researches into the archives of the Camera, which are kept partly in the Archivio Segreto Vaticano, partly in the Archivio di Stato at Rome.

27. ASF, *Mediceo avanti il Principato* (henceforth referred to as *MAP*), VII, 1 (in the same archive are found twenty-eight other letters of Bacci's, all of which are noted by Regoliosi, apart from *MAP*, V, 905, to Giuliano Piero de Medici, dated 16 March 1474).

28. On the Patriarch of Aquileia, long known under the mistaken name of Ludovico Scarampi-Mezzarota, see the seminal study by P. Paschini, *Lodovico cardinal camerlengo († 1465)*, Rome 1939 ('*Lateranum*', n.s., a. V, n. 1). He continued to be designated "patriarch" even after his appointment as Cardinal: for example, ASF, *Signori. Legazioni e commisarie. Elezioni, istruzioni, lettere*, n. 15, cc. 147*r*, 149*r*. I have been unable to discover exactly when Giovanni Bacci was expelled from the Camera: it was certainly before 1446 (see G. Bourgin, "La 'familia' pontifica sotto Eugenio IV", in *Archivio della Società romana di storia patria*, XXVII [1904], p. 215, where six clerks' names, not including Bacci's, are listed). On the presence of six clerks to the Camera Apostolica during certain periods of the pontificate of Eugenius IV (who had laid it down that their number should never exceed seven: see above, p. 28), see A. Gottlob, *Aus der Camera Apostolica des 15 Jahrhunderts. Ein Betrag zur Geschichte des päpstlichen Finanzwesens und des endenden Mittelalters*, Innsbruck 1889, p. 115.

29. Paschini, *Lodovico*.

30. Sannadini, "Briciole umanistiche", pp. 212-13.

31. Gamurrini, *Istoria*, III, p. 335. Tortelli, too, had followed Nicholas V to Fabriano: Mancini, "Giovanni Tortelli", p. 222. Cremona had been unsuccessfully besieged by Malatesta during his time as commander-in-chief of the Venetian army, and had only fallen as a result of the treachery of Carlo Gonzaga, the head of the Milanese forces.

32. ASF, *MAP*, XVII, 292 (letter dated from Cesena, 27 January 1461: Bacci signs himself "potestas Cesenae"; see also Regoliosi, "Nuove ricerche", p. 157). See ASC, *Riformanze*, 47, c. 12v (1 January 1461).

33. ASF, *MAP*, VII, 4; ASF, *MAP*, XXIV, 371. In a letter of 6 March 1473 (ASF, *MAP*, XXIX, 144), Giovanni Bacci names as among those who have protected him "in health and in sickness" Cosimo, Piero and Giovanni de Medici; Sforza; Borso d'Este; the other "*signori* of the Romagna"; and the Count of Urbino.

34. G. Vasari, *Le opere con nuove annotazioni ... di G. Milanesi*, II, Florence 1906 (anastatic reprint, Florence 1973), p. 491; this is available in English as Part II of vol. 1 of the Everyman 4 vol. edn of Vasari, A.B. Hinds,

trans., 1927. See also Gilbert (*Change*, pp. 51-2). Gilbert refers to the date (July 1451) of the lost fresco, evidently influenced by Piero, which Bono da Ferrara painted at the Eremitani.

35. C. Santoro, *Gli uffici del sominio sforzesco (1450-1500)*, Milan 1948, p. 142: the "eximius vir D. Iohannes de Barciis de Aretio" is appointed "iudex maleficiorum potestatis Mediolani", with a stipend of sixteen florins. The mistake ("de Barciis" for "de Bacciis") is corrected in C. Santoro, *I registri delle lettere ducali del periodo sforzesco*, Milan 1961, pp. 16, 27, 322, 324. The letter of appointment, dated 24 June 1451, was registered exactly a month later. Bacci's successor, Angelo da Viterbo, took his place on 21 May 1453. Bacci refers to his links with Francesco Sforza in a letter cited above (see n. 33). It is worth remarking that in the *Dizionario degli aretini illustri* compiled by the Aretine scholar F.A. Massetani, which was completed in 1940 and of which the typescript is kept in the Arezzo State Archives, we find the following entry for "Bacci (de) Giovanni (Messer)"; "Lawyer, poet. Served as junior judge to the Duke of Milan Gian Galeazzo Sforza in 1458, and was appointed by the latter, at his death, as lieutenant to the Dukedom. Wrote a poem on the Crusades and translated into Italian Giovanni Boccaccio's *De claris mulieribus*. We possess a letter written by him to Cosimo de Medici on 28 September 1449." Now this last item refers without doubt to the Bacci with whom we are concerned, as do the biographical data mistakenly given by Massetani under the entries for "Bacci (de) Giovanni (Mons.) di Francesco di Baccio" and "Bacci (de) Giovanni d'Angiol Antonio" (actually, Giovanni di Francesco). These are instances of the very numerous errors found in the *Dizionario*, a work which, though not without its uses, is certainly to be handled with the greatest caution. In the entry cited above, "Gian Galeazzo" should obviously read "Francesco". Moreover, there is no junior judge by the name of Bacci at the court of Milan in 1458 (unless there is some confusion here with the office of "iudex maleficiorum" held during an earlier period), nor do we encounter Bacci as ducal lieutenant on the death of Francesco Sforza. (It is odd that Goretti Miniati (*Aleuni ricordi*, p. 97) should just as groundlessly attribute similar duties, as podestà of Milan in 1453, to Giovanni *di Donato* Bacci.) No Bacci is recorded among these who translated the *De claris mulieribus* into the vulgar tongue (see A. Altamura, "Donato da Casentino. Un volgarizzamento trecentesco del 'De claris mulieribus' del Boccaccio (estratti da un codice inedito)", in *Atti e memorie della R. Accademia Petrarca*, n.s., XXV [1938], pp. 265-71; V. Zaccaria, "I volgarizzamenti del Boccaccio latino a Venezia", in *Studi sul Boccaccio*, X [1977-78], pp. 285-306). In these circumstances, the attribution to Giovanni Bacci of a poem on the Crusades appears unreliable, or at any rate unverifiable, pending evidence to the contrary (Massetani's bibliographical references are either mistaken, or else fail to justify the attribution). Were proof forthcoming, however, it would further confirm our interpretation of the iconography of the Arezzo cycle.

36. Longhi, *Piero*, pp. 100-1.

37. The Misericordia altarpiece, commissioned in 1445 and urgently requested ten years later, was finished, perhaps, around 1462; the altarpiece painted for the Augustinians was commissioned in 1454, and the last payment made for it only in 1469 (though in this case Piero had taken the precaution of asking eight years to complete it) (Longhi, *Piero*, pp. 100, 102: however, see below on the somewhat controversial question of the chronology of the Misericordia altarpiece).

38. Longhi, *Piero*, pp. 48-9, 51, 85.

39. Ibid., pp. 51, 53 (where the *Resurrection* is said to seem united by its style "rather with the mature work at Arezzo than with the slightly earlier frescoes").

40. Vasari, II, pp. 492-3.

41. See respectively Zippel, "Piero della Francesca a Roma" and the documents published by Battisti (II, p. 224). It is probable that Piero had already reached Rome by the autumn of 1458; for on 22 September, he granted power of attorney to his brother Marco, evidently because he was about to set out (Battisti, II, p. 223). On 24 October of the same year, moreover, are recorded the payments made for the scaffolding-wood needed for the Papal chamber to be decorated in fresco (it is for this work that Piero is paid in an entry of 12 April 1459): Zippel, "Piero della Francesca a Roma", p. 86.

42. Longhi, *Piero*, pp. 100-1, 214. It should be noted that these works are not unanimously attributed to Piero.

43. Ibid., p. 214. In the light of what is said in n. 41 above, Longhi's suggestion would make autumn 1458 the *terminus ante quem*.

44. Clark, pp. 38-9, 52. G. Robertson's review of Gilbert, *Change* (see *The Art Quarterly*, XXXIV [1971], pp. 356-8) misinterprets Longhi's position, confusing it with Clark's on this point. Clark's hypothesis that there were two scaffolds is accepted both by Robertson and by P. Hendy (in another review of Gilbert's book: *Burlington Magazine*, CXII [1970], pp. 469-70).

45. In all this, I am following the opinion of Longhi.

46. Clark, p. 52.

47. Battisti, II, pp. 23 ff.

48. G. Becatti, "Il Pothos di Scopa", in *Le arti*, III (1941), pp. 40ff (Gilbert notes this article in *Change*, pp. 71-2, n. 34). And see, now, R. Cocke, "Masaccio and the Spinario, Piero and the Pothos: Observations on the Reception of the Antique in Renaissance Painting", in *Zeitschrift für Kunstgeschichte*, 43 (1980), pp. 21-32.

49. The prevalence in fifteenth-century art of the classical motif of the vanquished warrior brought to his knees (of which Piero himself makes use in the *Defeat*) sufficiently demonstrates how untenable is the criterion invoked by Battisti in support of his proposed dating: see O.J. Brendel, "A Kneeling Persian: Migrations of a Motif", in *Essays in the History of Art Presented to Rudolf Wittkower*, London 1967, pp. 62-71; L. Fusco, "Antonio Pollaiuolo's Use of the Antique", in *Journal of the Warburg and Courtauld Institutes*, 42 (1979), pp. 259-60, esp. p. 260, n. 14.

50. Gilbert, *Change*, pp. 48-9 and *passim*.

51. Ibid., pp. 27 ff. Gilbert interprets correctly the date of the request, which Battisti misunderstands (cf. Beck, "Una data").

52. Gilbert, *Change*, pp. 88, n. 40.

53. Longhi, *Piero*, p. 82 (the phrase is in his 1950 essay on "Piero in Arezzo").

54. J. da Varazze, *Legenda aurea*, T. Graesse (ed.), 1890 (anastatic reprint: Osnabrück 1965), pp. 303-11, 605-11.

55. Longhi, *Piero*, pp. 82-3.

56. On the theme in general, see still P. Mazzoni, *La leggenda della Croce nell'arte italiana*, Florence 1914. On the Santa Croce cycle, B. Cole, *Agnolo Gaddi*, Oxford 1977; and see also M. Boskovits, "In margine alla bottega di Agnolo Gaddi", in *Paragone*, 355 (1979), pp. 54-62. On the relationship between Agnolo's cycle and that of Piero, see De Tolnay, "Conceptions religieuses", pp. 222-6, and Gilbert, *Change*, pp. 73-4, n. 36 (here, among other suggestions, Gilbert puts forward the view, for which there is no apparent evidence, that the left-hand lunette was begun by Bicci di Lorenzo).

57. Mazzoni, pp. 111-12.

58. Many scholars have tried to explain the lack of order among these scenes by recourse to supposed typological or other parallelisms: see M. Alpatov, "Les fresques de Piero della Francesca à Arezzo. Semantique et stylistique", in *Commentari*, XIV (1963), pp. 17-38; and L. Schneider, "The Iconography of Piero della Francesca's Frescoes Illustrating the Legend of the True Cross in the Church of San Francesco in Arezzo", in *The Art Quarterly*, XXXII (1969), pp. 22-48, esp. pp. 37-43 (neither essay is convincing: and the first — which would explain the frescoes' sequence by the notion that their hidden purpose is to narrate the history of humanity — is particularly implausible). A.W.G. Posèq (*The Lunette*, Jerusalem 1974, lithogr., p. 563) formulates the hypothesis of an iconographical change of plan. Freud's famous remark comes to mind: "The distortion of a text is rather like a murder. The difficulty lies not in the execution of the deed but in the doing away of the traces" (*Moses and Monotheism*, Katherine Jones trans., London 1939). Among the traces that we have left unexamined here is the blind Cupid on the left-hand pillar: his presence in the cycle remains unexplained, various speculations notwithstanding.

59. P. Schubring, *Cassoni*, Leipzig 1915, nos. 192-7, 425-6 etc., and pp. 111, 204.

60. See Warburg, "L'ingresso dello stile ideale", pp. 290 ff. on the contrast between the historic representation of antiquity (Piero) and the representation of antiquity in contemporary costume (exemplified by a wedding-chest by Benozzo Gozzoli). This contrast is somewhat obscured in E. Panofsky, *Renaissance and Renascences in Western Art*, Uppsala 1965, p. 172.

61. Schneider, "The Iconography".

62. R. Krautheimer and T. Krautheimer-Hess, *Lorenzo Ghiberti*, Princeton (N.J.) 1956, pp. 180-87.

63. Clark, pp. 38-9.

64. "... we are able to recognize in the features of Constantine's face ... a personage of the day who did indeed have the right to present himself in this guise: the Greek Emperor, John Palaeologus", writes Warburg ("L'ingresso dello stile ideale", p. 291; cf. by the same author: *Die Erneuerung*, pp. 390-91). None of the later commentators has gone beyond this observation that Constantine's portrayal as Palaeologus is consistent with the theme of a Crusade.

65. Salmi, "I Bacci di Arezzo", p. 236.

66. The first to suggest such a connection was, to the best of my knowledge, Marinesco, on the basis of the ties between Bessarion and Federigo da Montefeltro ("Echos byzantins", pp. 193, 202-3). The supposition that Piero may have met Bessarion at Urbino (p. 203) overlooks a possible occasion of their meeting in 1458-9, while Piero was in Rome (on this, see ch. 4 below). The reference (p. 202) to a lost portrait of Bessarion by Piero is based on a particularly confused passage in Vasari, on which see below, ch. 4. Marinesco sees Bessarion as having introduced Piero to certain themes of the Byzantine iconographic tradition. A different con-

nection is suggested by T. Gouma-Peterson, in an essay analysed later in the present work.

67. The most comprehensive work on Bessarion is still L. Mohler, *Kardinal Bessarion als Theologe, Humanist und Staatsmann*, Paderborn 1923, 1927, 1942: there is one volume of biography, and two of published and unpublished texts. This is brought up to date, not only bibliographically but in other respects, by L. Labowsky's excellent entry in the *Dizionario biografico degli italiani* (Rome 1967, pp. 686-96). On Bessarion's attitude during the Council, see J. Gill, "Was Bessarion a conciliarist or a unionist before the council of Florence?", in *Collectanea byzantina*, Rome 1977, pp. 201-19. For his relationship with John VIII, see also A. Gentilini, "Una consolatoria inedita del Bessarione", in *Scritti in onore di Carlo Diano*, Bologna 1975, pp. 149-64 (where there is a discussion of three *sermones* written on the occasion of the Empress Maria Comnena's death).

68. R. Loenertz, "Pour la biographie du cardinal Bessarion", in *Orientalia Christiana Periodica*, X (1944), p. 284.

69. G. Mercati, *Per la cronologia della vita e degli scritti di Niccolò Perotti arcivescovo di Siponto*, Rome 1925.

70. Gill, *The Council*, p. 376f.

71. See G.B. Schioppalalba (but publ. anonymously), *In perantiquam sacram tabulam Graecam insigni sodalitio sanctae Mariae Caritatis Venetiarum ab amplissimo Cardinali Bessarione dono datam dissertatio*, Venetiis 1767. See also G. Cozza Luzzi, "La croce a Venezia del card. Bessarione", in *Bessarione*, VIII (1904), pp. 1-8, 223-36; G. Fogolari, "La teca del Bessarione e la croce di san Teodoro di Venezia", in *Dedalo*, III (1922-3), pp. 139-60; E. Schaffran, "Gentile Bellini und das Bessarion-Reliquar", in *Das Münster*, 10 (1957), pp. 153-7.

72. A. Frolow, *La relique de la vraie Croix. Récherches sur le développement d'un culte*, Paris 1961, pp. 563-5 (and see also the same author's *Les reliquaires de la vraie Croix*, Paris 1965).

73. Schioppalalba, pp. 117-19.

74. Attention has recently been drawn to the importance of this for Piero's cycle by Battisti (I, p. 249) and by A. Chastel, *Fables, formes et figures*, Paris 1978, I, p. 58; Chastel follows up a hint of Schneider's (p. 46, n. 44). On the relics of the True Cross found in Italy, see A. Frolow's studies cited above.

75. G. Mercati, *Scritti d'Isidoro il cardinale Ruteno...*, Rome 1926, p. 134 and n. 6.

76. H. Vast, *Le cardinal Bessarion*, Paris 1878, p. 234; L. Mohler, I, p. 286.

77. Schioppalalba, pp. 118-19: Gregory "ante obitum suum ... reverendissimo D. Cardinali [i.e. Bessarion] ... absenti tunc, et in Mantuano conventu degenti legavit" (the passage is from the deed of gift to the Scuola Grande della Carità, and is given in Cozza Luzi pp. 3-6: "agenti" appears instead of "degenti").

78. Mercati, p. 134, n. 6.

79. Schioppalalba, p. 118.

80. On the date and antecedents of this medal, see the notes below.

81. The description found in a letter of 1551 to Cosimo I, is as follows: "I still possess a very beautiful medallion of Giovanni Paleologo, Emperor of Constantinople, with that odd Grecian-looking little cap the Emperors were wont to wear. And it was made by this same Pisano in Florence at the time of the Council of Eugenius, which was attended by the aforesaid Emperor; the reverse side bears the Cross of Christ, upheld by two hands, token of the Latin and Greek Churches" (G. Bottari and S. Ticozzi, *Raccolta di lettere sulla pittura*, Milan 1822, V, p. 83; Vasari also quotes the passage (III, p. 11). It has been maintained by J.A. Fasanelli on the basis of this passage (see "Some Notes on Pisanello and the Council of Florence", in *Master Drawings*, III (1965), pp. 36-47) that the medal was struck at Florence in commemoration of the Council's successful outcome, this being indicated by the symbol on the back of the version described by Giovio; he thus proposes a date for the two versions of the medal between 6 July (the act of union) and 26 August (the Emperor's departure) 1439. R. Weiss (*Pisanello's Medallion of the Emperor John VIII Palaeologus*, London 1966, pp. 16-17) has cast doubt on the existence of the version mentioned by Giovio, ruling out Pisanello's attendance at the Council in Florence on the grounds that he was in Mantua in May 1439; he argues that the medal of John VIII was struck at Ferrara in 1438, and commissioned by Leonello d'Este or by the Emperor himself. V. Juren ("A propos de la médaille de Jean VIII Paléologue par Pisanello", in *Revue numismatique*, s. 6ª, XV [1973], pp. 219-25) identifies the cross upheld by two arms as Bessarion's personal symbol, but disagrees with Fasanelli and Hill (*Pisanello*, London 1905, pp. 106-7; *Medals of the Renaissance*, G. Pollard (ed.), London, 1978, p. 36) in regarding the extant version of the medal of John VIII as the only one struck; for it, he proposes the *terminus ad quem* of August 1438, with convincing arguments. The article by M. Vickers ("Some Preparatory Drawings") has nothing new to tell us on the dating, or on the existence or otherwise, of the version in Giovio's description, and these are questions which must thus remain open for the present.

82. Cf. J. von Schlosser, 'Die Aeltesten Medaillen und die Antike', in *Jahrbuch der Kunsthistorischen Sammlungen des allerhöchsten Kaiserhauses*, 18 (1897), pp. 64-108, still a fundamental work (for the connection with the history of the cross, cf. pp. 77-78). On page 92 the two medals are defined as 'the oldest forgeries of

antiquity'. Cf. also O. Kurz, *Fakes*, New York 1967, p. 191.

83. Cf. J. von Schlosser, *Raccolte d'arte e di meraviglie del tardo Rinascimento*, Italian trans., Florence 1974, pp. 44-5 (the original German edn is of 1908). M. Jones also suggests the attribution to the Limbourgs, putting forward some new arguments, in "The First Cast Medals and the Limbourgs. The Iconography and Attribution of the Constantine and Heraclius Medals", in *Art History*, 2 (1979), pp. 35-44 (though Jones appears not to know of Schlosser's second contribution). That the Limbourgs should be identified as the authors of the drawings on which the medals were based (and not, as Schlosser and Jones would have it, of the medals themselves) had earlier been argued by C. Marinesco, "Deux empereurs byzantins. Manuel II et Jean VIII Paléologue, vus par des artistes parisiens et italiens", in *Bulletin de la Société nationale des antiquaires de France*, 1958, p. 38.

84. Cf. R. Weiss, 'The Medieval Medallions of Constantine and Heraclius', in *The Numismatic Chronicle*, 7, III (1963), pp. 129-44 (in particular p. 140); and see also M. Meiss, *French Painting in the Time of Jean de Berry*, London 1967, Vol. I, pp. 53-58.

85. Longhi, *Piero*, pp. 40, 212-13; and the same author's "Genio degli anonimi: Giovanni di Riamonte?" in *Fatti di Masolino e di Masaccio*, pp. 131-7.

86. Battisti, I, p. 133. It should be noted that in the essay just cited ("Genio degli anonimi"), Longhi himself does not speak of specific debts, in connection with the Città di Castello altarpiece, to the Arezzo frescoes — debts that one might legitimately expect to find if the latter had been commenced in 1452 or soon after.

87. In support of Longhi's proposed chronology, A. Conti has argued that a fragment of fresco by Parri Spinelli (d. 1453), now housed in the art gallery at Arezzo, derives from Piero's *Triumph of Constantine* (see "Le prospettive urbinati: tentativo di un bilancio ed abbozzo di una biliografia", in the section devoted to literature, etc., of the *Annali della Scuola Normale Superiore di Pisa*, s. III, VI [1976], p. 1214 n.). The undeniable link between the two works, which had already been remarked by P. Hendy (*Piero della Francesca and the Early Renaissance*, London 1968, p. 84), can, however, be interpreted in the inverse direction: see M.J. Zucker, *Parri Spinelli*, New York 1973 (typescript), pp. 316-17, who, on the basis of stylistic considerations, dates Parri's fresco to around 1435-40. It is interesting to note this fresco's original location — the monastery of Santa Fiora and Lucilla, whose abbot at the time was Aliotti, a friend of Giovanni Bacci and like him connected with Traversari.

III

The *Flagellation of Christ*

Every aspect of this famous small panel (58 cm by 81 cm) has been the subject of debate, except its authenticity. Doubt has never been raised about the signature to be read in Roman capitals on the step beneath Pilate's feet: "Opus Petri de Burgo Sancti Sepulcri". The rest — its patron, its date, the subject it represents — is uncertain. Innumerable commentaries, coming ever thicker and faster in recent years, have made the *Flagellation* one of the most controversial cases in the hermeneutics of art.

No record of the work is found for three centuries. In the eighteenth century it was kept in the sacristy of the Cathedral at Urbino. An inventory dated 1744 contains the following reference, one of the earliest that we have: "In the sacristy ... the Flagellation of Our Lord upon the column and, set apart, our most serene highnesses the Dukes Oddo Antonio, Federico and Guid'Ubaldo by Pietro Dall'Borgo"[1]. "Set apart": thus did Dean Ubaldo Tosi, who at the time was enlarging the inventory, distinguish the most exceptional feature of the painting (we shall return later to his suggested identification of the characters). The scene of Christ's flagellation is immediately recognizable, but it takes place in the background and to one side. A large distance, which Piero has rendered with an extraordinary command of perspective, separates the beaten Christ from the three mysterious figures in the foreground. Why is there such a distance between the two scenes?

The question, as will be seen, concerns not only the picture's formal peculiarity, but also its iconographic anomalies[2]. We shall thus be trying not just to solve an iconographic riddle, but to decipher an element crucial to an understanding of the work as a whole, in all its aspects — including its patron and its date.

In identifying the fundamental hermeneutical problem, we also provide ourselves with a criterion with which to analyse the principal interpretations of the *Flagellation* put forward hitherto. Rather than reviewing these in the order in which they were first advanced, we shall divide them into three distinct groups: 1) those which state that there is no significant connection between the group in the foreground and the flagellation of Christ, which are purely and simply juxtaposed; 2) those which hold that the characters in the foreground form an organic part of the scene of Christ's flagellation; 3) those which hold that the two scenes are separated (even in the time of their occurrence), and that there exists between them a relation that has to be determined. For the moment, we will simply give the essence of the principal interpretations, taking up later, where relevant, more detailed points of individual scholarship.

The first thesis is elliptically maintained by Toesca in his claim that Piero here manifests "sovereign disinterest . . . in the principal subject" (that is, in the flagellation of Christ)[3]. Creighton Gilbert formerly argued (though he has subsequently changed his views) for a still more anachronistic interpretation, taking the three men in the foreground to be anonymous passers-by, and viewing the picture itself as a "slice of life", prefiguring Tintoretto and Degas[4].

The second thesis has been far more widely accepted. Gombrich surmised that the bearded man was Judas, in the act of giving back to the members of the Sanhedrin the price paid for his treachery: however (as Gombrich himself acknowledges), the picture contains no trace of the thirty pieces of silver[5]. In a second contribution, Gilbert based his analysis on the phrase "Convenerunt in unum", which, according to Passavant (1839), used formerly to accompany the painting (today, the inscription has disappeared, together with the frame to which it was probably attached)[6]. This is a reference to the second verse of Psalm 2: "Adstiterunt reges terrae, et principes convenerunt in unum adversus Dominum et adversus Christum eius"(The kings of the earth set themselves in array and the rulers were gathered together against the Lord and against his Anointed). In the Acts of the Apostles (iv. 26-7), the psalm is quoted in reference to Christ's passion: "Convenerunt in unum adversus Dominum et adversus Christus eius. Convenerunt enim . . . Herodes, et Pontius Pilatus, cum gentibus et populis Israel." Gilbert, following an observation of P. Running's[7], has identified the latter passage as the textual basis of Piero's *Flagellation*. This would then depict, apart, of course, from Pilate on his throne, Herod (the turbaned man whose back is turned towards us and who faces Christ) and, in the foreground, from left to right, a gentile, a soldier, and Joseph of Arimathea. According to Gilbert, the picture's iconography is by no means novel: in other pictures of similar subject-matter (and of Sienese provenance) — such as Pietro Lorenzetti's fresco in the lower church at Assisi, or the small panel by the so-called Maestro dell'Osservanza found today in the Vatican Gallery[8] — groups of people present at Christ's torment, and standing a little apart, are to be found. However, neither of these comparisons is very convincing: in Piero's *Flagellation*, the three men in the foreground are much farther away from the scene of Christ surrounded by his tormentors, on which, moreover (and this is the most telling point), they have turned their backs.

A similar attempt to find a scriptural correspondence that will explain Piero's entire composition has been made recently by L. Borgo[9]. He draws attention to the passage in the Gospel of St John (xviii. 28) in which we are told that the members of the Sanhedrin remained outside Pilate's palace in order not to contaminate themselves before Passover. This textual correspondence, precise though it seems to be, none the less leaves several features unexplained: why, for example, is the young man in the centre wearing a tunic, and why does he go barefoot, while the two men are shod and wear modern clothes? Borgo sets out, by way of some very frail arguments[10], to trace three more or less analogous characters in various flagellations, some earlier and some later than Piero's; and he explains this iconographic tradition by reference to a ninth-century Hebrew text concerning Jesus' trial. In this, three opponents of Pilate's are mentioned — a priest, an old man, and someone called "the gardener" because it was in his garden that Jesus was eventually buried. Apart from the difficulty (acknowledged by Borgo himself) of identifying the barefoot young man as "the gardener", there is another and graver

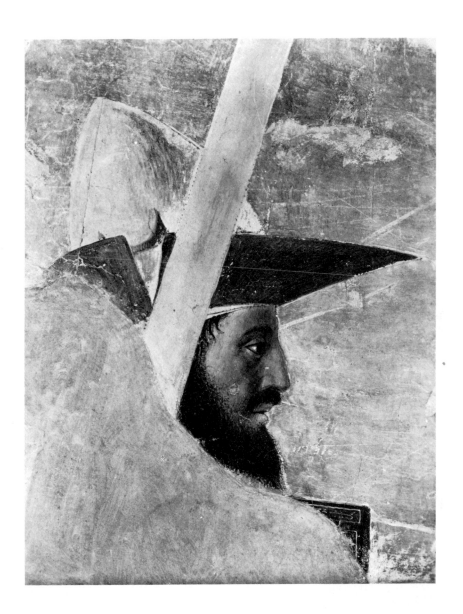

1. PIERO DELLA FRANCESCA, *Triumph of Constantine* (DETAIL).

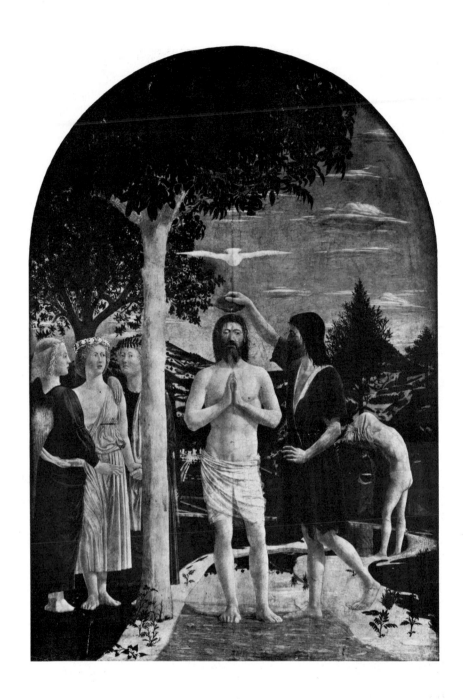

2-3. PIERO DELLA FRANCESCA, *Baptism of Christ*, (AND DETAIL).

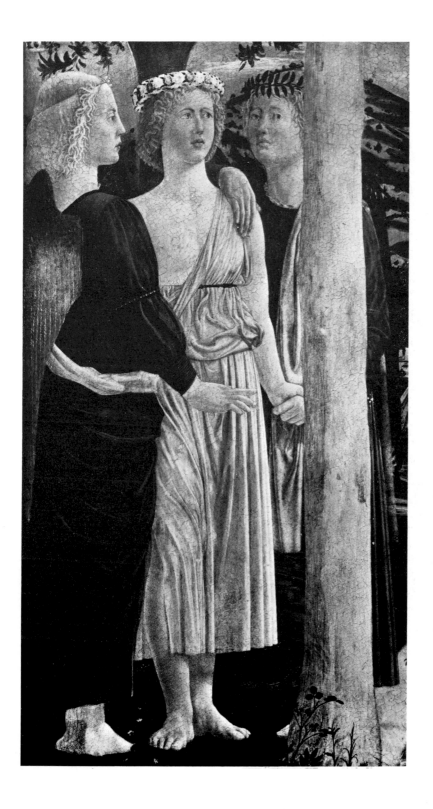

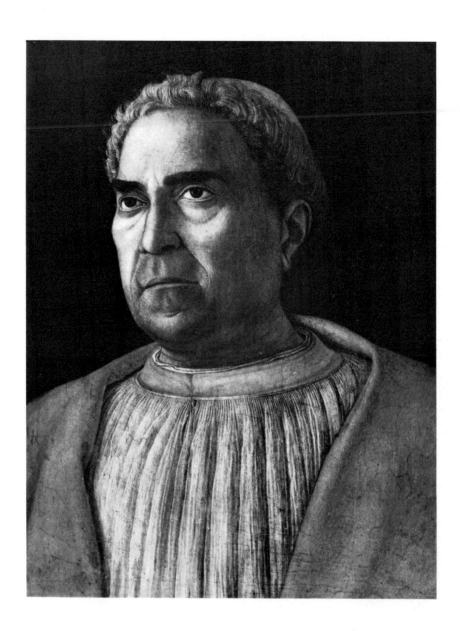

4. ANDREA MANTEGNA, *Cardinal Ludovico.*

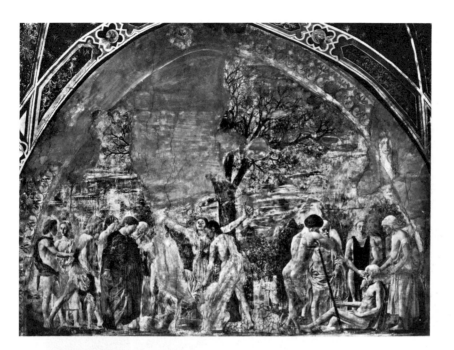

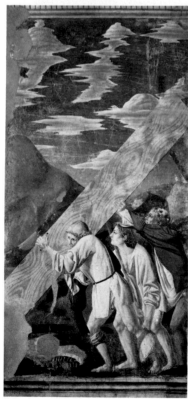

PIERO DELLA FRANCESCA,
5. *Death of Adam.*
6. *Raising of the Wood.*

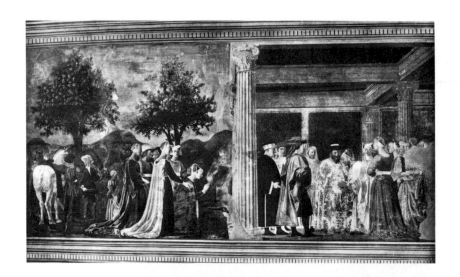

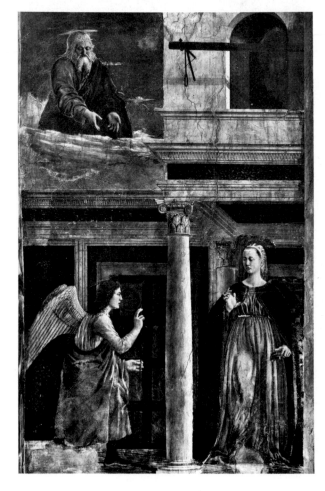

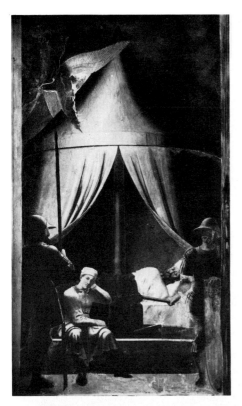

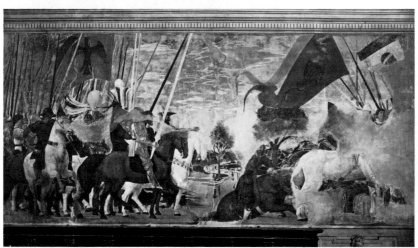

PIERO DELLA FRANCESCA,
7. *Queen of Sheba and her Retinue. Solomon Receiving the Queen of Sheba.*
8. *Annunciation.*
9. *Dream of Constantine.*
10. *Triumph of Constantine.*

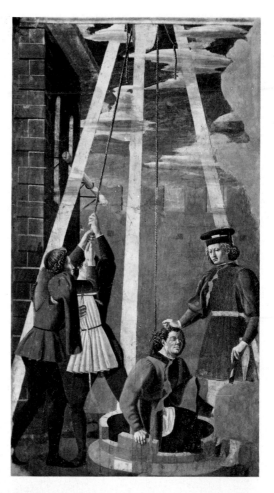

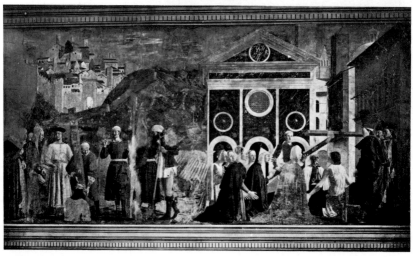

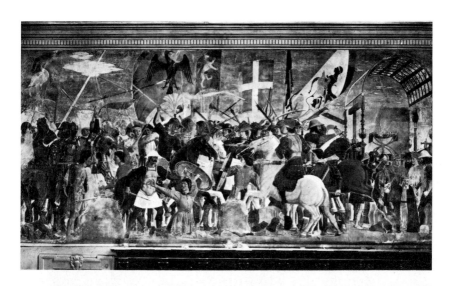

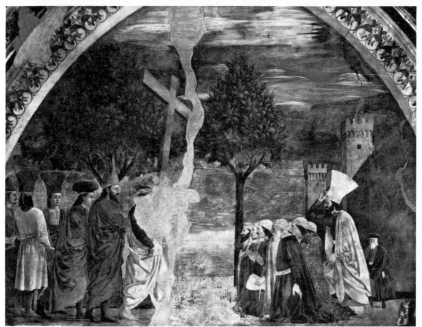

PIERO DELLA FRANCESCA,
11. *Torture of the Jew.*
12. *Discovery and Proof of the Cross.*
13. *Defeat of Chosroes.*
14. *Exaltation of the Cross.*

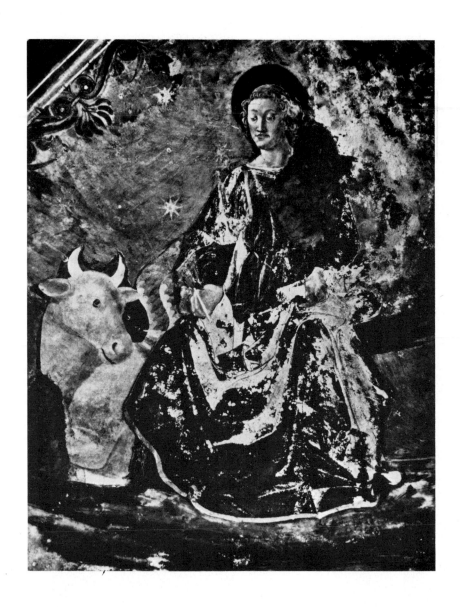

15. PIERO DELLA FRANCESCA, *St Luke the Evangelist*.

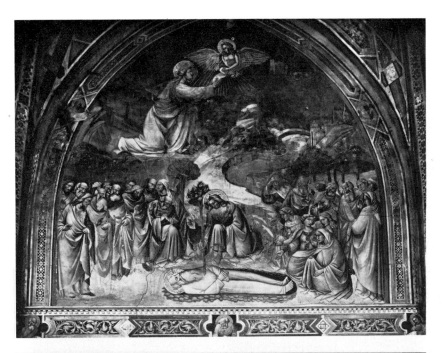

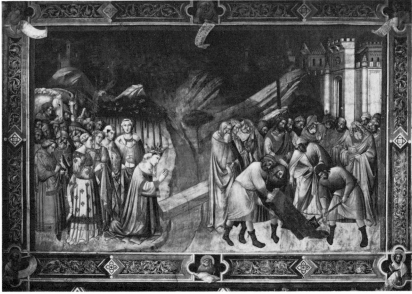

AGNOLO GADDI,

16. *Death of Adam.*

17. *Queen of Sheba Kneeling before the Wood of the Cross. Solomon Burying the Wood.*

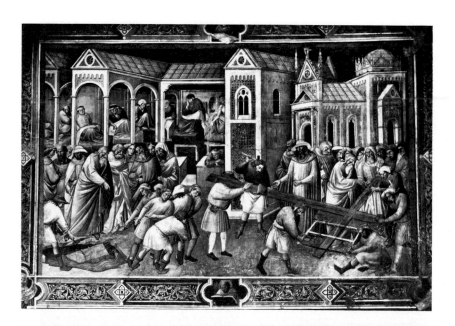

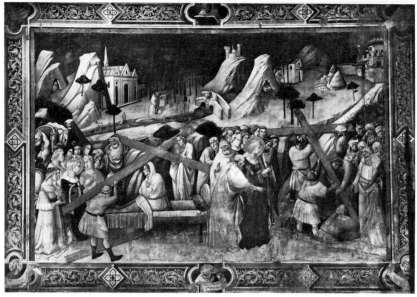

AGNOLO GADDI.
18. *Making of the Cross.*
19. *Empress Helena Making Proof of the Three Crosses.*

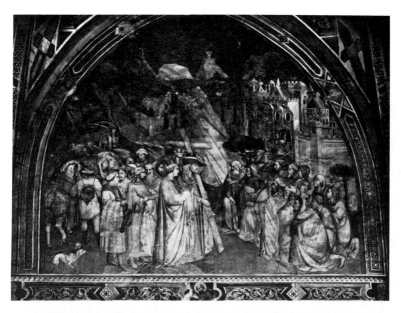

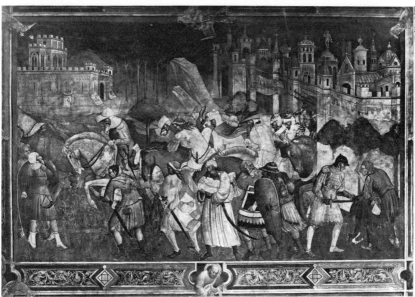

AGNOLO GADDI,
20. *Empress Helena Taking the Cross to Jerusalem.*
21. *Chosroes Removing the Cross from Jerusalem.*

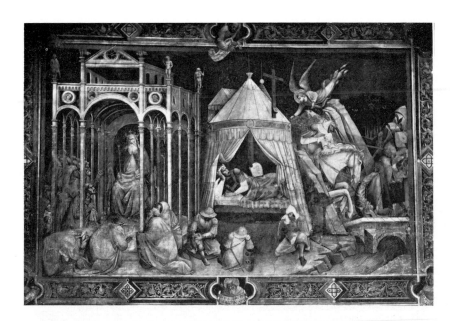

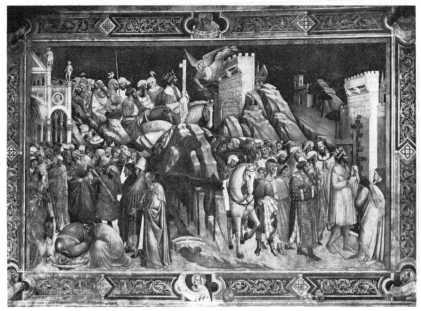

AGNOLO GADDI.
22. *Chosroes Worshipped by His Subjects. Dream of Heraclius.*
23. *Beheading of Chosroes. Heraclius Returning the Cross to Jerusalem.*

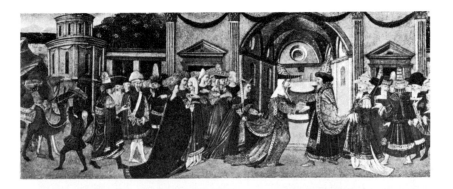

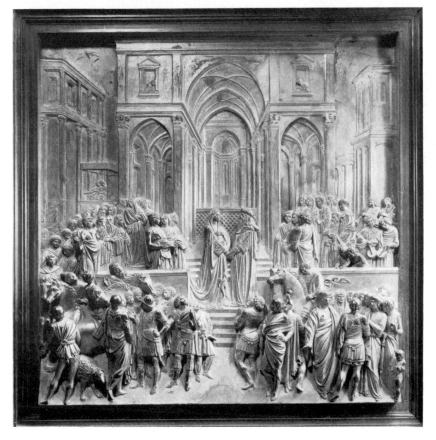

24. FLORENTINE WEDDING-CHEST PAINTING, *Solomon and the Queen of Sheba* (DETAIL).

25. LORENZO GHIBERTI, *Solomon and the Queen of Sheba*.

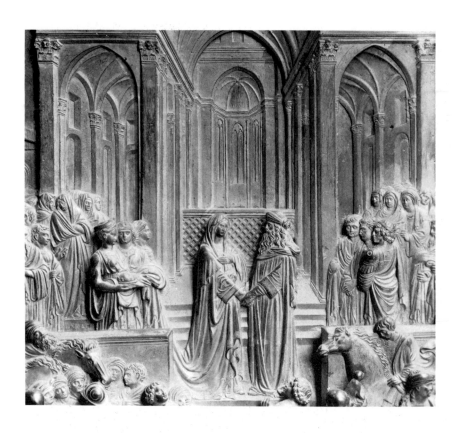

26. LORENZO GHIBERTI, *Solomon and the Queen of Sheba* (DETAIL).

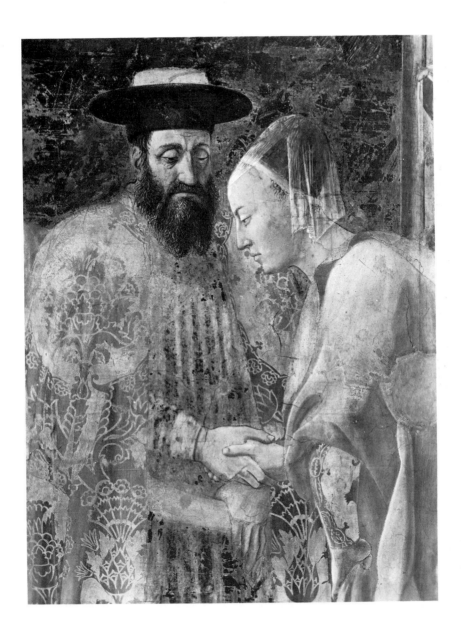

27. PIERO DELLA FRANCESCA, *Solomon Receiving the Queen of Sheba* (DETAIL).

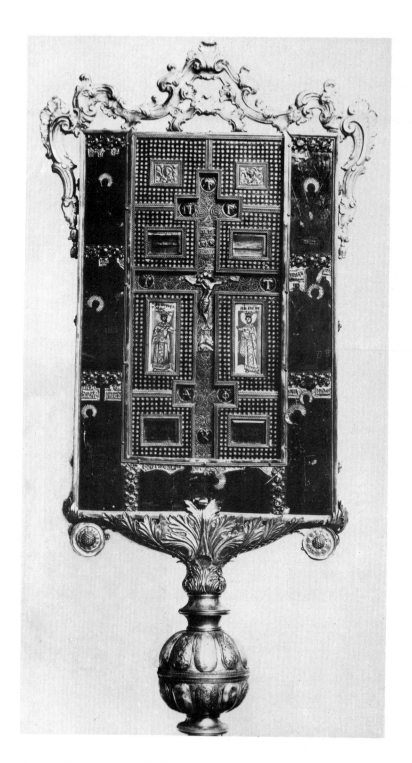

28. CASKET, ONCE THE PROPERTY OF CARDINAL BESSARION.

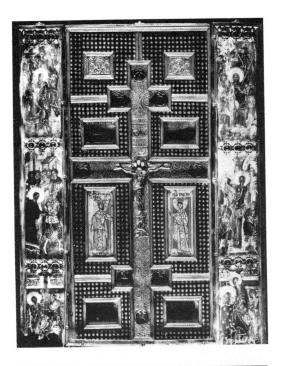

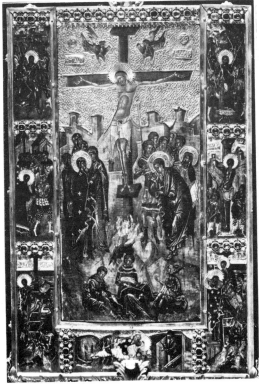

29-30. BESSARION'S CASKET (CLOSED
AND OPEN).

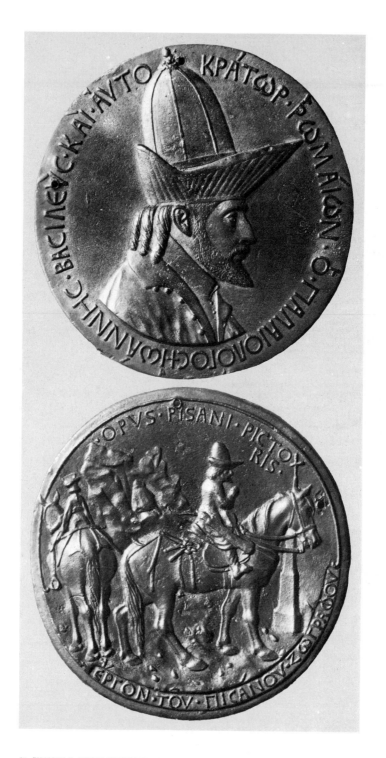

31. PISANELLO, MEDAL OF JOHN VIII PALAEOLOGUS.

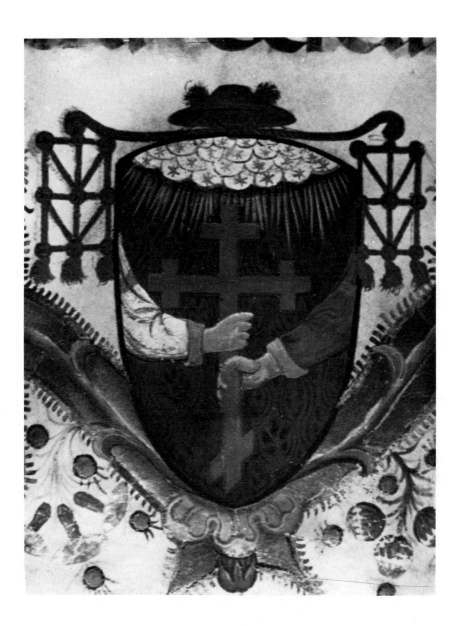

32. ANTHEM-BOOK GIVEN BY BESSARION, NO. 2 IN SERIES (DETAIL).

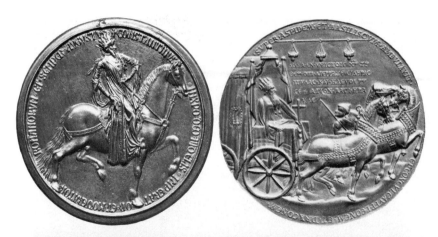

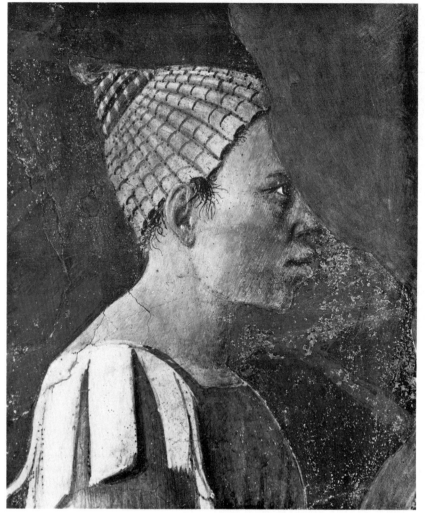

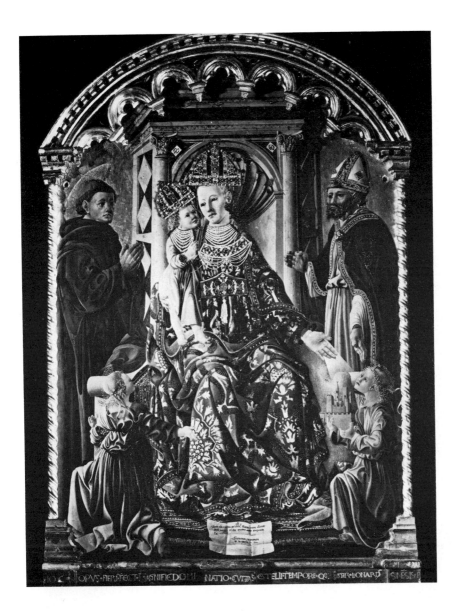

33. MEDAL OF CONSTANTINE (FACE).

34. MEDAL OF HERACLIUS (REVERSE SIDE).

35. PIERO DELLA FRANCESCA, *Queen of Sheba and her Retinue* (DETAIL).

36. GIOVANNI DI PIAMONTE, *Madonna Enthroned and Saints.*

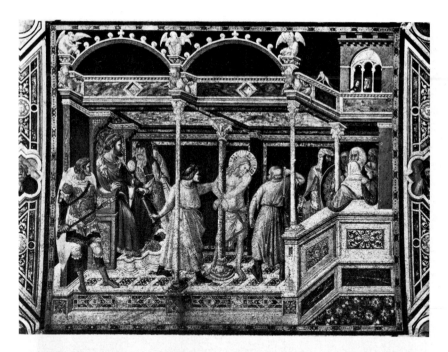

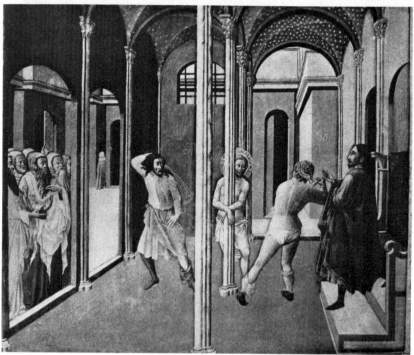

37. PIETRO LORENZETTI, *Flagellation of Christ.*
38. MAESTRO DELL'OSSERVANZA, *Flagellation of Christ.*

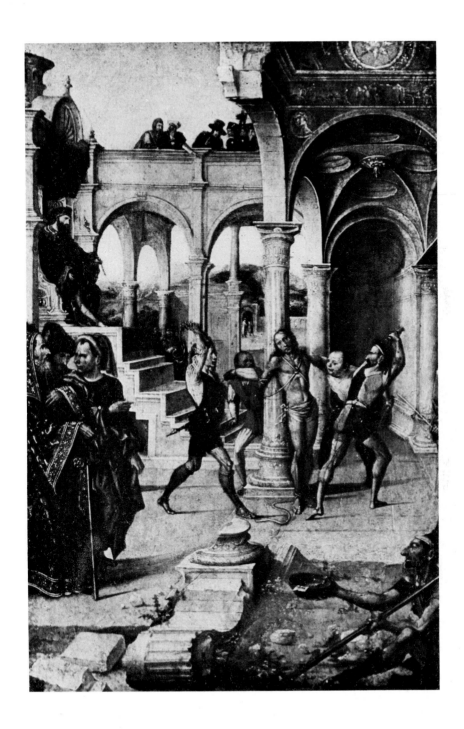

39. ALEJO FERNANDEZ (?), *Flagellation of Christ*.

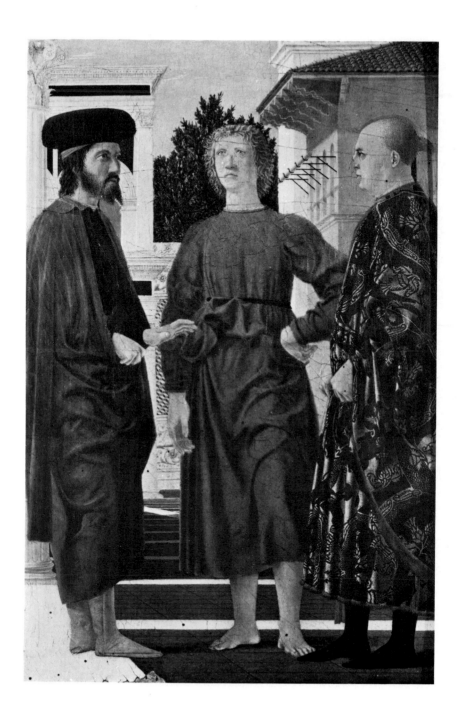

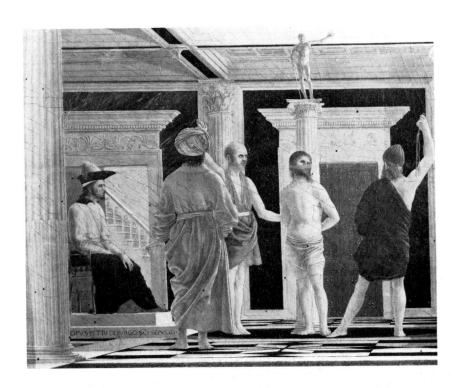

40-41. PIERO DELLA FRANCESCA, *Flagellation of Christ* (DETAILS).

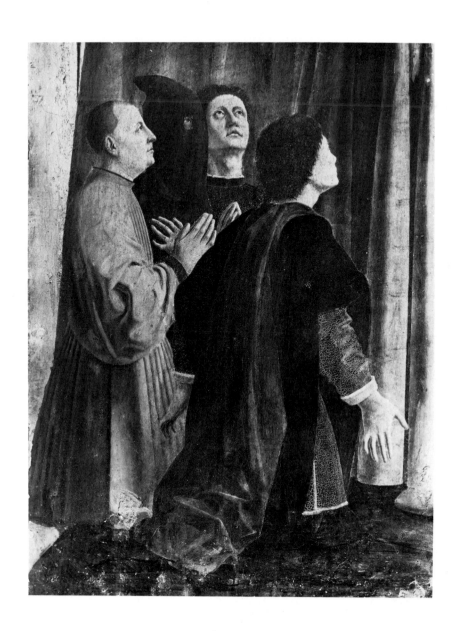

42. PIERO DELLA FRANCESCA, *Madonna of the Misericordia* (DETAIL).

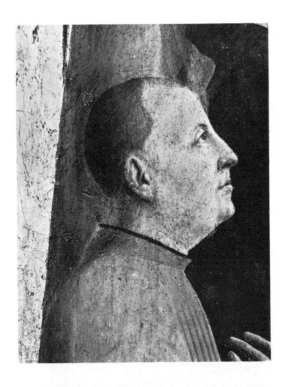

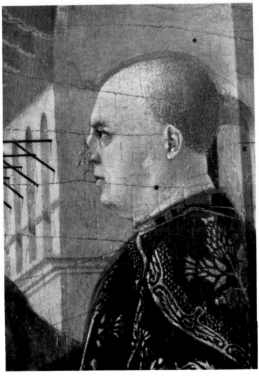

PIERO DELLA FRANCESCA,
43. *Madonna della Misericordia*
(DETAIL).
44. *Flagellation of Christ* (DETAIL).

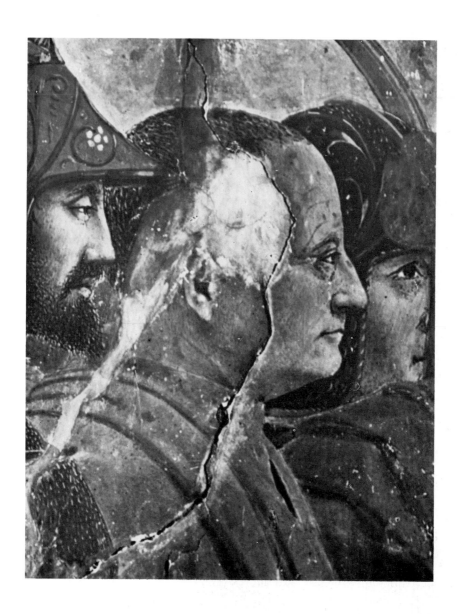

45. PIERO DELLA FRANCESCA, *Defeat of Chosroes* (DETAIL).

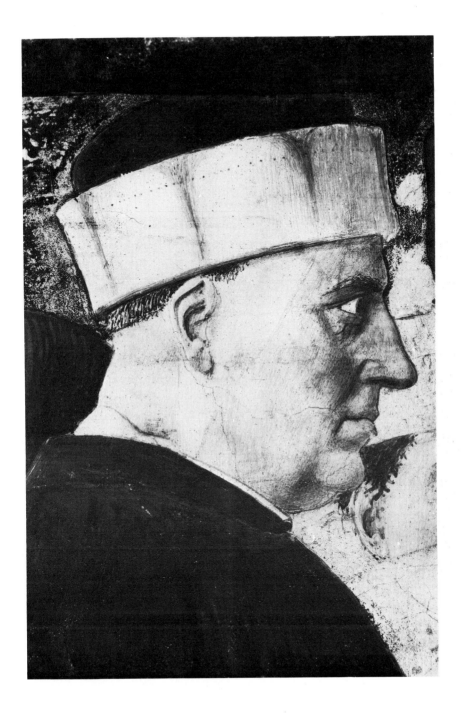

46. PIERO DELLA FRANCESCA, *Solomon Receiving the Queen of Sheba* (DETAIL).

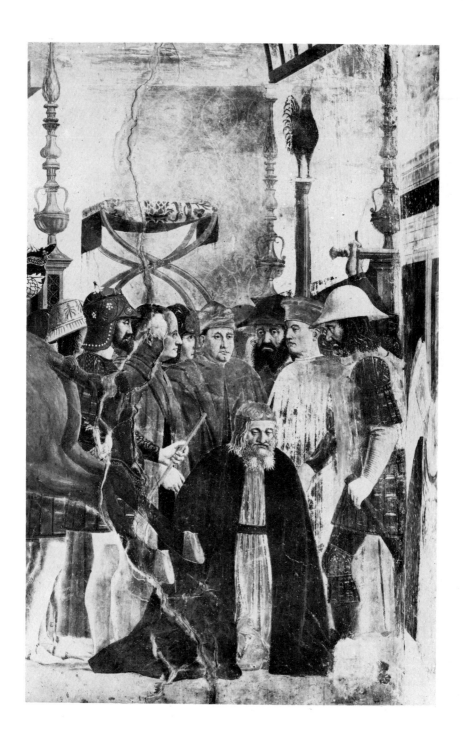

47. PIERO DELLA FRANCESCA, *Defeat of Chosroes* (DETAIL).

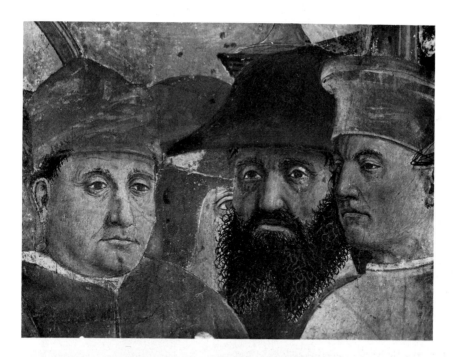

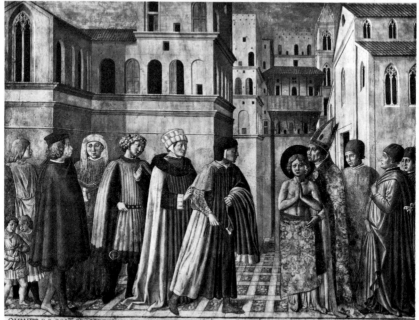

Q·VALITER·B·F·CORA·EPISCOPO·ASISII·RENVIT·PATRI·HEREDITATEM·PATERNAM·ET·OMIA·VESTIMENTA·ET·FEMORALIA·B·TRI·REIECIT

48. PIERO DELLA FRANCESCA, , *Defeat of Chosroes* (DETAIL).
49. BENOZZO GOZZOLI, *St Francis Stripping Himself of his Possessions.*

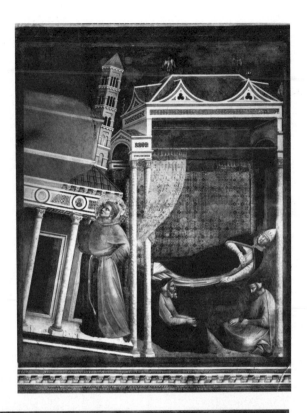

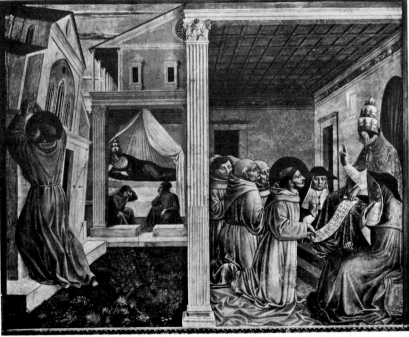

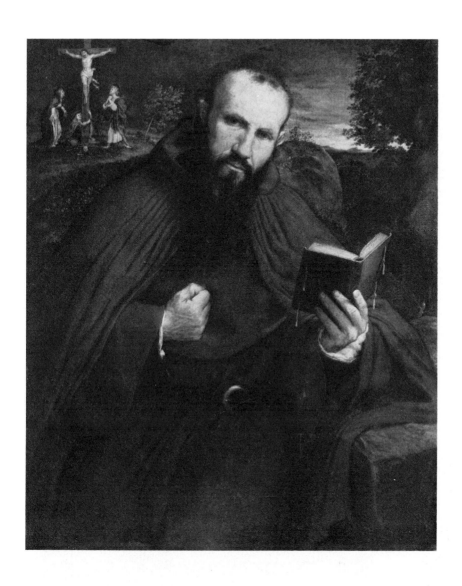

50. GIOTTO, *Dream of Innocent III*.
51. BENOZZO GOZZOLI, *Dream of Innocent III*.
52. LORENZO LOTTO, *Brother Gregorio Belo of Vicenza*.

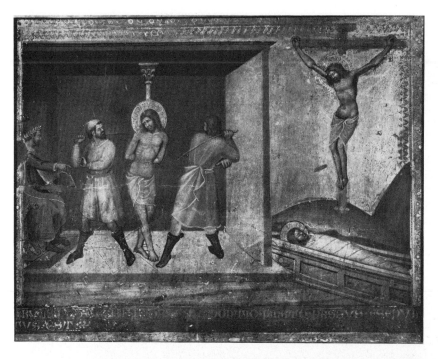

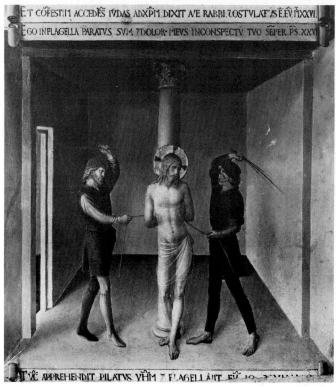

ET CŌFESTIM ACCEDĒS IVDAS ADXPM DIXIT AVE RABBI: 70STVLAF IS Ē EV MXXVI.
EGO INFLAGELLA PARATVS SVM 7DOLOR MEVS INCONSPECTV TVO SEPER PS XXVI

TVC APPREHENDIT PILATVS VHM 7 FLAGELLANT EVIO XVIII

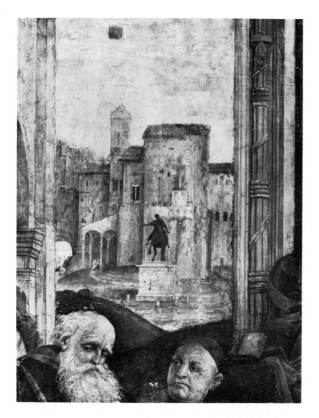

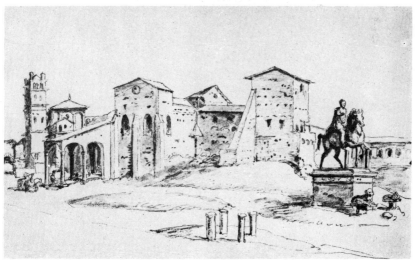

53. TADDEO DI BARTOLO (?), *Flagellation of Christ.*
54. BEATO ANGELICO, *Flagellation of Christ.*
55. FILIPPINO LIPPI, *Triumph of St Thomas* (DETAIL).
56. MARTEN VAN HEEMSKERK, *View of the Lateran.*

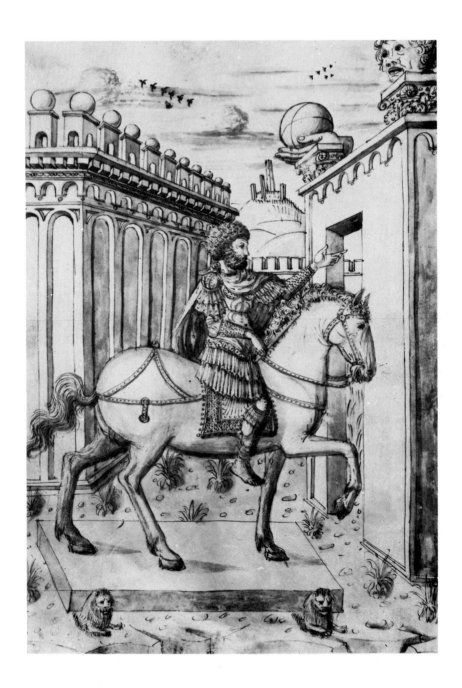

57. GIOVANNI MARCANOVA, *Antiquitates:* VIEW OF THE LATERAN.

58. HEAD OF CONSTANTINE.

59. HAND OF CONSTANTINE.

60. SPHERE, ONCE PART OF THE STATUE OF CONSTANTINE.

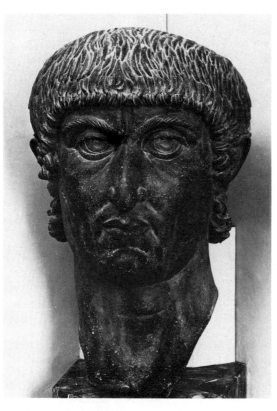

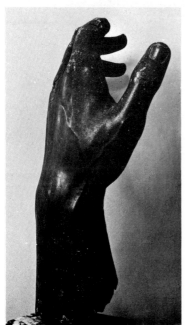

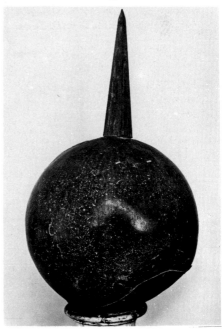

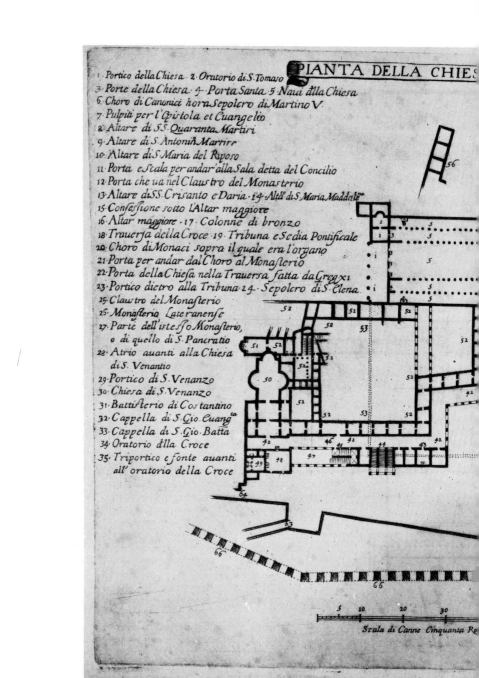

PIANTA DELLA CHIES[

1. Portico della Chiesa 2. Oratorio di S. Tomaso
3. Porte della Chiesa 4. Porta Santa 5. Naui dlla Chiesa
6. Choro di Canonici hora Sepolcro di Martino V.
7. Pulpiti per l'Epistola et Euangelio
8. Altare di SS. Quaranta Martiri
9. Altare di S. Antonin Martire
10. Altare di S. Maria del Riposo
11. Porta e Scala per andar alla Sala detta del Concilio
12. Porta che ua nel Claustro del Monasterio
13. Altare di SS. Crisanto e Daria. 14. Altâ di S. Maria Maddal.ᵉ
15. Confessione sotto l'Altar maggiore
16. Altar maggiore. 17. Colonne di bronzo
18. Trauersa della Croce. 19. Tribuna e Sedia Pontificale
20. Choro di Monaci sopra il quale era l'organo
21. Porta per andar dal Choro al Monasterio
22. Porta della Chiesa nella Trauersa fatta da Greg. x1
23. Portico dietro alla Tribuna 24. Sepolcro di S. Elena
25. Claustro del Monasterio
26. Monasterio Lateranense
27. Parte dell'istesso Monasterio,
    o di quello di S. Pancratio
28. Atrio auanti alla Chiesa
    di S. Venantio
29. Portico di S. Venanzo
30. Chiesa di S. Venanzo
31. Battisterio di Costantino
32. Cappella di S. Gio. Euangᵗᵃ
33. Cappella di S. Gio. Batta
34. Oratorio dlla Croce
35. Triportico e fonte auanti
    all'oratorio della Croce

5 10 20 30
Scala di Canne Cinquanta R[

61. PLAN OF THE LATERAN (FROM SEVERANO'S *Memorie sacre*).

36. Portico nouo e loggia della Benedittione
37. Sala detta del Concilio. 38. Tribuna colla mesura di n.ro Sig.
39. Tramezo doue erano le Porte dette Sante
40. Altare della B.Vergine
41. Loggia e Pulpito di Bonifatio per la Benedittione
42. Corridori del Palazzo Lateranense
43. Cappella di S. Siluestro 44. Luogo doue erano le scale sant
45. Scale e Porta del Palazo Lateranense
46. Porta interiore del Palazzo
47. Portico del Palazzo. 48. Vestibolo auanti alla Cappella di SS. SS.
49. Cappella di S. Lorenzo detta Santta Sanctorum
50. Triclinio di S. Leone. 3. rinouato dal Card. Francesco Barbe.
51. Oratorio di S. Nicolo. 52. Siti degli altri Oratorij Basiliche e
    del Palazzo Lateranense
53. Palazzo nuouo fatto da Sisto V.
54. Luogo della Guglia 55. Torre de gli Anibaldi
56. Vestigij e Sito delle Biblioteche: della Chiesa di
    S. Angelo: dell'Oratorio di S. Stefano e di altre
    fabriche uicin' alla chiesa di S. Gio: delle
    quali si fa mentione nel libro
57. Strada che uiene da S. Sebastiano
58. Monasterio di SS. Bartolomeo et Andrea
    hora Hospidale di S. Gio
59. Strada che uiene da S. Stefano
    Rotondo
60. Strada che uiene da SS. Quattro
61. Strada che uiene dal Coliseo
62. Strada che uiene da S. Maria Maggior
63. Strada antica che uiene dalla med.ª
64. Strada che ua a S. Croce
65. Sito di fabriche et Habitationi di
    Palatini
66. Acquedotti di Claudio

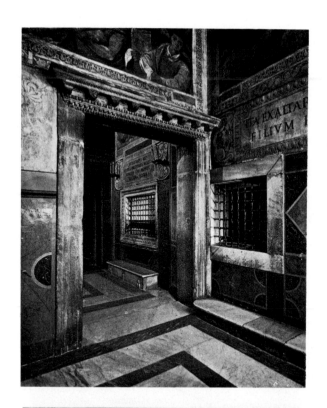

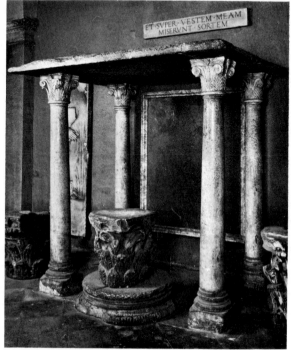

62. "PILATE'S DOORWAYS",
NEAR THE SCALA SANTA.
63. STONE, AND COLUMN WITH
"MENSURA CHRISTI", FROM THE
CLOISTER OF ST JOHN
LATERAN.

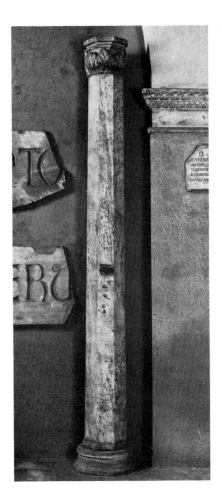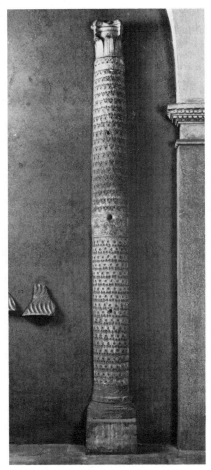

64. "PILATE'S COLUMN", FROM THE CLOISTER OF ST JOHN LATERAN.

65. ANOTHER "PILATE'S COLUMN" FROM THE CLOISTER OF ST JOHN LATERAN.

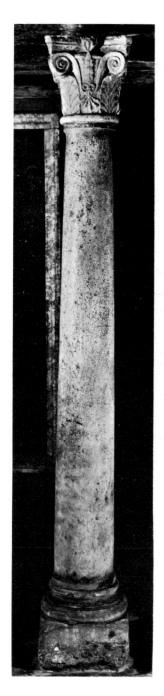
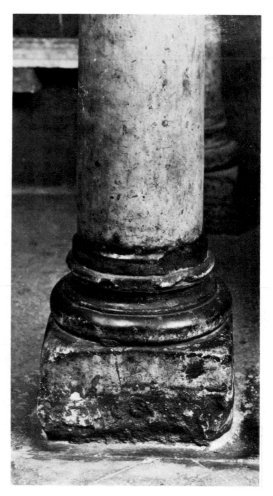

66-7. COLUMN WITH "MENSURA CHRISTI" FROM THE CLOISTER OF ST JOHN LATERAN, AND DETAIL.

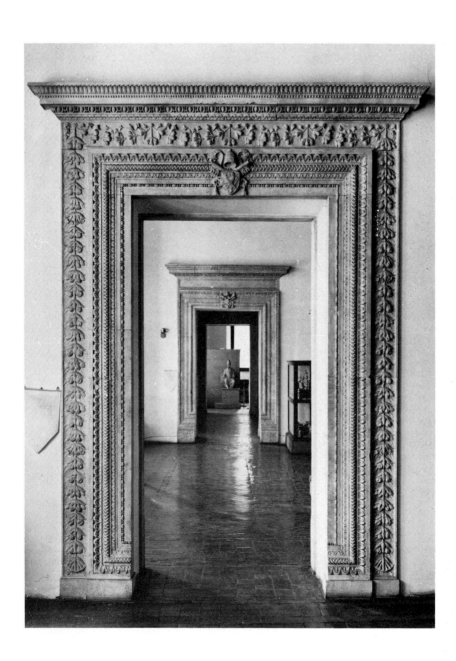

68. DOORWAY IN THE PALAZZO VENEZIA.

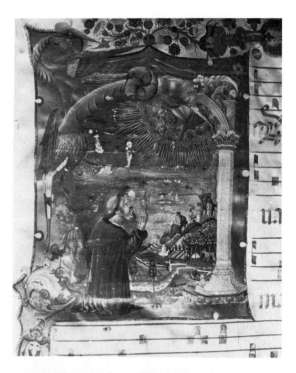

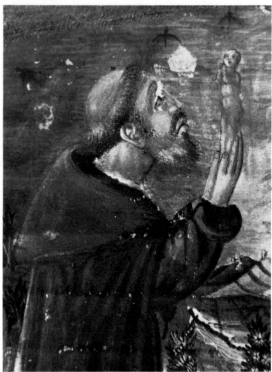

69-70. ANTHEM-BOOK GIVEN BY
BESSARION, NO. 2 IN SERIES,
FRONTISPIECE, AND DETAIL.

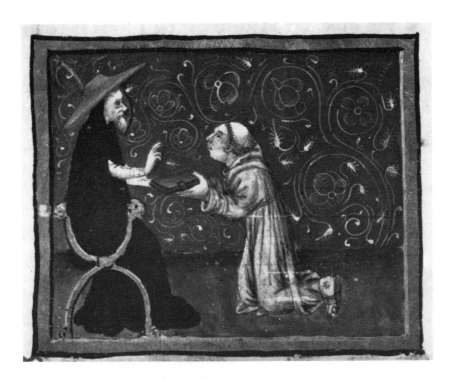

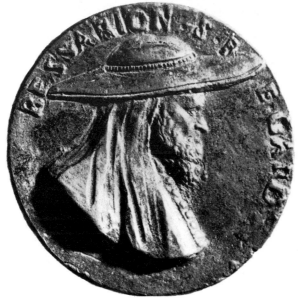

71. GRAZIANO THE MINORITE, *Summa de casibus conscientiae*, FRONTISPIECE (DETAIL).
72. MEDAL OF BESSARION (FACE).

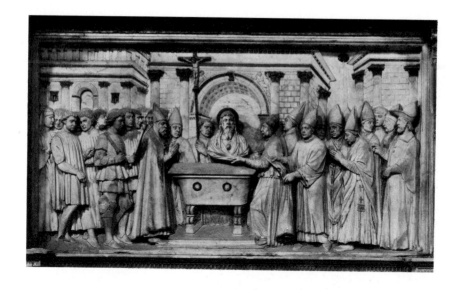

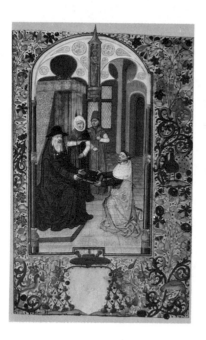
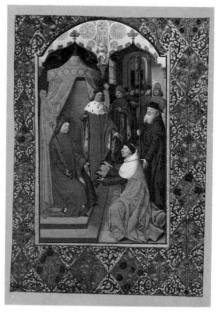

73. PAOLO ROMANO (COMPLETED BY A FOLLOWER OF ANDREA BREGNO), FUNERAL MONUMENT OF
    PIUS II: THE GIFT OF THE RELIC OF ST ANDREW'S HEAD.

74. GUILLAUME FICHET, *Rhetorica*, FRONTISPIECE.

75. BESSARION, *Epistolae et orationes*, FRONTISPIECE.

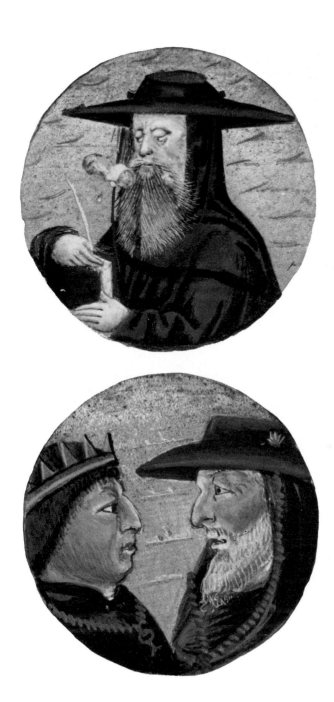

76. ANDREA CONTRARIO, *Obiurgatio in Platonis calumniatorem* (DETAIL).
77. BESSARION, *Adversus calumniatorem Platonis* (DETAIL).

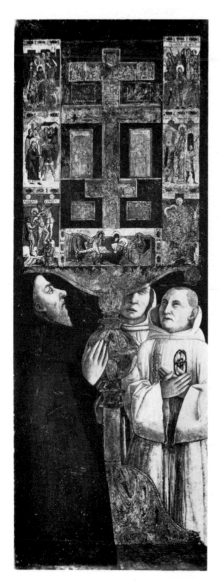
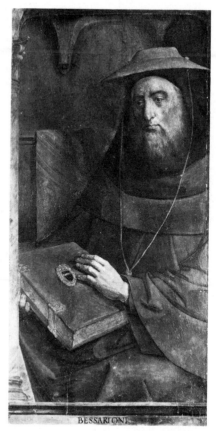

78. GENTILE BELLINI, *Bessarion kneeling before the casket given to the Scuola Grande della Carità.*

79. PEDRO BERRUGUETE (?), *Bessarion.*

80. 16th-CENTURY ANONYMOUS PAINTER (AFTER GENTILE BELLINI?), *Bessarion.*

81. DIPTYCH OF BESSARION.

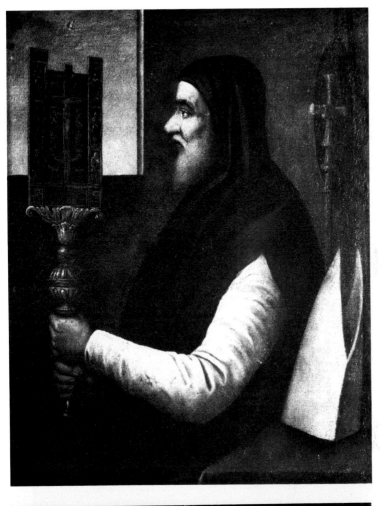

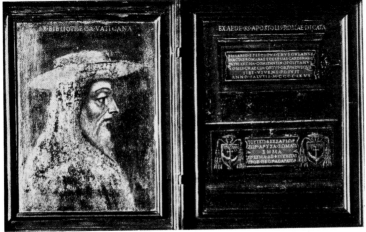

82. CRISTOFORO ALTISSIMO, *Bessarion*.

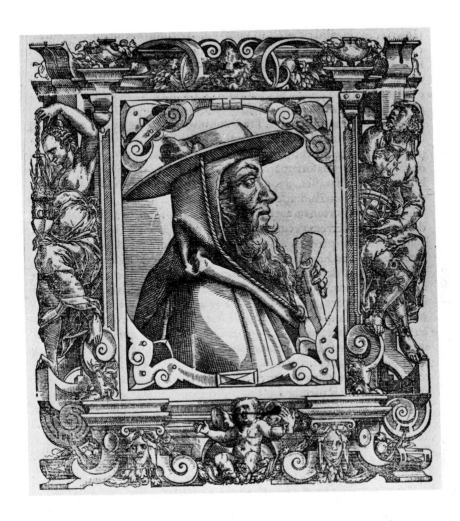

83. *Bessarion* (FROM GIOVIO'S *Elogia virorum literis illustrium*).

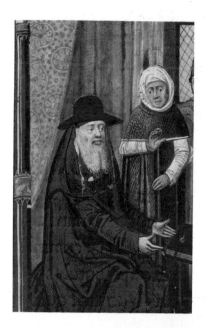
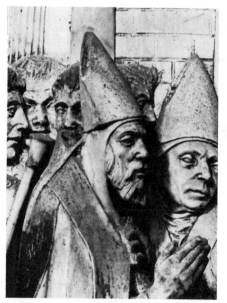
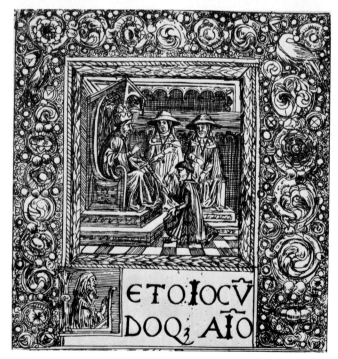

84. GUILLAUME FICHET, *Rhetorica*, FRONTISPIECE (DETAIL).

85. PAOLO ROMANO (COMPLETED BY A FOLLOWER OF ANDREA BREGNO), FUNERAL MONUMENT OF
PIUS II: THE GIFT OF THE RELIC OF ST ANDREW'S HEAD (DETAIL).

86. ILLUMINATED INITIAL WITH PORTRAIT OF BESSARION (FROM *Ludovici Bentivoli virtutis, et nobilitatis
insignia*).

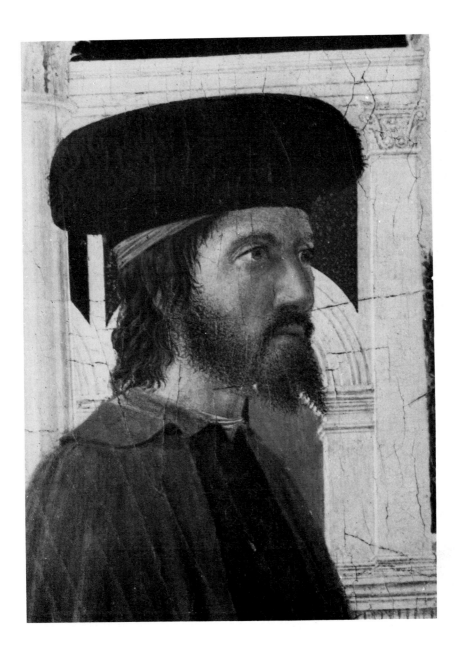

87. PIERO DELLA FRANCESCA, *Flagellation of Christ* (DETAIL).

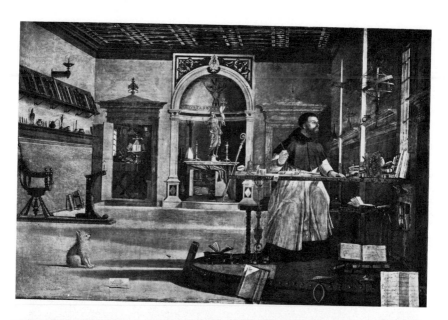

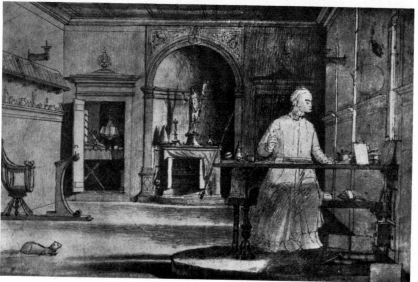

VITTORE CARPACCIO,

88. *Vision of St Augustine.*

89. DRAWING.

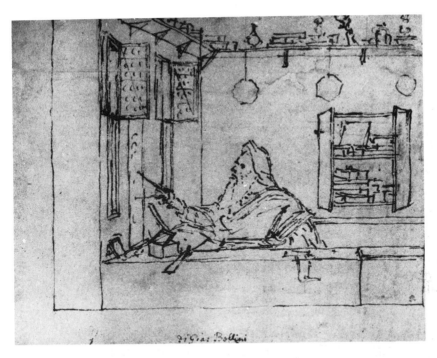

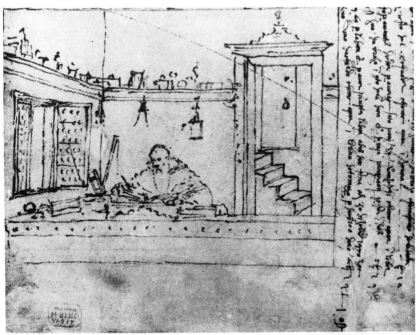

90-91. VITTORE CARPACCIO, DRAWINGS.

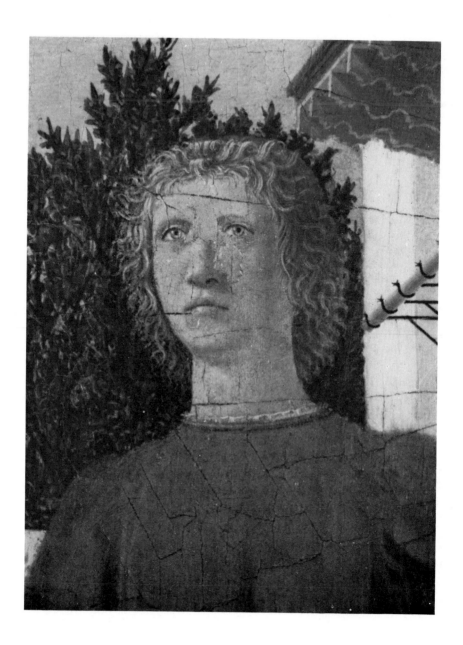

92. PIERO DELLA FRANCESCA, *Flagellation of Christ* (DETAIL).

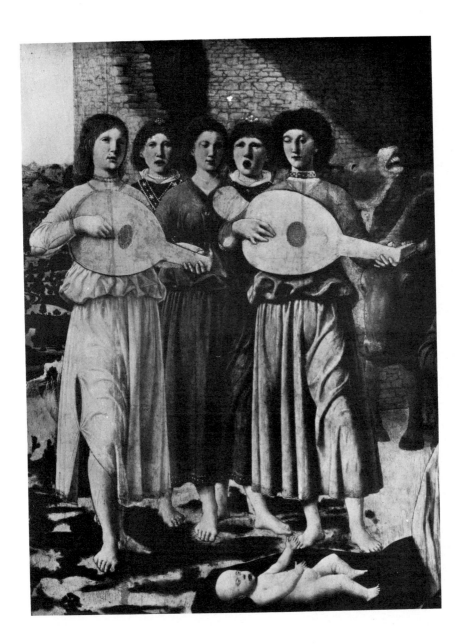

93. PIERO DELLA FRANCESCA, *Nativity* (DETAIL).

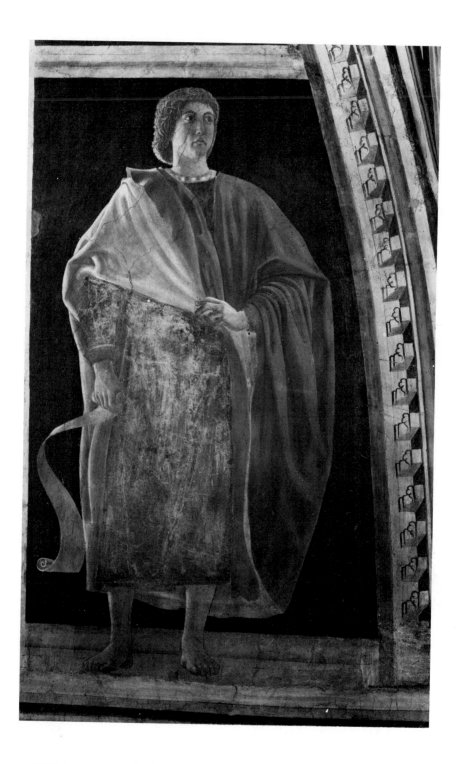

94. PIERO DELLA FRANCESCA, *Prophet*.

objection: we don't have any evidence that this Hebrew text can have circulated in fifteenth-century Italy. Borgo is thus obliged to postulate a missing source, connected in some way with this Hebrew tradition, on which Piero's picture may have been based. But why should the members of the Sanhedrin be placed in the foreground? Borgo argues that Piero drew his inspiration from the lost *Flagellation* of Andrea del Castagno in Santa Croce. The fact that this fresco had been "scratched and spoiled" (as Vasari wrote) "by children and other simpletons, who have scratched out all the heads and the arms and almost all the remainder of the figures of the Jews"[11] is meant to prove not only that these latter were fully visible, but even that they were most probably "situated to some significant extent towards the foreground" of the composition. Leaving aside the captiousness of this conclusion, it seems clear that Borgo's edifice of interpretation rests on two rather shaky pillars: a text we cannot trace, and a lost fresco.

It is true that a *Flagellation* does exist which would seem at first sight to confirm Borgo's hypothesis of an iconographic tradition that singled out three well-characterized figures from among Pilate's interlocutors. This is an anonymous small panel painted in oils, probably in the early decades of the sixteenth century, and kept today in the Prado in Madrid. We see Christ being beaten by his tormentors in an open gallery, while outside it, a little set apart from Pilate's throne, three men are standing by: an old man with a beard (clearly a priest), a middle-aged man and a youth. Are these R. Joshua ben Perachiah, Marinus, and the "gardener", R. Judah, mentioned in the ninth-century Hebrew text, and did this text also make its way, by unknown intermediate stages, to the knowledge of Piero, or of whoever commissioned him[12]? The explanation is probably simpler. The Prado *Flagellation* has been attributed, at various times, to different artists — to a Spanish follower of Bosch, to Juan de Flandes, to Alejo Fernandez or a painter of his circle. The question remains open, in any case. But the great prominence given to the architecture has led scholars to suppose that the painting was inspired by some Italian model (in the past, significantly, it was attributed to Antonello da Messina). It has been remarked that the ruined building that is the scene of Christ's martyrdom derives from a well-known engraving bearing Bramante's signature[13]. This name we associate with Urbino — and with Piero (by whom Bramante was later said to have been "created"): and Post has indeed invoked Piero's *Flagellation* in connection with the Prado panel, surmising that its painter had travelled in central Italy[14]. Some connection between the two works, direct or indirect (perhaps by way of Pedro Berruguete, who worked at Urbino and who completed the altarpiece by Piero, now in the Brera, showing Federico da Montefeltro's coat of arms), does indeed seem plausible. The positioning of the three men seems to echo that of the three characters in the foreground of Piero's painting: more specifically, the brocade mantle of the old priest in the Madrid painting irresistibly recalls that worn by the old man in Urbino. To be sure, their physiognomies are quite different; and the gestures and clothes of the two outside figures have been, so to speak, reversed. Above all, we seem able to make out in the Madrid panel a desire to normalize the iconography of Piero's *Flagellation*[15]: the three men stand to one side of Christ, rather than turning their backs on him at a distance (and one of them is actually pointing to him, turning toward the other two); the richly clad old man has been given a long beard, identifying him as a Hebrew priest and placing him unambiguously in the sacred scene;

the middle-aged man, who is speaking, wears a black cap, rather than an oriental hat; the young man has neither tunic nor bare feet. Whether or not it is connected in some way with Piero's *Flagellation*, this *Flagellation* in the Prado in any case confirms its absolute iconographic uniqueness.

It is precisely this singularity that is denied by those who see Piero's picture as a variant of the normal flagellations. Their efforts, however, are confounded not only by the painting's overall compositional structure, but by something else: the physiognomical individualization and contemporary clothes of two of the three men in the foreground. The possibility that these may be portraits leads us at once to ask who the persons depicted may be, and by what link they are connected with the flagellation scene in the background. And this brings us to the third, and most numerous, group of interpretations.

Among these is included the oldest interpretation, formulated during the eighteenth century by Urbino scholars, and found as part of the entry in the 1744 inventory that we have already quoted. According to this, the three in the foreground are Oddantonio, Count of Urbino (in the middle), his brother Federico (on the right), and the latter's son, Guidubaldo (on the left). This triple identification, which is patently absurd, since the respective ages of the persons shown are not congruous with it and since Federico's unmistakable features are conspicuous by their absence, was later corrected. Oddantonio, the sole survivor from the first hypothesis, was now thought to be flanked by the wicked counsellors Manfredo dei Pio and Tommasso dell'Agnello, who were killed together with Oddantonio himself in the plot of 1444[16]. Further confirmation for this interpretation was found in the phrase from Psalm 2 that we have already discussed, "Convenerunt in unum". The words were applied not only to Christ but also to the murdered Duke, and a relation of analogy thus proposed between the scene in the foreground and that in the background. This iconographic decoding gave rise to a *terminus post quem* — 1444, the year of the conspiracy and of Oddantonio's death — which was deemed to be probably very close to the date of the painting's actual execution, since its presumed patron, Federico da Montefeltro, would hardly have delayed long in commemorating his murdered brother.

To date the picture this early, and thus to set it among the earliest of Piero's works to have come down to us, raises quite serious stylistic difficulties, of which Longhi himself was ultimately forced to take cognizance, despite his long-held commitment to the view (together with all its implications) that the picture portrayed Oddantonio[17]. From a strictly iconographic point of view, the interpretation appears altogether baseless, since the identification of the figures came very late[18], the parallel between Oddantonio and Christ seems implausible, and the verse of the Psalm recalled by the phrase "convenerunt in unum" is singularly ill-adapted to its supposed evocation of the counsels of the two wicked ministers (and still less appropriate as a reference to the plot), speaking as it does of "reges terrae, et principes".

Despite this, the interpretation went unchallenged until the middle of the present century. (Toesca's solitary dissenting view, expressed, as we have seen, in somewhat crudely anti-historical terms, found no supporters.) In 1951, Clark refuted it, quietly but effectively setting out the grounds for an altogether different reading[19]. It is worth remarking that his argument's point of departure was not iconographic but stylistic: the echoes of Alberti's architecture, and more especially of the porticos of San Pancrazio and Santo Sepolcro Rucellai, which are discernible in Pilate's loggia (itself in turn compared to the loggia where Solomon greets the Queen of Sheba in the Arezzo fresco). Thus the date implied by the identification of the young man as Oddantonio (1444 or very soon afterwards) was rejected, being too early in terms of Alberti's stylistic development; and the identification itself was refuted, on the grounds that a tyrant such as Oddantonio was hardly likely to have been shown with bare feet, or more generally to have been commemorated at all following the conspiracy that had killed him. Instead, the hypothesis was put forward that the three figures were intently meditating on Christ's sufferings, which were a symbol of the tribulations undergone by the Church at the hands of the Turks (evoked by the turbaned figure with his back towards us). A similar meaning was to be found in the verse "Convenerunt in unum", which is part of the liturgy for Good Friday[20] and which in the Books of Hours often accompanies images of the flagellation. All this formed the basis of a broader suggested dating of the work — roughly between 1455 and 1460 — as well as of two more specific suggestions: that the picture was painted in 1459, on the occasion of the assembly called to Mantua by Pius II to exhort the Christian princes to the Crusade, or else in 1461, when Thomas Palaeologus, brother of the dead Emperor John VIII, conveyed to Rome the famous relic of the apostle Andrew[21]. Clark in fact discerned "a certain resemblance" to the Palaeologi in the bearded man, but he none the less admitted that this interpretation left unresolved the identity of the richly dressed figure (certainly a portrait) in the foreground, and the significance of the "arcadian youth" at his side.

Clark's contribution marked an important date in the history of the Urbino picture's interpretation — both for its intrinsic value, and because in its complete rebuttal of the hitherto accepted thesis it opened the way for a debate that has now extended over thirty years. We have already considered the group of suggestions that attempt, as if in reaction to Clark, to replace Piero's picture within the more or less canonical iconography of the flagellation of Christ. Meanwhile, other scholars have tried to effect a compromise between Clark's thesis and the traditional one. Siebenhüner identifies the three characters, from the left, as John VIII Palaeologus, Oddantonio and Guidantonio da Montefeltro: he holds the picture to be connected with Pius II's projects for a Crusade, to have been commissioned by Federico da Montefeltro, and to have been executed in 1464-65[22]. According to Battisti, the three are (from the left) a Byzantine ambassador, Oddantonio, and either Filippo Maria Visconti or (if you prefer) Francesco Sforza; the patron was Federico da Montefeltro, who was seeking to rehabilitate Oddantonio's memory; and the date is 1474, or 1463, or else an intermediate date (1465-69)[23].

These identifications rest, for the most part, on little or no documentary basis. More analytic, but no less unacceptable, is M. Aronberg Lavin's lengthy essay[24], which puts forward an altogether new interpretation. She argues that Piero depicts, on the left,

Ottaviano Ubaldini della Carda — a courtier of Federico da Montefeltro, and the painting's patron — in conversation with Ludovico Gonzaga, the Marquis of Mantua (on the right). They are talking, Lavin argues, about the family misfortunes which both had suffered: the death of the former's son (1458), and the illness of the latter's nephew (1456-60). The central figure depicts this nephew before he became ill. Ubaldini, it is argued, is exhorting Ludovico to resignation, and reminding him, by way of the example of the flagellation evoked in the background, that Christian glory is higher than earthly woes. This interpretation, as several critics have insisted[25], is altogether baseless taken as a whole; but it does contain some useful hints, to which we shall return.

T. Gouma-Peterson's rewarding essay[26], on the other hand, returns to the line of interpretation opened up by Clark, deepening it in certain respects. Her scholarly analysis begins with the identification of Pilate with John VIII Palaeologus (an identification already put forward by Babelon which nobody had followed up). This is definitively confirmed by the detail of the crimson stockings, which formed part of the regalia of the Eastern emperors. Christ's flagellation is held to symbolize (as Clark had suggested) the sufferings of the Church at the hands of the Turks. Pilate's inaction — for he does nothing to halt these sufferings — is matched by that of the right-hand figure in the foreground, whom Gouma-Peterson sees as a "western prince", without identifying him more precisely. The bearded man stands between these two; he is a Greek, as shown by his clothes and his hat, and possibly an ambassador. His position in the picture seems to mark him out as a mediator between East (Pilate-John VIII) and West (the "prince" in the foreground). The young man, on the other hand, is to be seen as an allegorical figure, the "champion of virtue" ready to do battle. And he is exhorting the bearded Greek himself to battle against the Turks (depicted in the background), so that Christ's sufferings may be relieved. The latter are represented as an "archetypal event inserted into the context of historical reality"[27]. The gap between the two worlds, that of the present (the figures in the foreground) and that of the past (the flagellation), is emphasized, not only by the spatial distance, but also by the existence of two different light-sources (respectively on the left and on the right). Gouma-Peterson follows Lavin in attributing to this feature an expressive and even a symbolic value[28]. The picture would thus have a decidedly political meaning. Gouma-Peterson argues that it was commissioned by Cardinal Bessarion, who then sent it to Federico da Montefeltro (with whom he was very closely linked) to convince him of the necessity of a Crusade against the Turks. Its dating may fall within either of two periods, 1459-64 or 1459-72, since at these times plans were being laid (by Paul II and Sixtus IV respectively) for Crusades — plans which Bessarion warmly supported. Gouma-Peterson asks whether we should not see the bearded Greek in the foreground as a portrait of Bessarion. Her reply is in the negative: the bearded man's face is unlike Bessarion's, and besides he wears neither the insignia of a Cardinal nor the habit of a monk of St Basil in which Bessarion is generally portrayed. She concludes that we are to see this as a "crypto-portrait" of Bessarion, in the guise of a Byzantine ambassador.

It is not clear how we are meant to take this last expression: how can one speak of a portrait, if the data are inconsistent with those which ought to characterize the person in

41

question? We shall see below whether a less contradictory conclusion cannot be reached on this point.

This review of the scholarly literature, summary and incomplete as it is, should suffice to show that the same ingredients, cooked in different hermeneutic sauces, can produce concoctions of very varying flavour. One might be pardoned for a somewhat sceptical reaction to this spectacle of thirty years of extremely close discussion about the *Flagellation*, which have failed to result in even the most minimal agreement about the painting's date, or its patron, or the subject that it represents.

This last element is the key in the present case. Since no documents have been traced on the painting's commissioning, or even its original location, scholars have had to couple their various hypotheses about its patron to the identification of its subject. The same has gone, at least in most cases, for its dating: leaving aside the interpretative line that manages to see Piero's painting as just one more flagellation more or less conforming to the norm, all the other iconographic suggestions have also implied a dating, more or less elastic and conjectural.

What this means is that the contest over the *Flagellation* is played out entirely on the terrain of iconographic decoding. And the briefest glance at the series of interpretations hitherto advanced shows that some progress, despite everything, has been made. If we leave aside the most improbable and unfounded theses (including the traditional identification of Oddantonio as one of the painting's subjects), then the competing interpretations can be reduced to two. First we have Gilbert's suggestions, put forward in his second contribution, that Piero's *Flagellation* must be placed in a pre-existing iconographic series — which then makes it a picture of a sacred subject, where every figure depicted plays a role in an episode of Christ's passion. Alternatively, there is the hypothesis put forward by Clark and considerably modified by Gouma-Peterson, which proposes a decidedly anomalous iconography — the picture refers to contemporary political and religious events, just as it depicts, in the foreground, contemporary personages (apart from the young man, whom Gouma-Peterson regards as an allegorical figure); and the scene of the flagellation represents the subject of their reflections (Clark), or an archetypal event (Gouma-Peterson), alluding symbolically to the sufferings inflicted by the Turks upon the Church of Christ.

These two overall views give rise, as we have seen, to completely different interpretations of every element (this is no exaggeration) making up the picture. However, the enigma of its iconography remains unresolved. We must now take up our position on the basic options we have outlined, in order to offer, if possible, an analytic interpretation more convincing than those put forward so far.

Notes

1. BUU, *Fondo del Commune*, ms. 93 (miscell.), c. 224 r. The passage forms part of a "Catalogue of paintings preserved in the metropolitan city of Urbino, with information on their authors". Systematic research into the pastoral visitations might establish whether the *Flagellation* was always kept in the Metropolitan sacristy. The visitation of 1636 makes this seem questionable: on 16 September, after having forbidden the "deambulationes, nugas, circulos, negociationes" that were occurring in the Metropolitan sacristy, it was ordered that seats should be brought into it "ubi sacerdotes missae sacrum facturi genuflectere ac sese colligere et orare valeant, *proposita desuper crucifixi effigie aut aliqua alia pia immagine*" (ACAU, *Fondo visite pastorali*; italics added). The last phrase suggests that the sacristy walls were not at this time hung with any paintings of religious subject-matter. L. Pungileoni (*Elogio storico di Giovanni Santi*, Urbino 1822, p. 97) refers to a much earlier document, an "inventory of things to be found in this Metropolitan made in 1504 by the Notary Federico di Paolo", as containing "a note on the paintings, too, but ... scanty and disordered". It is possible that this inventory still forms part of the deeds drawn up by this same lawyer (Federico di Paolo Guidicci), which are kept in the Urbino state archives, but I have been unable to find it. Today, Piero's *Flagellation* is to be seen (or rather, half-seen, since it is protected from projectiles by a thick screen of greenish glass) in the Galleria Nazionale delle Marche at Urbino.

2. C. Gilbert insists on this point in "On Subject and Not-Subject in Italian Renaissance Pictures", in *The Art Bulletin*, XXXIV (1952), p. 208, n. 21; however, as argued below, his suggested solution is unacceptable.

3. P. Toesca, "Piero della Francesca", in *Enciclopedia italiana*, Rome 1935, XXVII, p. 211.

4. Gilbert, "On Subject" pp. 208-9.

5. E.H. Gombrich, in his review of Clark's *Piero*, *Burlington Magazine*, 94 (1952), pp. 176-8; and "The Repentance of Judas in Piero della Francesca's 'Flagellation of Christ'", *Journal of the Warburg and Courtauld Institutes*, XXII (1959), pp. 105-7.

6. C. Gilbert, "Piero della Francesca's 'Flagellation': The Figures in the Foreground", in *The Art Bulletin*, LIII (1971), p. 41, n. 5. The "gilded frame", now lost, is mentioned in an inventory of 1754 (BUU, *Fondo di Urbino*, ms. 93, c. 386r, for the date, see c. 388r).

7. P.D. Running, in *The Art Bulletin* XXV (1953), p. 85 and Gilbert, "Figures", pp. 41-51.

8. On the "maestro dell'Osservanza", see Longhi, "Fatti di Masolino e di Massaccio", p. 60; A. Graziani, *Il Maestro dell'Osservanza*, Florence 1948 (extract from *Proporzioni*); F. Zeri, "Il Maestro dell'Osservanza; una 'Crocefissione'," in *Paragone*, 49 (1954), pp. 43-4; E. Carli, *Sassetta e il Maestro dell'Osservanza*, Milan 1957, pp. 89 ff.

9. L. Borgo, "New Questions for Piero's 'Flagellation'", *Burlington Magazine*, 121 (1979), pp. 547-53. The argument of this essay has been countered in criticisms by M. Aronberg Lavin (ibid., p. 801) and by C.H. Clough (ibid., 122 [1980], pp. 575-7).

10. See Clough's observations, ibid., p. 577.

11. See Vasari, II, pp. 672-3; and Borgo, "New Questions", pp. 550-51.

12. Ibid., p. 548.

13. D. Angúlo Iñiguez, "Bramante et la 'Flagellation' du musée du Prado", in *Gazette des Beaux-Arts*, vol. XLII, a. 95 (1953), pp. 5-8. The engraving is actually the work of B. Prevedari: cf. E. Borea, "Stampa figurativa e pubblico", in *Storia dell'arte italiana*, I, 2, pp. 346-7.

14. It was Sabba da Castiglione who described Bramante as having been "created" by Piero (see Longhi, *Piero*, p. 117); Post's reference to Piero in connection with the Prado painting — attributed, uncertainly, to Alejo Fernandez — is in C.R. Post, *History of Spanish Painting*, Cambridge (Mass.) 1950, X. p. 90.

15. Something of the same intention is discernible in Bartolomeo della Gatta's illumination for the Urbino *Antifonario*, depicting the martyrdom of St Agatha (cf. M. Salmi, *La miniatura italiana*, Milan 1956, p.

50 and illustr. XLIV). Gilbert (*Change*, p. 106) supposes this to derive directly from Piero's *Flagellation*: it shows three onlookers facing towards and pointing at the saint bound to the column.

16. The details of this interpretation, and its history, are charted in M. Aronberg Lavin, "Piero della Francesca's 'Flagellation': the Triumph of Christian Glory", in *Art Bulletin*, L (1968), pp. 321-42.

17. Ibid., pp. 6 ff.

18. See n. 21 below.

19. C. Clark, *Piero*, (1st edn), pp. 19-21.

20. They are the antiphon of the first nocturn for Good Friday, at Matins: so far as I know, this was first pointed out by W. Bombe, "Die Kunst am Hofe Federigos von Urbino", in *Monatshefte für Kunstwissenschaft*, V (1912), p. 470.

21. The second hypothesis was put forward by Clark in the revised (1969) edn of his *Piero*, pp. 34-5.

22. C.H. Siebenhüner, "Die Bedeutung des Rimini–Freskos und der Geisselung Christi des Piero della Francescas", in *Kunstchronik*, 7 (1954), pp. 124-5. Siebenhüner identifies Oddantonio by referring to a late fifteenth-century portrait, today at Vienna, which comes from the Ambras collection; in it, the Duke, named as such by a prominent inscription, does indeed have features very similar to those of the young man in the *Flagellation*. F. Kenner, who published a reproduction of the portrait, supposed it to have been copied from a lost original by Gentile da Fabriano (see "Die Porträtsammlung des Erzherzogs Ferdinand von Tirol", in *Jahrbüch der Kunsthistorischen Sammlungen des allerhöchsten Kaiserhauses*, 17 (1896), pp. 269-70. Bombe ("Die Kunst", p. 470) who later substituted for Gentile's name that of Piero, attributed the copy to Alessandro Allori.

23. Battisti, I, pp. 318ff; there is a reference (involving some bibliographical confusion) to the portrait formerly in the possession of the Archduke of the Tyrol on p. 324.

24. Aronberg Lavin, "Triumph"; this article, together with a hypothesis on the painting's original destination, appears in book form in Lavin's *Piero della Francesca: the Flagellation* (New York 1972).

25. See Gilbert's detailed discussion, in "Figures" and B. Cole's review of the book mentioned in n. 24 in *Burlington Magazine*, 115 (1973), pp. 749-50.

26. T. Gouma-Peterson, "Piero della Francesca's 'Flagellation': an Historical Interpretation", in *Storia dell'arte*, 28 (1976), pp. 217-33.

27. Ibid., p. 229. On Babelon's contribution, see Ch. 4, n. 92.

28. Aronberg Lavin, "Triumph", p. 330; the point is reasserted in the course of a polemic against Borgo (*Burlington Magazine*, 121 [1979], p. 801). It should be noted, however, that when Lavin also speaks of an "effect of a mystical radiance emanating upward from Christ", she is crediting with symbolic value a feature actually due to the unfortunate intervention of a restorer, who lightened part of the lacunar ceiling: see C. Brandi, "Restauri a Piero della Francesca", in *Bollettino dell'Istituto Centrale del Restauro*, 17-18 (1954), p. 91. Brandi had already noted the existence of two light-sources, but he drew no interpretative conclusions from his observation.

IV

Further Thoughts on the *Flagellation*

The presence, or otherwise, of portraits of contemporary people in Piero's picture is evidently of decisive importance in understanding its iconographic implications. The existence of any such portraits has often been flatly denied. When Gilbert put forward the thesis (which he himself later refuted) that the three men in the foreground were mere passers-by, arrived by chance at the scene of Christ's flagellation, he stated that their faces corresponded to physiognomical types recurrent in Piero's work. This was proved, he argued, by the fact that the man in the brocade cloak appears again among the kneeling figures at the Madonna's feet in the Misericordia altarpiece in San Sepolcro, and that the blond youth has the same face as one of the angels in the *Baptism* in the National Gallery, London[1].

Both comparisons are undeniably valid. However, the conclusions that Gilbert draws from them are quite illogical. It is clear, first of all, that the powerful facial individuality of the man in the brocade cloak is quite another matter from the youth's angelic aspect – which is generically typical (and sublimely so). Only in the first case can we suppose that we are looking at a portrait. Gilbert however rules this out, because 1) the man in the Misericordia altarpiece is not a portrait[2]; and 2) supposing he were one, this would make the figure in the *Flagellation* a citizen of San Sepolcro, not a chancellor of Federico da Montefeltro. But there is no basis for the first statement; and the second puts forward (even if only as a *per absurdum* hypothesis) a gratuitous choice of alternatives. Actually, *tertium datur*: there is a third alternative, and things are more complicated.

It is absolutely certain that the man kneeling at the feet of the Madonna della Misericordia and the man in the brocade cloak in the *Flagellation* are one and the same person. The decisive proof (not that this is needed, given the evident resemblance) lies in the identical modification made in both cases to alter the outline, and slightly reduce the dimensions, of the unknown person's cranium[3]. This can only reflect the artist's scrupulous determination, not just to paint a portrait, but to render with the greatest precision the features of his model.

Piero, moreover, painted this same person on a third occasion, in one of the Arezzo frescoes. In a note which (unless I am mistaken) has escaped the attention of subsequent researchers[4], Clark pointed out that, notoriously risky though it is to identify resemblances, there can be no doubt that the man seen in profile to the left of Chosroes is the same person, grown a little heavier with age, whom we see at the feet of the Madonna della Misericordia. Bringing this identification together with the one (not mentioned by Clark) between the Misericordia portrait and the man in the brocade cloak, we must conclude that we are dealing with the same individual in all three cases. It is enough to note the thick neck, with its deep fold of skin; the chin, the mouth, the eyes; above all, the very unusual ear, sharply pointed and indented at the top, fleshy at the lobe. On the basis of these characteristics, of which he gives a point-by-point list, F. Hartt[5] has compared the man in the *Flagellation*, the man in the Misericordia altarpiece, and one of the figures in Solomon's retinue in *Solomon Receiving the Queen of Sheba*. However, the inclusion of this last figure is a little less convincing: his profile differs from the others in being slightly indented at the top of the nose and in having a rather more prominent upper lip. We shall play safe and limit our series of profiles to the three already identified: those in the *Flagellation*, the Misericordia altarpiece, and the *Defeat of Chosroes*.

In his second discussion of the *Flagellation*, Gilbert correctly refuted Lavin's mistaken identification of the man in the brocade cloak as Ludovico Gonzaga, supporting instead his own suggestions and those of Hartt. However, this did not lead him to reject his earlier thesis that the character in the *Flagellation* is a physiognomic type recurrent in Piero's work: it was just that the casual passer-by had now become Joseph of Arimathea[6].

In actual fact, the figure in question was a man well known to Piero, whose name we can discover from his presence in the *Defeat of Chosroes*. In the final fresco, gathered about the defeated king, Piero portrayed the patrons of the Arezzo cycle. "And so for this work," wrote Vasari, "he deserved to be richly rewarded by Luigi Bacci (whom he drew therein, standing by at the beheading of a King, together with Carlo and other of his brothers, and many citizens of Arezzo who at that time excelled for their learning)."[7] However, as often happens, Vasari is a little inexact here — rather oddly, in the present case, since (as Salmi points out) he had married a descendant of the family, Nicolosa Bacci. But Salmi's researches into the Bacci family tree have brought to light neither a Luigi nor a Carlo. He therefore suggests that the man in profile beside Chosroes should be identified as Francesco Bacci, and the two men on either side of him as his nephews, Andrea and Agnolo. This identification is conjectural, since we have no other portrait of any of these three. Salmi's choice of names was prompted by a document from which we learn that in September 1447 Francesco Bacci, the uncle, and his two nephews had sold a vineyard in order to pay "the painter whom he has chosen to paint our great chapel of San Francesco"[8]. This "painter", as we know, was the artist who began the work, that is to say Bicci di Lorenzo.

Salmi's hypothesis is unlikely, however. In the *Defeat of Chosroes* Piero painted the portraits, not of those who had paid for his predecessor's work, but of representatives of the three generations of the Bacci family who had conceived the project of decorating the chapel, had had the work begun, and had seen it finished — that is to say (from left to right) of Baccio, who decided on 5 August 1416 "that we shall have adorned with figurative painting the whole of the great chapel of the church of San Francesco at Arezzo"; of his son, Francesco, who had the work begun in 1447; and of Francesco's son, Giovanni, who oversaw its completion following his father's death in 1459. In the case of grandfather and son, the identification, though highly probable, is conjectural; but it is certain in the case of the grandson, Giovanni. He was the man who had himself painted in profile near Chosroes. "Piero," wrote Longhi, "did not judge even his patrons at Arezzo to be worthy of his own brush, except to a very small extent."[9] This "very small extent" comprises, we are claiming, the splendid profile of Giovanni, to whom Piero had prob-

46

47, 48

ably been linked for some years, and who at that moment was responsible for the decoration of the chapel. Assistants, on the other hand, could quite well be entrusted with the portrayal of the father and the grandfather, who were both dead.

The physiognomical identity of the patron of the Arezzo cycle (seen in profile) and the man in the brocade cloak of the *Flagellation* irresistibly suggests the name of Giovanni Bacci. We quoted earlier from his letter of 1461, which mentions the names of Federico da Montefeltro and Borso d'Este, described by Bacci as "in their manner of life wiser and more refined than any other gentlemen of Italy"[10]. This description was based on personal experience: for three terms, from January 1456 until June 1457 (an unusually long period), Giovanni Bacci held the office of *podestà* at Gubbio, at that time under the rule of the Montefeltro family. He held the same post again from June to November of 1468[11]. The *Flagellation* was certainly commissioned by him, as a gift to Federico.

The identification of the man in the brocade cloak as Giovanni Bacci scotches once and for all any interpretation of Piero's *Flagellation* as a variant of the usual treatments of Christ's flagellation. Bacci, the painting's donor, is certainly not depicted as a by-stander at an episode in Christ's life. The flagellation is relegated to the background. What links it to the scene taking place in the foreground?

Attempts to answer this question have been made by those who see in the picture the depiction of two distinct scenes, rather than a single scene based on a scriptural subject. According to Clark, Christ's flagellation is expressive of the thoughts of the three foreground figures[12]. Lavin sees the flagellation as an "apparition", whose meaning Ottaviano Ubaldini is elucidating to the Marquis of Mantua[13]. For Gouma-Peterson, it is an "archetypal event", whose contemporary political and religious significance the Greek ambassador is explaining to the Western prince[14]. These interpretations, various as they are, all emphasize one common element: the distance between the two scenes not just in physical but (we might say) in ontological terms. As we have noted, Lavin, followed by Gouma-Peterson, has observed that this gap is accentuated by the different lighting, which falls upon the event taking place beneath the loggia not from the left but from the right.

The representation of different levels of reality within the framework of a single pictorial entity (a painting or a fresco-cycle) is common in European art from the fifteenth century onwards. Sandström's researches[15] have shown how, as artists mastered the illusionistic resources of pictorial representation, they came to make use of a variety of means — from *grisaille* to light-effects — to depict the gap between reality and fiction, or between natural and supernatural reality. In the *Flagellation*, Piero not only employed different light-sources; he also used perspective. The grasp of perspective displayed in the Urbino painting is not offered (as is commonly held) as a virtuoso performance. It represents a deliberate expressive choice.

In making it, Piero was following the example of Benozzo Gozzoli, at Montefalco. To suggest such an influence may seem surprising, for the great disparity in the quality of the two painters' work has meant that Benozzo has been seen as Piero's debtor in every respect. The possibility of a reverse indebtedness has been ruled out *a priori*, despite the contrary evidence of chronology. Once again we see how hard it is to dispel certain ideas about how genius works. In fact, even if we follow the hypothesis of Longhi and others in dating the *beginning* of Piero's work on the Arezzo frescoes to 1452, they cannot possibly have influenced Benozzo's depiction of the life of St Francis at Montefalco, for an inscription roundly states that the latter work was *finished* in 1452. Borrowings from Piero are indeed discernible in it, but from the Piero of the *Baptism of Christ*, which was painted shortly after 1440 and which is echoed in the gesture of St Francis as he strips himself of his possessions; not, assuredly, from the Piero of the Arezzo cycle[16]. Piero must have turned off to Montefalco in the autumn of 1458 (if not earlier), as he travelled down the Tiber valley from Borgo San Sepolcro towards Rome. There, he would have seen among other frescoes one depicting the *Dream of Innocent III*. At Assisi, Giotto had expressed the gap between the everyday reality of the sleeping Pope on the one hand, and his vision on the other, by tilting at an angle of forty-five degrees the image of Francis supporting the Lateran. Benozzo, however, had recourse to a more modern language, relegating the Pope to the background while propelling St Francis right into the foreground. In his *Flagellation*, Piero used the same perspective device, but in reverse: everyday reality is shown in the foreground, while the *other* reality (we shall see how to define it shortly) is projected onto the background.

Between the two planes is a distance which, as we have said, is not only physical but ontological. What, in the sphere of everyday reality, has evoked the depiction of Christ's martyrdom? In Benozzo's fresco, the vision appears to the sleeping Pope. Here, there are neither sleepers nor apparitions such as sleepers see. And Clark's hypothesis — that it is the thoughts of the three in the foreground that are expressed in the flagellation — ignores the variety of their attitudes. The bearded man is actually speaking: his mouth is half-open, his left hand is lifted to waist-height in a gesture accompanying some statement[17]. He is undoubtedly talking about Christ's flagellation (Lorenzo Lotto, less than a century later, was to depict in similar fashion the sermon on the Crucifixion given by Gregorio Belo of the brotherhood of St Vincent: the portrait is now in New York). Giovanni Bacci is listening, his gaze fixed on the speaker. But the bearded man does not return Bacci's look; his eyes are turned to the right, outside the picture. Between the two, the youth's clear and unmoving eyes are fixed on a point to the spectator's left. We are thus excluded from this play of intersecting and diverging glances. None the less, the bearded man's words summon up the scene of the flagellation before us: and the Turk, seen from the back, virtually compels us to participate in it[18]. What holds the whole composition together, in narrative terms, is the gesture of the man who is speaking.

We know that at the beginning of the nineteenth century a written phrase, "Convenerunt in unum", accompanied the picture. In Covi's view, this was inauthentic, since the phrase must have been attached to the frame, a rare practice in Piero's day. However, it was not unheard of: we might cite the lines from the Credo that accompany the panels (*ante* 1412) attributed to Taddeo di Bartolo. Gilbert, moreover, has pertinently drawn attention to the example of reliquaries, a class of images to which the *Flagellation* seems to belong by its shape, its iconography and its provenance (the sacristy of a church). Angelico's silver-reliquary (*c.* 1450) is accompanied by Biblical passages written on mock frames[19]. There is thus no reason to doubt the lost inscription's authenticity. As we have already stressed, it was perfectly suited to a representation of Christ's flagellation: the antiphon read for the first nocturn at matins on Good Friday consists, precisely, of the words "Convenerunt in unum", which open the second verse of Psalm 2[20]. At this point, however, a difficulty arises: since we have ruled out the idea that Piero's picture is an ordinary flagellation, what significance should we give to the words "Convenerunt in unum"? They must clearly refer not just to the scene of the flagellation, which as we have seen constitutes the picture's secondary subject, but also to the principal subject, namely the mysterious scene in the foreground. In other words, the caption suggested to the spectator the theme on which the bearded man, his mouth half-open, is speaking as he invokes Christ's flagellation in illustration of the verse "Convenerunt in unum".

54

This interpretation is confirmed by the presence of the turbaned Turk, seen from the back, who is attending the flagellation (and may indeed have commanded it); and also by the depiction of Pilate wearing the cap and the crimson stockings of the Byzantine emperors[21]. These are the kings and princes mentioned in the psalm: the bearded man is commenting on that psalm, with reference to contemporary reality. Clark originally surmised an allusion to the council called by Pius II at Mantua, in 1459, to resist the Turkish threat.

If there is a gap between the group in the foreground and the flagellation taking place in the background, it cannot be ruled out that the bearded man's speech is being delivered at a precise and identifiable time and place. Let us begin with the place.

The loggia that is the site of Christ's flagellation is clearly an imaginary building. Clark, it will be remembered, referred to its Albertian characteristics as evidence that the picture should be dated around 1459-60. Lavin supposes that Piero may also have drawn upon the information (which is actually very vague) given about "the houses of Pilate" in a contemporary traveller's account of a voyage to the Holy Land[22]. More recently, Borgo (followed by Lavin) has indicated another possible source of Piero's inspiration in a reference in the *Jewish Wars* of Flavius Josephus to the "towers" of the Antonia Fortress, which was thought to have been the site of Pilate's praetorium[23]. This reference is very fleeting; and in any case, Piero never seems to have attempted exact archaeological reconstruction of the kind undertaken by Mantegna[24]. Much more illuminating is another suggestion of Lavin's: that the staircase visible through the doorway before which Pilate sits in the *Flagellation* implies an allusion to the Scala Santa[25].

The Scala Santa has occupied its present site only since the demolition of the ancient patriarchal court, carried out by order of Sixtus V to make room for the new Lateran Palace. At that time, the Scala Santa was transferred to below the Santa Sanctorum, and housed in Domenico Fontana's specially constructed building. Previously, however, it had been situated — as Severano wrote almost half a century after the thorough reconstruction of the Lateran — "near the gate of the new Lateran Palace, which looks north towards the *tramontana*"[26]. All earlier evidence agrees on this point. Some idea of how the Papal building's northern façade looked at that time can be gained from a detail in Filippino Lippi's *Triumph of St Thomas*, painted in fresco in the Caraffa chapel at Santa Maria sopra Minerva (1489-93), and from a drawing by Marten van Heemskerck (1532-36)[27].

55, 56

The relic had been greatly venerated since the jubilee of 1450. It was commonly known as the "scala di Pilato", *scala Pilati*, probably a corruption of *scala Palatii*, "scala del Palazzo" (the staircase of the palace). Saint Helena, the Emperor Constantine's mother, was traditionally held to have brought it to Rome from Pilate's praetorium, where Christ was supposed to have climbed it three times before being led away to Calvary. Giovanni Rucellai, who was in Rome for the jubilee of 1450, gives in his *Zibaldone* one of the earliest accounts of the veneration of the relic, and of the custom (still flourishing) by which pilgrims climbed the stairs on their knees during Holy Week. After mentioning the "pleasant chapel ... called Sancto Sanctorum", situated "outside the body of the church" of St John, Rucellai continues:

"Item, near the said chapel of Sancto Sanctorum there is a staircase descending into the Piazza of St John, six *braccia* in width and with steps cut from a single piece of marble, and this was the staircase of Pilate's palace at Jerusalem, where Christ stood when sentence of death was passed on him, and it came from Jerusalem; and the more to show their devotion, those who come to the jubilee, and especially those from beyond the mountains, climb it upon their knees ... ". He then refers to the statue of Marcus Aurelius on horseback (believed at that time to be a statue of Constantine) which stood in front of the Lateran and which is now in the Piazza del Campidoglio, and adds:

"Item, in this piazza, upon a piece of a column, a giant's head in bronze and an arm with a bronze ball."[28]

Here we can recognize the original of the statue on top of the column to which Christ is bound in the *Flagellation*. As W. Haftmann first noted[29], Piero indeed drew his inspiration for this from the remnants of a giant statue that used to stand in front of the Lateran, as we know from travellers' accounts from the twelfth century on, and later from successive editions of the *Mirabilia Urbis*. According to legendary tradition, it was originally housed in the Temple of the Sun, its remains later being removed by Pope Silvester to their site outside the Lateran. One of the illustrations to the copy of Giovanni Marcanova's *Antiquitates* belonging to the Dukes of Este shows the fragments' situation in the mid-fifteenth century. Although it is largely imaginary, and quite different from the precise and almost contemporaneous description in Giovanni Rucellai's *Zibaldone*, it does place them (on the basis, evidently, of verbal descriptions) before the northern façade of the Papal buildings, not far from the equestrian statue of Marcus Aurelius[30]. At the end of the century, the head, the hand, and the ball (popularly known as the "palla Sansonis") were removed to the Campidoglio and placed together first outside and then within the Palazzo dei Conservatori, where they are still to be found. They are now generally thought to be fragments of a gilded bronze statue, about three metres high, which represented, as has recently been shown, the Emperor Constantine[31].

57

58-60

So specific an allusion cannot have predated Piero's journey to Rome — the journey, that is, for which we have documentary evidence, and which took place during the pontificate of Pius II, for until we have evidence to the contrary the other visit, under Nicholas V, must be regarded as a figment of Vasari's confusion. This means that the *Flagellation* may have been painted at Rome, between the autumn of 1458 and that of 1459, and then moved elsewhere, presumably to Urbino; or it may have been painted at some later period. This rules out suggestions of an early date, beginning with Longhi's proposal; it is congruent with the later date (1458-59) put forward, on other grounds, by Clark.

The Scala Santa was not the only relic from Pilate's praetorium kept in the northern part of the Lateran Papal buildings. There were also two doors and three columns traditionally held to have been brought to Rome by Saint Helena, the mother of Constantine[32]. To reconstruct the history of their removal, we can bring together a series of documentary accounts with the very accurate plan of the Lateran drawn up at the beginning of the seventeenth century by the architect Contini[33]. According to the   61 *Tabula magna continens elenchum reliquiarum et indulgentiarum sacrosanctae ecclesiae Lateranensis*, drawn up in 1518, the three doors used to stand in a "*capella*" (chapel) or "*aula*" (hall), of which no further details are given. The same document informs us, however, that another famous relic was kept nearby: the stone upon which Judas's thirty pieces of silver were counted out, and upon which the soldiers later diced for Christ's clothes. This was supported by four marble columns supposedly of the same height as Christ[34]. Now we know that this "mensura Christi" was to be found — after 1484, at any rate — in the so-called Council Chamber or *aula del Concilio*, which was in the Palazzo Nuovo built by command of Boniface VIII, behind the loggia from which benedictions were given and which opened onto the Piazza (*see* Contini's plan, nos. 37-39). During the coronation ceremony for Innocent VIII, in fact, the Pope's seat was placed just in front of the relic[35]. Its cult was certainly long established, given the aura that surrounded it. Lauer thought that the stone supported by the columns was a relic of the table of the Last Supper, bearing the inscription "*mesa Christi*", which was later misinterpreted as "*mensura Christi*". This hypothesis seems to be confirmed by the mention of a *mensa domini* in the inventory of Lateran relics drawn up by Giovanni Diacono in 1170[36]. There is no reason to think this relic was situated elsewhere in the middle of the fifteenth century. In the same hall were kept two octagonal columns "with some rings of iron ... which they say stood once in Pilate's palace in Jerusalem."[37] In the reorganization of the Lateran carried out under Sixtus V, the relics were variously dispersed. We have spoken already of the Scala Santa.   62 The doors were removed into the corridor running along the front of the Sancta Sanctorum; the "mensura Christi" and the two columns, however, were placed in the cloisters, together with two other columns, known as "Pilate's columns" (which were cylindrical, and decorated with ivy leaves)[38].   63-65

There can be no doubt that Piero drew inspiration for his *Flagellation* from this group of Lateran relics. The proof of this does not lie principally in the fact that the two doors ("Pilate's" doors) served as starting-points for his depiction of the two doorways at the back of the loggia where Christ's martyrdom takes place; it lies, rather, in the other relic kept in the *aula del Concilio* — the "mensura Christi".

In a famous essay, Wittkower and Carter identified the modular unit underlying the architecture of the *Flagellation*[39]. This module is one-fifth of the unit proposed by

Pacioli in his *De divina proportione*, it measures 1.85 *pollici*, or 4.699 centimetres. Carter points out, however, that another, separate unit of measurement also plays a central part in the picture's formal organization: the height of Christ[40]. This is equal to 17.8 centimetres. Now, the columns that formerly stood near the Scala Santa, and which were thought to be exactly equivalent in height to Christ, measure 187 centimetres. But an inspection of their base reveals clearly the line that separates the column properly so-called from the rougher part, which in the past was driven into the earth. If we eliminate this part, which was formerly invisible, then we have a column 178 centimetres high[41]. Thus, irrespective of the fact that Piero measured not in centimetres and metres but in *piedi* and *braccia*, there is a 1:10 relation between the height of Christ in the *Flagellation* and the height attributed to him by the tradition based on the Lateran columns. Taking Christ's height in the *Flagellation* (17.8 cm.) as the unit of measurement, then the picture's breadth works out at 4½ times that unit; its height, at 3¼ times; the height of the columns in the foreground, at 2½ times; and the distance between their bases, at 2 times.

66, 67

Piero, then, built his picture with scrupulous accuracy on the basis of what he clearly saw as a pricelessly valuable piece of evidence — the evidence of the exact measure of the stature of the Man–God, model of perfection in his bodily form as in all else. Priceless evidence; but hardly unique, for written and monumental documents of the same period gave other measurements of Christ's height, differing more or less from that derived from the Lateran columns[42]. We hear, a little later, of the scores of men and women who would stick up "behind the door of the house or in the shop" a printed prayer-sheet containing an image of Christ together with a length accompanied by the following words: "This is the measurement of our blessed Saviour Jesus Christ; who was fifteen times as high as this is long" — giving him, in this case, a height of 150 centimetres, or a little under 5 feet[43].

7

The Corinthian columns that stand out in the Arezzo fresco of *Solomon Receiving the Queen of Sheba* were described by Vasari as "divinely measured"[44]. Clark, in his discussion of the *Flagellation*, speaks of the "*mystique* of measurement"[45]. These phrases must now be understood literally as well as metaphorically.

Many features of its iconography, as well as the actual formal construction of the *Flagellation*, are thus closely linked with monuments situated on the northern side of the Lateran, or opposite it: the Scala Santa, the fragments of the statue of Constantine, "Pilate's" doors, and the "mensura Christi" (*see* Contini's plan, nos. 45, 65, 38 and 39). There are thus two possibilities: either Piero used material from the Lateran in depicting an evocation of Christ's flagellation that takes place in some unspecified place; or the place is in fact the Lateran, and the scene in the foreground is set in front of the Scala Santa.

The second hypothesis seems improbable, because the marble constructions in the background and the same rose-tinted building in the foreground cannot possibly be identified with the medieval Papal buildings. We fall back on an attempt to make the first hypothesis more precise, using time as the index of place — which means that we must seek to specify the moment at which the bearded man is evoking the flagellation of Christ.

But we have not yet ascertained the identity of the bearded man who is speaking. There are those, it must be said, who regard this as an inadmissible question: however, having recognized the man in the brocade cloak as Giovanni Bacci, we are now justified in pushing this line of enquiry further.

In the course of his justified rebuttal of Lavin's identification of the man as Ottavio Ubaldini, Gilbert notes that, other considerations apart, the fact that the figure is bearded makes it impossible that we are dealing with a portrait: at the period in question, men went clean-shaven in Italy. "Without exception," he writes, "beards are worn only by (a) figures from the past, for example Christ and Constantine, (b) foreigners, especially Greeks such as the Emperor John Palaeologus, (c) Italians after *circa* 1485, when the fashion for beards slowly revived[46]." But the man in the *Flagellation* falls, precisely, into category (b). As has often been pointed out (most recently by Borgo, who however draws conclusions quite different from our own[47]), his long-sleeved gown and his forked beard mark him out immediately as one of the Greek prelates who came to Italy for the Council of 1438-39.

One of them — or, better, the most famous of them, Bessarion. Gouma-Peterson, it will be remembered, was on the verge of reaching the same conclusion, but then returned to her thesis that the figure was a "crypto-portrait". This, as we have said, is historically and logically untenable — besides being based on a cursory, and partial, survey of the existing evidence. It will be necessary to re-examine this evidence.

Two photographs of the same person may, as we know, differ to an extraordinary degree; how much more so two paintings or two bas-reliefs. We must proceed, here, with great caution, for in Bessarion's case the surviving portraits present us (as Gouma-Peterson herself has noted[48]) with very marked physiognomical differences.

Unfortunately, most of the iconographic evidence about Bessarion has disappeared. Galasso's fresco in the church of the Madonna del Monte at Bologna — in which Bessarion, then a Papal legate, had himself portrayed beside Nicholas V, together with his own secretary Niccolò Perotti (whom we met with earlier) — has been destroyed[49]. The painting by Gentile Bellini for the *sala* of the great Council chamber at Venice, which showed Bessarion with the Pope and the Doge in the act of sending an embassy to the Emperor Frederick, exists no longer. A portrait also by Bellini and kept in the same room was burned in 1546[50]. On the other hand, there is very little in common, physiognomically, apart from the long beard, in the many paintings of the Venetian school where Bessarion (according to Vast) appears in the guise of St Jerome[51]. Leaving aside portraits that are either doubtful or of too late a date[52], we are left with the following list (which, however, is certainly not complete):

a) a miniature contained in the second of the eighteen anthem-books made for Bessarion in 1455, which he subsequently gave to the convent of the Observant Friars at

69, 70

Cesena. Bessarion (identified by Weiss[53]) wears Franciscan dress; kneeling, and wearing on his head his Cardinal's hat, he is in the act of offering up to God his soul in the form of a new-born child.

71   b) the tiny miniature at the beginning of the *Summa de casibus conscientiae* of Graziano the Minorite (Paris, Bibilothèque Nationale, nouv. acq. lat. 1002). Bessarion, in the habit of a monk of St Basil, and wearing a Cardinal's hat, is receiving the book as a gift from the author, who kneels at his feet. The manuscript is dated 14 October 1461[54].

72   c) a fifteenth-century medal, undated, belonging to Goethe's collection and now in the Weimar museum. Here, too, Bessarion is seen in profile, wearing a Cardinal's hat. This medal was probably the source of the portrait incorporated in the monument which Bessarion, during his lifetime, had built in the basilica of the Holy Apostles. The portrait has disappeared (together with the monument, which was replaced by an inscription
81   dated 1682); but a copy remains — a copper diptych, sent to Venice from the Vatican library in 1592[55].

73   d) a bas-relief that forms part of the funeral monument of Pius II, originally in St Peter's and now in Sant'Andrea del Valle. Bessarion, in the costume of a bishop, is shown giving the Pope the relic of St Andrew's head. This ceremony took place in 1462; Pius II died in 1464. The monument, begun by Paolo Romano, may have been finished by a pupil of Andrea Bregno, and dates from 1465-70[56].

74   e) the miniature that stands at the front of the copy of Guillaume Fichet's *Rhetorica*, dedicated, and given to Bessarion. This was printed in Paris in 1471 (Venice, Biblioteca Marciana, membr. 53): the miniature shows the author presenting his book to Bessarion, who is in the habit of a monk of St Basil, and has a Cardinal's hat on his head[57].

75   f) the illuminated frontispiece of the dedicatory copy of Bessarion's *Epistulae et orationes*, presented to Edward IV of England (Vat. lat. 3586: the book is a parchment incunabulum, printed in Paris in 1471[58]). Bessarion, in the black cloak of a monk of St Basil and wearing the Cardinal's hat, lays his hand in a protective gesture on Guillaume Fichet's shoulder, while the latter offers the King the volume whose publication he had overseen.

76   g) an illuminated portrait of Bessarion, whose figure, with those of six other philosophers, frames the *incipit* of Andrea Contrario's *Obiurgatio in Platonis calumniatorem* (Paris, Bibliothèque Nationale, lat. 12947, c. 11r.)[59].

77   h) a medal, framed in laurel, which depicts Bessarion and King Ferdinand of Aragon, both in profile: this is a miniature framing the *incipit* of a Parisian manuscript (Bibliothèque Nationale, lat. 12946, c. 29r) of the *Adversus calumniatorem Platonis* written by Bessarion himself and completed in Naples in 1476[60]. Both in this miniature and in the preceding one, he has the Cardinal's hat upon his head.

78   i) Gentile Bellini's painting in the Vienna Kunsthistorisches Museum, which was probably executed shortly after the death of Bessarion[61], who is shown in the habit of a monk of St Basil kneeling before the casket we have already mentioned, which he gave to the Scuola Grande della Carità.

79   j) a painting, probably the work of Pedro Berruguete, based on a drawing by Justus of Ghent, and painted around 1480 for the study of Federico da Montefeltro. This is now in the Louvre[62].

This *corpus* of images is very heterogeneous in form, in the materials employed, in destination and in quality. What information does it give us about Bessarion's features?

One point springs to our eyes at once. The Louvre portrait is completely unlike the series as a whole from the point of view of physiognomy. The Bessarion depicted in it is a creature of the imagination, painted soon after his death by someone who probably never met him. It is very remarkable that such a painting should have been destined for the court of Urbino, with which Bessarion was so long and so closely connected: but we must accept the evidence. Now it is precisely this portrait that constitutes the principal basis on which Gouma-Peterson (who even provides a full-page reproduction of it) rules out the possibility that the bearded man in the *Flagellation* can be identified as Bessarion.

In terms of physiognomy, the rest of the series of portraits is fairly uniform. There is one element, however, — the nose — that is subject to varying degrees of alteration. It is slightly humped, and rounded towards the end, in Pius II's funeral monument and in all   85
the miniatures we have listed — apart from that contained in the *Summa* of Graziano the   71
Minorite, on which (given its dimensions) we can place less reliance, physiognomically, and where there is no trace of any hump, while the tip is particularly fleshy. In the Weimar medal, it is decidedly humped, while the tip becomes sharp and downward-   72
pointing. In these last two images, we might say, one characteristic (the humped appearance or the fleshiness) is accentuated to the prejudice of the other. Two physiognomical traditions stem from this, both posthumous (and this cannot be a matter of coincidence). Evidence of the first can be seen in the painting by Gentile Bellini that is now in Vienna: here, Bessarion is given a very pronounced nose, with no hump whatever, and in the   80
sixteenth-century copy now in the Accademia, which was painted from memory of a portrait by Gentile Bellini that was stolen in 1540[63], it has become a veritable snub nose. In the second tradition, exemplified by the picture that is now in the Marciana, Bessarion has a straight, almost Grecian nose. In similar fashion, two non-identical profiles derive   81
from copies of portraits of Bessarion now kept in the Museo Gioviano di Como, the work respectively of Cristoforo Altissimo in 1566, and of an unknown engraver for the   82
edition of Giovio's *Elogia virorum literis illustrium*, which appeared at Basel in 1577. We   83
are dealing here with copies of a copy — a copy commissioned by Raphael (so Vasari informs us) from Giulio Romano of Bramantino's frescoes, now lost, in the Vatican, where Bessarion's portrait appeared as one in a series of famous men. Vasari is, however, undoubtedly mistaken in attributing the work to Bramantino[64]. The original (whoever the artist may have been) probably dates back to the mid-fifteenth century. These copies, to be sure, are not much to be relied upon in matters of physiognomy. None the less, they do confirm the tendency of copyists, however close to a common source, to simplify Bessarion's profile along divergent lines.

The conjectural reconstruction of this *stemma nasorum* may strike some as an unprofitable, even trivial, exercise. But our roamings in this forest of noses — painted, sculpted and illuminated — have not been without their purpose, for they have enabled us to single out those portraits of Bessarion that are most reliable from a physiognomical point of view. They are, it may be concluded, the first eight of the series, all of which were produced when he was alive.

Can we add to them the bearded man in the *Flagellation*? Some features of his face   84-87 are undoubtedly very similar to those found in the portraits of Bessarion: the sunken eye-sockets; the heavy eyelids; the prominent nose, slightly arched, with its rounded tip and deeply incised nostrils; the full lips, their corners turning down; the forked beard, which is evident for example in the Marciana miniature[65]. In the latter, as in the Cesena miniature and in Pius II's funeral monument, we find exactly the same carriage of the head, with the neck stretched slightly forward.

All this should incline us to an affirmative conclusion. In particular, the comparison with the medallion-shaped illumination of the Parisian codex of the *Adversus calumniatorem Platonis* seems almost decisive from a physiognomical point of view. However, there are two extremely serious difficulties. The first, already pointed out by Gouma-Peterson, concerns the costume: Piero's figure, unlike other portraits of Bessarion, is not wearing the black habit of a Basilican monk, nor does he bear any of the insignia of a Cardinal[66]. The second concerns age: in 1459, Bessarion was fifty-six. Now the bearded man in the *Flagellation* is clearly much younger — younger, even, than the kneeling monk in the Cesena miniature, recognized by Weiss as a very rare image of Bessarion at a relatively early age[67]. Neither of these difficulties, however, presents itself if, adhering to the date proposed for the *Flagellation*, we suppose Piero to have depicted Bessarion *prior* to his appointment as a Cardinal.

Bessarion was made Cardinal on 18 December 1439. On 4 January 1440, he received the title of the Holy Apostles *in absentia*. By that time, along with the other Greeks returning from the Council[68], he was already sailing towards Constantinople, where he arrived on 1 February 1440 after an exceptionally long voyage lasting three and a half months. It is generally held that he had not been informed of his appointment even though on 11 August of the previous year, Pope Eugenius IV had offered him a handsome pension on condition that he moved to Italy, and possibly to Rome. Sometime during 1440 (and at any rate after 4 May, when he took part in the election of the New Patriarch) Bessarion left Constantinople for good; on 10 December he received his Cardinal's beret at Florence[69]. Obviously, he had by then been officially informed of his appointment. When, and by whom, we do not know. We propose to identify the bearer of this news as Giovanni Bacci, and to suggest that, in commissioning Piero's painting, he was commemorating, at a distance of twenty years, the crowning moment of his political career.

In the very brief autobiographical note (the earliest we possess) compiled in the mid-seventeenth century by Alessandro Certini of Citta di Castello, Giovanni Bacci is described as "clerk to the Camera, nuncio to Caesar, most celebrated jurisconsult."[70] The otherwise incomprehensible formula "nuncio to Caesar" is very readily explained if, in 1440, Bacci had received a mission from the Pope to travel to Constantinople as nuncio extraordinary to give Bessarion the solemn news of his appointment as Cardinal. At that date, Bacci was clerk to the Camera Apostolica and in favour with Eugenius IV, partly because of his kinship with Giovanni Tortelli, who had but lately returned from a political and religious (as well as cultural) mission to Greece and Constantinople.

We are dealing, for the time being, with a hypothesis only, though one that is backed, as we have seen, by a measure of documentary evidence. At all events, it allows us to explain a series of features of Piero's painting, notably: 1) the youthful appearance of Bessarion, who in 1440 was thirty-seven years old (one might also note that his beard is shorter than in later paintings); 2) the fact that he wears none of the insignia of a Cardinal; 3) the splendour of Bacci's robes, which would certainly be appropriate to a Papal messenger. (Again, the vitality of his expression — very much in contrast to his somewhat lifeless appearance in the profiles at San Sepolcro and Arezzo — could also be due to Piero's desire to portray his model as he was at an earlier stage of his life.); 4) the long red scarf, unobtrusively but clearly visible, which hangs down from Bacci's right shoulder almost to his ankle. This can be identified as the Cardinal's scarf, which Bacci is shortly to bestow upon Bessarion as a symbol of the office conferred on him in his absence by the Pope[71].

Piero's painting should therefore be understood as doubly evocative: of Bacci's mission to Constantinople (the scene in the foreground) and of the flagellation of Christ (the scene in the background). Bessarion's words, which connect the two scenes, summon up — metaphorically for Giovanni Bacci; physically for us — the spectators observing the events, Pilate, the tormentors, Christ bound to the column. The distance of perspective expresses a distance at once temporal and ontological — between profane and sacred history, between reality and its verbal evocation[72]. The relics of Pilate's palace conserved in the Lateran and the other antiquities situated in front of it are projected upon an imagined Constantinople, thus creating an architecture both visionary and prescient, from which the probable constructor of the Palazzo Venezia, Francesco del Borgo, fellow-townsman of Piero, was to draw inspiration (the door-frames, for example)[73].

The scene in the background thus translates in visual terms the speech delivered by Bessarion when he accepted his appointment as Cardinal of the Holy Roman Church, and thus of his decision to abandon (permanently, as it proved) Constantinople and the Greek church of which he was one of the most illustrious representatives. His words can be construed as follows: the reigning Emperor, John VIII Palaeologus, is to be compared to Pilate in his comportment, since this makes him an accomplice in the martyrdom the Turks are preparing to inflict on the Christians of the East, of whom Christ bound to the column is the symbol. To both figures — the Emperor and the Turk — Bessarion applies the phrase "Convenerunt in unum", thus justifying his acceptance of the appointment announced to him by Giovanni Bacci. In the face of the calamities assailing Christianity, only a choice in favour of Rome could keep alive the flickering ideal of unity between the Christian churches.

This interpretation removes a difficulty: the presence of John VIII in the guise of Pilate[74]. Bessarion had maintained very close links with him since his youth. The fact that he prevailed upon Giovanni Bacci to have John VIII celebrated as Constantine in the Arezzo cycle testifies to his loyalty to his memory. Is it possible that in a contemporaneous painting — commissioned by Bacci, but certainly not in conflict with Bessarion's ideas — John VIII can have been accorded so dishonourable a role? But the contradiction lessens if one thinks of the different destinations of the two works. The Arezzo fresco was a public tribute; the *Flagellation* was a picture for private use, in which it was possible to hint at a negative political judgement on the Emperor's character. On his return to Constantinople from the Council, John VIII had been reluctant to take sides in the bitter struggles between those who favoured and those who opposed union with Rome. As a result, the decree proclaimed at Florence in 1439 lost all effect, and the Emperor was politically isolated[75]. It is more than plausible that Bessarion, who from the time of the Council of Florence had been among the most ardent advocates of union with Rome, saw John VIII's attitude as comparable to that of Pilate: both, through their inaction, had given consent to Christ's martyrdom.

The allusion to the Good Friday liturgy, which includes the phrase "Convenerunt in unum" that was placed over the painting, allows us to date the scene precisely: 25 March 1440. It is a plausible date: given that Bessarion was appointed Cardinal on 18 December 1439, one may presume that the messenger made responsible for conveying news of this to him had left Italy a little earlier and arrived in Constantinople (supposing a voyage of average duration) towards the middle of March.

But why — if we allow that our proposed interpretation is so far accurate — should Giovanni Bacci have commissioned from Piero a re-evocation of his mission to Constantinople twenty years previously, in order to then present it to Federico da Montefeltro? Bacci's motive was certainly not a simple desire to gratify personal vanity. In reality, the time elapsed since the scene depicted had taken place converts the speech attributed to Bessarion at the moment when he receives the news of his appointment from Bacci into a sort of "prophecy with hindsight", rich in allusions to the contemporary political and religious situation. The marble palaces of Constantinople indirectly evoke their destruction by the Turks during the invasion of 1453; Christ's flagellation betokens the sufferings undergone by the Christians of the East up to the time of the very recent invasion of the land of the Moors in 1458-59. The *Flagellation* thus becomes a silent appeal to the Crusade addressed to Federico da Montefeltro, the absent interlocutor, by Bessarion, who probably inspired — in accord with Bacci — the iconography of the painting[76].

We have already supposed that a meeting took place between Bessarion, Giovanni Bacci and Piero della Francesca — in all likelihood between the end of 1458 and the first months of 1459 — in connection with the alteration of the Arezzo cycle's iconographic scheme. During this period, Bessarion's thoughts were all of the Crusade. News had reached Rome of the Turkish army's Moorish invasion, in which they were later opposed, during the early months of 1459, by the despot Thomas Palaeologus[77]. Pope Pius II decided, above all because of the pressure he was under from Bessarion, to convene a diet at Mantua to persuade the Christian princes of the need to move against the Turks. On 22 January he had left Rome, accompanied by six Cardinals, planning to move northwards at a leisurely pace[78]. It was intended that the rest of the Sacred College, comprised of men who were sickly or advanced in years, should make the journey in a more favourable season[79]. Bessarion, who was delicate in health, must have begun his journey in spring: what is known for certain is that on 7 March, preceding the Papal procession by two days, he entered Bologna alone "to be met by the entire city"[80]. But before his departure from Rome, in discussions whose content we can only imagine, the plan of a painting to be delivered to Federico da Montefeltro must have taken shape.

Christ's flagellation on the orders of the man with the turban evokes, as we have already pointed out, the sufferings of the Christians, especially of the Greeks, under Turkish rule. We said above that the classical-style gallery beneath which Christ's martyrdom takes place was not inspired by any archaeological concern to reconstruct Pilate's praetorium exactly as it was. May we perhaps discern in it a symbolic meaning? For humanists such as Bessarion or Pius II, the fall of Constantinople to the Turks had an additional meaning: as well as being a political disaster and a religious profanation, it was the final disappearance of classical Greece. "O nobilis Graecia ecce nunc tuum finem, nunc demum mortua es?", Piccolomini had asked, before he became Pius II, in his oration *De Constantinopolitana clade et bello contra Turcos congregando*. "Heu quot olim urbes fama rebusque potentes sunt extinctae. Ubi nunc Thebae, ubi Athenae, ubi Mycenae, ubi Larissa, ubi Lacaedemon, ubi Corinthiorum civitas, ubi alia memoranda oppida, quorum si muros queras, nec ruinas invenias? Nemo solum, in quo iacuerunt, queat ostendere. Graeciam saepe nostri in ipsa Graecia requirunt, sola ex tot cadaveribus civitatum Constantinopolis supererat ... "[81]. But even Constantinople now survived no longer.

But the painting commissioned of Piero was not simply commemorative of past events and expressive of the pain caused by present misfortunes. The second psalm, moreover, in which the phrase "Convenerunt in unum" recurs, is not just an expression of anguish in the face of the assaults against the Messiah that the Kings and Princes have inspired. The verse quoted is followed immediately by a call to battle: "Dirumpamus vincula eorum et priociamus a nobis iugum ipsorum"[82]. Four years later, Bessarion, in an *Instructio pro praedicatoribus per eum deputatis ad predicandum crucem*, advised that Psalm 129 should be read as an exhortation to the Crusade: "Saepe expugnaverunt me a iuventute mea, dicat nunc Israël: saepe expugnaverunt a iuventute mea; etenim non potuerunt mihi. (...) Dominus iustus concidit cervices peccatorum. Confundantur et convertantur retrorsum omnes qui oderunt Sion, fiant sicut faenum tectorum, quod priusquam evellatur exaruit ... "[83]. He did not hesitate, however, to make use also of more concrete arguments. On 20 May he wrote from Ferrara, where he was staying with the Papal family en route for Mantua, a long letter to Fra Giacomo della Marca, the Provincial of the Franciscans of the March of Ancona (who was later made a saint). In this he encourages Fra Giacomo to gather together an army of Crusaders, who were to go to the land of the Moors, where a fresh Turkish offensive was feared. The letter opens with a description of Moorish riches: there is abundance of "panem, vinum, carnes, caseum, lanam, bombicem, linum, setam, chremisinum, granum, uvas passas parvas, per quas fit tinctura ... Frumenti dantur pro uno ducato duo staria magna Marchesana ... " It concludes with an exhortation to make haste: better to have five, four, even three hundred men at once, than many thousands later[84].

Bessarion does not dwell on the more properly religious themes that would have been involved in preaching the Crusade in the March. These, clearly, could be taken for granted. In the *Flagellation*, however, they are invoked, and from this point of view the picture can be regarded as a figurative sermon, addressed to anyone who appeared to underestimate the gravity of the Turkish threat.

That Piero's picture was meant for Urbino is certain, at any rate, until proof to the contrary is offered. Now Gouma-Peterson has pertinently observed that Federico da Montefeltro was anything but favourably disposed to plans for the Crusade: in 1457, he had gone so far as to prohibit any collecting of money for such a project in his dominions, leading Pope Callistus III to threaten him with excommunication in consequence[85]. The danger that the Turks might invade Moorish territory, which led Bessarion to plead, in the summer of 1459, for a Crusading force to be equipped in the March of Ancona, obviously also made it advisable to put pressure on Federico. This was very probably another motive (though not, as we shall see, the only motive) for the picture's being sent in that same year.

It is certain, anyway, that Bacci commissioned it (for otherwise it would be impossible to explain why it contains his portrait). His links with Federico da Montefeltro, as evidenced by his having been appointed *podestà* at Gubbio three years earlier, thanks to the intercession of the Medici[86], provided ample reason for Bacci to send a painting to Urbino. In the letter of 1472 from which we have already quoted, Giovanni Bacci, having mentioned the gentlemen to whom he had been "very dear", went on to offer his own services to Lorenzo de Medici in the following words: "Once again I would remind your Majesty to select someone whom you make bold to refer to and to speak to you on every matter. Lacking such guidance, people have often fallen into grave misfortunes. Our present Pope (Sixtus IV) knows that I alone had the courage to write to Pope Paul on every issue, and so I have done also with the above named Lords."[87] Among these Lords, it will be remembered, was Federico da Montefeltro: we can imagine him receiving the *Flagellation* together with a letter in which Bacci "made so bold" as to insist on the necessity of a Crusade. A gesture of that kind would have been consistent with his (largely frustrated) ambitions as a political counsellor.

The idea of putting the figurative sermon on the flagellation into the mouth of Bessarion was justified by the Cardinal's links with the picture's patron and, above all, with its recipient. We have already proved that the former links existed, in our analysis of the iconographic transformation that affected the Arezzo cycle during the break in the work coincident with Piero's stay in Rome. (It is to be noted that this is, indeed, a proof, rather than a presupposition based upon the *Flagellation* — which, given the doubts about the identification of Bessarion, would have involved us in a truly vicious circle.) The links with Federico go back at least to 1445, in which year Bessarion was appointed commendatory abbot of the abbey of Castel Durante, in the dominions of the Montefeltro family[88]. In the years that followed, he stayed many times at the court of Urbino, forming a deep friendship with Federico and enjoying particularly affectionate relations with his sons, Buonconte and Antonio. On the death of Bessarion, a miniature of him (the one by Berruguete that we mentioned earlier) was included in the series of famous men that adorned Federico's study; with it was an inscription dedicated "amico sapientissimo optimoque"[89].

Giovanni Bacci, Federico da Montefeltro and Bessarion were joined, then in a mutually interlocking network of relations. How intimate they were we cannot say with any certainty, but they were quite close enough to lend credence to the reconstruction we are putting forward. There is, however, one figure in the picture which our account has deliberately ignored hitherto: the mysterious blond youth.

None of the very numerous interpretations proposed over the years has offered an acceptable explanation of his presence. His clothes, his face and his attitude all seem incongruous with what is going on around him. Barefoot, clad in a simple tunic, he stands between two men who are shod and wearing elaborate modern dress. He neither speaks (like the man on his right) nor listens (like the man on his left)[90]. The former's solemn gravity, like the latter's attentiveness, leaves him unmoved. His beautiful face is un-ruffled by any recognizable emotion or sentiment. His eyes are fixed upon something that we cannot see.

The young man is dead.

Hitherto, we have been trying to decode the political and religious implications of the *Flagellation*. Now we have arrived at its most intimate and private core. We propose to identify the young man as Buonconte da Montefeltro, the illegitimate son of Federico, who was made legitimate in 1454 and who died of the plague at Aversa in the autumn of 1458, aged seventeen[91].

Enamoured as he was of manuscripts and of classical antiquity, Federico had given the young man whom he intended to be his heir a complete humanistic education. In 1453 Bessarion and Flavio Biondo were staying at Urbino. While they were at table (so Biondo, writing a few years later, relates), Federico showed Buonconte a letter that was written in "vulgari materno" (the vulgar mother-tongue) and common in its expression. Buonconte, then twelve years of age, translated it into an elegant Latin. Already at this time, perhaps, or anyway not much later, Federico had appointed as his son's tutor the peasant-humanist, Martino Filetico da Filettino[92].

Bessarion was struck by the boy's intellectual precocity; and when he received a letter from him written in Latin and in Greek, he in turn replied in Greek. This undated letter of Bessarion's now survives only in a Latin translation, made by his secretary, Niccolò Perotti — who himself in due course sent a note to Buonconte[93]. It was a miracle, wrote Bessarion, that a boy, still of tender years, should know Latin and Greek — truly a divine gift, a comfort to his father and to his father's friends, and an extra-ordinary hope for the future. He urged Buonconte to attend to his father's example, and to imitate his virtues: wisdom, prudence, courage, justice, honesty, mercy, loyalty, magnanimity. With these he should combine, Bessarion advised, the study of letters, for this (as the divine Plato had said) was God's greatest blessing. And Bessarion also expressed the wish that he might confirm Buonconte, thus giving a further, spiritual strength to the bond of friendship that joined him to the boy's father. In this way (observed Bessarion) Buonconte, Federico's son in the flesh, would become his own son in the spirit. He thus promised to come to Urbino as soon as possible: and he invited Buonconte to learn by heart the letter that he was sending him, so that he would be able to repeat not just isolated words, but whole phrases, in Greek or Latin, as he chose. He must have questioned the boy closely on it all[94].

Bessarion, no doubt, was deeply impressed by the fact that Federico's son was learning Greek as well as Latin. The same admiration was felt, however, by others who occasionally visited the court at Urbino, such as Biondo, as well as by professional eulogizers such as the humanist, Porcellio, in whose epigrams Buonconte is lauded for his beauty, his genius, his strength and his skill: "Vera Iovis soboles forma facieque decora/ Et mira ingenii nobilitate puer,/Romano eloquio indulget pariter Pelasgo/Dulceque mellifluo stillat ab ore melos./Aeacides qualis micuit Chirone magistro/Ense, oculis, dextra, mobilitate pedum/Talis in arma puer, vel si contenderet arcu/Et calamis Phrygium vinceret ille Parim./Nunc spumantis equi duro premit ilia clavo/Dirigit in girum Tyndaridae assimilis./Hic cantu hic choreis hic clarus in arte palestrae/Clarus et arte pilae, clarus et arte lirae ... "[95].

Buonconte, although still very young, soon began to take a part in the responsibilities of government. In 1457, during his father's absence, he wrote to Sigismondo Malatesta to deplore the damage done by soldiers near Sassoferrato[96]. The following summer, he left Urbino in company with Bernardino, the son of Ottaviano Ubaldini della Carda, and travelled to the Aragonese court at Naples. On their way through Rome, they were received by the Pope: "and he was astonished," wrote Guerriero da Gubbio in his chronicle, "as were the other Cardinals, to find so great a cleverness in so small an age"[97]. Bessarion must surely have been proud of his pupil.

From Rome, the two young men went on to Naples. At Aversa, they fell victim to the plague. Buonconte died at once; Bernardino on the journey home, at Castel Durante, not far from Urbino. When this happened, we do not precisely know: but Biondo, in a letter to Galeazzo Sforza, Count of Pavia, dated 22 November 1458, speaks of Buonconte's death as a recent event ("nuper defuncto") which had caused a great stir throughout Italy[98].

The virtues of Buonconte and Bernardino, and their untimely deaths, were recorded in the chronicles of Giovanni Santi and Guerriero da Gubbio, and in Porcellio's epigrams[99]. Federico da Montefeltro's reply to Francesco Sforza's letter of condolence survives today: "... certainly it was a great comfort in my grief. My Lord I know that because of my sins our Lord God has plucked out my eye and this little son who was my life and contentment and that of my subjects, of whom I never required anything but that it was done according to my desire. Nor can I have a greater joy than to remember that he never displeased me in anything"[100].

No portraits exist of Buonconte[101]. To identify him as the young man is thus to offer a conjecture. However, various features do make the identification probable. First of all, there is his angelic aspect, which assimilates him to the dead: as has been noted, his bare feet and his tunic recall Piero's angels, whether those in the *Baptism* or those in the 93 *Nativity* in the National Gallery, London. There is his pallor, which contrasts with the athletic solidity of his body and calls to mind the similar unnatural pallor which indicates, in the portrait of Battista Sforza in the Uffizi, that the portrait is posthumous[102]. There is his detachment from his surroundings — a detachment not merely psychological but existential, so to speak, as of one who does not see and cannot be seen[103]. There is the date: if, as is shown by the interconnected features that we have pointed out in the course of our discussion, the painting was made in 1459, Buonconte had been dead for about a year. There are the links between Buonconte and the inspirer and the recipient of the pictures, respectively his spiritual father and his father in the flesh: through Giovanni Bacci, Bessarion was sending Federico a remembered image of the young man whom they had both loved while he was alive, and whose recent death they both mourned. Finally, there is the theme of the flagellation, which is appropriate, as has been remarked, to a funerary purpose, and perhaps to the decoration of a reliquary[104].

The young man's attitude, however, recalls the attitude of Christ bound to the column. Through this analogy with the Christian archetype of pain, the sufferings of Buonconte (the potential soldier of Christ cut down by an early death) were assimilated to those of the Greeks languishing beneath the oppression of the Turks, and Federico's private grief to the grievances of the Church. This network of references to personal feeling and to pressures for political and military intervention itself made Piero's *Flagellation* a difficult image to decipher. It is not surprising that a century after the representation of Federico's dead son the painting came to be wrongly interpreted as a portrait of his brother, Oddantonio[105], giving rise to a fictitious account of it that is still in circulation. And the difficulty of decoding the subject of the picture was heightened by its formal characteristics, which hinge upon the contrast between the perspectival unity and the ontological heterogeneity of the reality it depicts. The dead youth, whose sufferings are compared to Christ's, is spiritually present, but invisible to the two men in the foreground. Equally present and equally invisible is the flagellation evoked by Bessarion's words. Only for the painter (and for us the spectators) is this contrast resolved in a higher unity, which is first of all a spatial unity.

Against all this, it might be objected that, even if we accept that the young man represents someone who is dead, it is by no means uncontroversial to identify him as Buonconte; in assuming that he is, we must also in the last analysis assume the bearded man to be Bessarion — and this itself, as we have seen, poses some problems. These have been resolved through recourse to a hypothesis for which, as yet, there is no decisive documentary proof. If, on the other hand, having put forward the identification of Buonconte on the basis of that of Bessarion, we then appeal to the latter as evidence of the identity of the former, we are clearly arguing in a vicious circle. Only if we were to establish with certainty that the description "nuncio to Caesar", used of Giovanni Bacci by his biographer, referred to a mission undertaken to Constantinople in 1440, could the enigma posed by the *Flagellation* by resolved beyond all doubt.

This does not mean, however, that the whole reconstruction put forward here would be doomed to collapse should the identification of the bearded man as Bessarion turn out to be mistaken. The elements of which it is composed — the portrait of Giovanni Bacci, the relation between foreground and background, the allusions to the

Turkish invasion, the references to the relics in the Lateran — all these are independent of the suggestion that we can trace Bessarion's portrait in the picture; and if they are to be confuted, it must be on equally independent lines. There is one exception: the presence of Buonconte. If we have been led to place him in the painting's context, that is because of his relations with Bessarion. By placing him there, we have arrived at a very concise and coherent overall interpretation. Interpretative coherence, however, cannot have the certainty of factual verification. Documentary evidence about commissioning and location — such as allowed us in the case of the *Baptism* to test Tanner's iconographical account — has not yet come to light for the *Flagellation*, let us hope it will do so, some day. Pending new documentary discoveries, we have to admit that our proposed interpretation is in large part conjectural. Given the picture's iconographical anomalies, and our ignorance of its original recipient and location, it would probably have been difficult to proceed in any other way.

When and where was the *Flagellation* painted? Here, too, lack of documentary evidence means that we are confined to conjectures. Since the painting is small, Piero could well have begun it at Rome and finished it at Arezzo. Such a hypothesis is favoured, moreover, by the curve that we remarked in the profile of Giovanni Bacci's cranium. Giovanni must have been recalled to Arezzo, if he was not there already, by the news of his father's death, at the beginning of April; at the same period, Bessarion left Rome for Mantua. Piero probably began work on the painting soon afterwards, on the basis of their joint instructions. On returning to San Sepolcro on the occasion of his mother's death (6 November 1459), he saw Giovanni Bacci again, and was able to correct his portrait from life. We have seen that he introduced similar corrections in the portrait of Bacci in profile which is found, for reasons unknown, at the feet of the Madonna della Misericordia in the San Sepolcro altarpiece, which was completed or nearing completion at this time[106]. In Bessarion's case, however, no such checking against reality took place: Piero had already been gone from Rome some time when Bessarion, who after the diet at Mantua went first to Venice, then on to Germany, returned there in November 1461.

The completion of the *Flagellation* would thus coincide with Piero's resumption of work on the Arezzo frescoes following the hiatus of his Roman visit. This perhaps allows us to identify the exact point at which he had left off painting them. Longhi, in a famous essay of his youth, drew attention to the extraordinary formal similarity between the young man in the *Flagellation* and the prophet situated at Arezzo, to the right of the choir window — the only one of the two painted by Piero himself[107]. This is a similarity upon which the datings later proposed by Longhi (c. 1445 for the *Flagellation*, 1452 — ante 1459 for the Arezzo frescoes) can shed very little light, but which is most readily explained adopting the reconstruction we have proposed. The two figures are in fact exactly contemporaneous: they are cut, we might say, from the same cloth. This claim is to be taken literally: "Piero", Vassari tells us, "was in the habit of making clay figurines, which he then covered in densely pleated pieces of cloth, as aids to his drawing."[108] A procedure of just this kind seems to be discernible behind the two figures.

If this reconstruction is correct, Piero finished the *Flagellation* and painted the right-hand prophet between late 1459 and early 1460. It is certain that the architectural forms that appear in the middle row of frescoes — *Solomon Receiving the Queen of Sheba* and the *Discovery and Proof of the Cross* — closely echo those found in the Urbino painting[109].

7, 12

For nearly three centuries prior to its reappearance in the Urbino inventories in the mid-eighteenth century, we have no records concerning the *Flagellation*. But its extraordinary originality must have exercised a certain influence. The series painted by Carpaccio for the Scuola di San Giorgio degli Schiavoni, includes a canvas traditionally known by the title of *St Jerome's Study*. Not many years ago, a most detailed iconographic analysis showed that the subject represented is in fact a different one — the *Vision of St Augustine*. According to a legend current at the end of the fifteenth century, St Augustine, while he was writing a letter to St Jerome, saw a sudden light. A voice from beyond the grave — the voice, in fact, of St Jerome — announced the speaker's death, which had recently occurred; it then gave answers to a variety of questions about the Trinity, the procession of the Son from the Father, and the angelic hierarchy. On the basis of his resemblance (which is actually no more than generic) to certain existing portraits, Perocco had already previously suggested that Carpaccio intended this saintly humanist, immersed in books and codices, as a depiction of Bessarion, who had granted an indulgence to the Scuola di San Giorgio in 1464. This brilliant hypothesis was then proved definitively by Branca, who recognized the half-effaced seal in the foreground to be unmistakably that of Bessarion[110].

Since Bessarion had been dead more than thirty years when this picture was painted, there is nothing surprising about the portrait's lack of physiognomical fidelity. It is more surprising, however, that nobody (as far as I am aware) has pointed out the close links between this famous work of Carpaccio's and Piero's *Flagellation*[111].

There is, in the first place, the comparison between the decorated ceiling of the *St Augustine* and the lacunar ceiling in the *Flagellation*: both are at the same angle of perspective. The two doors in the back wall of the saint's study are near copies of those in Pilate's loggia; in both cases, moreover, the left-hand doorway is open, and reveals an illuminated interior. The statue of Christ in the Venetian painting is the Christianized mirror-image of the idol on top of the column in the picture at Urbino. The empty seat that stands next to St Augustine's prie-dieu is almost identical in form to the chair Pilate sits on. And there is something more: like Piero in the *Flagellation*, Carpaccio also introduces into his picture two contrasting light-sources, one natural and the other supernatural. The room that we can see through the open door is lit from the left; the saint's study, by contrast, is lit from the right. This contrast provides a very simple device by which the spectator is impressed with the marvellous nature of the event that has suddenly distracted St Augustine from his work. Here, too, as in the *Flagellation*, we are witnessing the juxtaposition, in a single scene, of the two ontologically distinct levels of reality.

All this implies that Carpaccio was acquainted with the *Flagellation*. By what means did he come by this knowledge? Perocco, although he does not refer to the picture at

Urbino, has already answered this question in his suggestion, made with reference to the *St Augustine*, that Carpaccio came to know of Piero's researches into perspective by way of Luca Pacioli, who was teaching mathematics in Venice soon after 1470. We can add to the detail of this conjecture. Pacioli was a fellow-countryman of "maestro Pietro de'Franceschi", and an admirer and plagiarist of his work, who described him (in a dedicatory message to Guidubaldo, Duke of Urbino) as "the reigning painter of our time". After his youthful sojourn in Venice, he became a friar and embarked on a wandering life that took him, among other places, to Perugia, to the court of Urbino, to Florence, where he taught from 1500 to 1507, and back to Venice. There, on 11 August 1508, he delivered, to a packed audience in the church of San Bartolomeo di Rialto, the introductory lecture to a course on the second book of Euclid[112]. The last of the paintings destined for the Scuola di San Giorgio — the *St Augustine* included among them[113] — have been attributed to the same period (the dates proposed vary between 1507 and 1511). In the dedication that precedes the *Summa de Arithmetica* of 1494, Pacioli records the discussions on perspective that he had had with Gentile and Giovanni Bellini; those which he probably held with Carpaccio, during his later Venetian stay, would surely have been equally fruitful. It is very probable that a copy of the masterpiece of perspective which Piero had painted and which belonged to the Montefeltro family would have been displayed and commented upon in their discussions. In establishing a connection between the *Vision of St Augustine* and the *Flagellation* we provide a concrete basis for the debt, so often emphasized, that Carpaccio owes to Piero. We also confirm Perocco's hypothesis that Carpaccio's education and development included a distinctive Urbino element[114]. And perhaps the fact that Carpaccio, wanting to portray Bessarion, turned precisely to Piero's painting for inspiration, is not a pure coincidence, but an additional — if hypothetical — element favouring the identification we have previously advanced of the bearded man in the *Flagellation*. It is true that there is no physiognomical resemblance between St Augustine and the bearded man in the *Flagellation* — even though the two heads are almost at the same angle (St Augustine holding his slightly farther forward). But if it was by way of Pacioli that Carpaccio came to know of Piero's painting, then he would have had directly before him a drawing that emphasized its compositional elements, not the physiognomical details of the people depicted in it.

90, 91   The drawings connected with the *Vision of St Augustine* confirm this hypothesis precisely, and allow us to trace step-by-step the way in which Carpaccio modified his plans. In the drawing now in the Pushkin Museum in Moscow, an old man with a beard sits on the right. He has a pair of compasses in his hand, and is turning to the left. His study is furnished with codices and antiquities that bring to mind those of the *St Augustine*; but the expression of his face is altogether different, and lacks, above all, any recollection of Piero's *Flagellation*. That Carpaccio was indirectly acquainted with the work is apparent, however, on the verso of the same sheet: at the back of the elderly bearded man, who sits writing, appears for the first time one of the two doors of the open gallery where Christ's flagellation takes place — the open door, to be more exact, through which can be seen Pilate's staircase, which is very clearly visible in this drawing[115]. Here, we have a precise borrowing, later dropped by Carpaccio, who replaced it with the no less

89   precise derivative features we have listed above. A drawing kept today in the British

Museum documents a much more advanced stage of the work, just prior to its completion. Some parts barely sketched in, correspond to equivalent alterations made in the final drawing: the animal on the left in the foreground, which is not a dog but a ferret, and the figure of the saint. The latter's face, which is no more than outlined, is quite different either from those in the earlier drawings, or from that in the picture: it does not even have a beard. Muraro has made the very reasonable suggestion that this drawing in London constitutes a draft that Carpaccio prepared while he was waiting, perhaps, for the instructions he needed before he could portray Bessarion's face[116]. It is none the less true that the final result offers no more than a generic resemblance to the existing portraits of Bessarion: at this point we may perhaps be allowed to make the point that the bearded man in the *Flagellation* is much closer to these, from the point of view of physiognomy, than is Carpaccio's *St Augustine*, where the identity of the person depicted is avouched by the presence of the Cardinal's seal. Pacioli, who along with Piero had been a "sedulous" courtier at Urbino[117], thus assured that his colleague's painting, destined though it was for purely private consumption, enjoyed the posterity it deserved.

Notes

1. Gilbert, "On Subject", p. 208. Aronberg Lavin ("Triumph", p. 335, n. 71) will admit to no more than a typological similarity with the man in the Sansepolcro altarpiece, proposing instead a comparison with the kneeling donor at the feet of the *St Jerome* in the Accademia, which may have derived from the same cartoon: but Lavin herself owns that the similarity holds "except for the face".

2. The emphatic tone of this denial is, however, immediately softened in the footnote (Gilbert, "On Subject", p. 208, n. 22).

3. Lavin notes the alteration to the *Flagellation*, but offers an historically untenable explanation for it ("Triumph", p. 335): "These changes could have been for aesthetic reasons in relating this curve to the arching top of the window in the palace backdrop." Another similar observation of Lavin's is rejected by Gilbert ("Figures", p. 43). The alteration to the Misericordia altarpiece is noted by Battisti (II, p. 92). I do not know of any discussion analysing these two alterations in the same context.

4. Clark, *Piero* (1969 edn), p. 79, n. 36.

5. F. Hartt, *History of Italian Renaissance Art*, New York n.d. (but publ. 1970), p. 244.

6. Gilbert, "Figures", p. 43: "These persons are not portraits, but men who participate in scenes as in the *Flagellation*" (and see the whole of this essay).

7. Vasari, II, p. 497.

8. Salmi, *I Bacci di Arezzo*, pp. 229, 231-2.

9. Ibid., p. 233; Longhi, *Piero*, p. 45.

10. See ch. 2, n. 33.

11. ASG, *Riformanze*, reg. 25, cc. 110*v*-111*v*, "Noticia ellectionis domini Johannis de Baccis de Aretio potestatis Eugubii" (12 January 1456); reg. 26, c. 35*v* (21 June 1457: appointment of the accountants and auditors responsible for checking Bacci's work during the preceding period); reg. 27, c. 109*v* (10 June 1468: swearing in of Battista de Torcellis, adjutant of the *podestà*, Giovanni Bacci); reg. 28, c. 8*r* (17 November 1468: presentation of the *libri malleficiorum* for the period of Bacci's tenure of the *podestà*); reg. 28, c. 13*r* (21 and 28 November 1468: election of the auditor and accountants responsible for checking Bacci's work). I am grateful to Dr. P.L. Menichetti for kindly allowing me to consult the card-index he is preparing on the *podestà* of Gubbio. A note on his appointment as *podestà* of Gubbio is found in a letter from Bacci to Cosimo de Medici (ASF, *MAP*, VII, 3).

12. Clark, *Piero*, p. 34.

13. Aronberg Lavin, "Triumph", p. 339.

14. Gouma-Peterson, "Historical Interpretation", p. 229.

15. S. Sanström, *Levels of Unreality*, Uppsala 1964 (for the period 1470-1524); and the same author's "Présence médiate et immédiate", in *Archives de l'art français*, XXV (1978), pp. 407-17 (which discusses instances as late as Gauguin and Redon). For another angle, see also M. Meiss, *Giovanni Bellini's St Francis in the Frick Collection*, Princeton (N.J.) 1964. It is worth considering these pieces of research in the light of Italo Calvino's essay on "I livelli della realtà in letteratura", in *Una pietra sopra*, Turin 1980, pp. 310-23.

16. A. Padoa Rizzo, *Benozzo Gozzoli pittore fiorentino*, Florence 1972, pp. 41-2 (which points out the borrowing from the London *Baptism*). After having dated the *Flagellation* to 1451 and the commissioning of the Arezzo cycle to 1452, Rizzo notes (p. 42, n. 87) "the speed with which Benozzo absorbed the lesson of Piero's art", but does not go so far as to reverse the standard account of the relations of influence between the two painters.

17. Baxandall, p. 61.

18. This is pointed out by Gouma-Peterson ("Historical Interpretation", p. 229). S. Settis informs me that on this point one should see a work with which I am not acquainted, M. Koch's *Die Rückenfigur im Bild*, Recklinghausen 1965.

19. E. Carli, *Il Duomo di Siena*, Siena 1979, p. 87 (on the *Credo* panels, with a sketch of earlier attributions); Gilbert, "Figures", p. 41, n. 5. On the surmise that the *Flagellation* may have constituted one of the panels of a reliquary, see Gilbert, "Change", p. 107.

20. See ch. 3, n. 20.

21. This detail was ascertained by Gouma-Peterson ("Historical Interpretation", pp. 219ff.).

22. Aronberg Lavin, "Triumph", pp. 324-5.

23. Borgo, "New Questions", p. 550; and Aronberg Lavin, in *Burlington Magazine*, 121 (1979), p. 801.

24. See also in the same journal the remarks of C.H. Clough, 122 (1980), p. 577.

25. Aronberg Lavin, "Triumph", p. 325. We may note, incidentally, that this same detail probably inspired Luca Signorelli to introduce into one of his frescoes at Monte Oliveto the device of an open door in the background (cf. A. Chastel, "La figure dans l'encadrement de la porte", in *Fables*, II, pp. 145-54, esp. p. 151).

26. G. Severano, *Memorie sacre delle sette chiese di Roma*, Rome 1630, I, p. 543. Severano speaks of "*scale sante*" (in the plural), referring to the two sets of steps that flanked the principal stairway, as well as to the latter — on which see also the useful summary of M. Cempenari and T. Amodei, *La Scala Santa*, Rome 1974 (2nd edn).

27. Both are reproduced in P. Lauer, *Le palais du Latran*, figs. 10, 114. On the former, see C. Bertelli, "Filippino Lippi riscoperto", in *Il Veltro*, VII (1963), pp. 59-60. On the latter, see C. Huelsen and H. Egger, *Die Römischen Skizzenbücher von Marten van Heemskerck*, Berlin 1913-16 (anastatic reprint, Soest 1975), I, pp. 36-9; and, in general, the study by J.M. Veldman, *Marten van Heemskerck and Dutch Humanism in the Sixteenth Century*, English trans., Maarssen 1977 (with bibliography).

28. *Giovanni Rucellai e il suo Zibaldone*, I, *Il Zibaldone Quaresimale*, A. Perosa (ed.), London 1960, pp. 70-1. Giovanni Rucellai and Giovanni Bacci, let us note, knew each other well. The latter wrote to one of the Medici (9 November 1473) that "the nature of all we *Bacceschi* can be known from your Giovanni Rucellai, and from a great many other learned and perfect men besides" (ASF, *MAP*, XXIX, 982).

29. W. Haftmann, *Das italienische Saülenmonument* ... , Leipzig and Berlin 1939, pp. 95-7; and see also W.S. Heckscher, *Sixtus IIII Aeneas Insignes Statuas Romano Populo Restituendas Censuit*, 's Gravenhage [1955], with English summary on pp. 46-7. Battisti (I, p. 320) sees a connection between the idol and the remains of the statue fronting the Lateran; he refers, however, to C. Vermeule, *European Art and the Classical Past* (Cambridge, Mass. 1964, p. 40), where a different and unconvincing derivation is actually suggested.

30. *Codex Urbis Romae Topographicus*, K.L. Urlichs (ed.), Würzburg 1871, pp. 121, 136, 160; *Codice topografico della città di Roma*, B. Valentini and G. Zucchetti (eds.), III, Rome 1953, pp. 196, 353; E. Stevenson, *Scoperte di antichi edifici al Laterano*, extracted from the *Annali dell'Instituto di corrispondenza archeologica*, Rome 1877, p. 52 (for the tradition concerning the Temple of the Sun); Lauer, pp. 24-5; P. Borchardt, "The sculpture in front of the Lateran as described by Benjamin of Tudela and Magister Gregorius", in *Journal of Roman Studies*, XXVI (1936), pp. 68 ff. On the drawing that illustrates Marcanova's *Antiquitates*, see C. Huelsen, *La Roma antica di Ciriaco di Ancona*, Rome 1907, p. 29 and Plate VII. On the copy of this work at Este, see A. Campana, "Biblioteche della provincia di Forlí", in *Tesori delle biblioteche d'Italia, Emilia-Romagna*, D. Fava (ed.), Milan 1932, p. 97. On the copy now at Princeton, see H. Van Mater Dennis, "The Garrett Manuscript of Marcanova", in *Memoirs of the American Academy in Rome*, VI (1927), pp. 113-26. On the illustrations in both, see E.B. Lawrence, "The Illustrations of the Garrett and Modena Manuscripts of Marcanova", ibid., pp. 127-31. Huelsen's thesis that the illustrations derive from designs by Ciriaco has since been called in question (cf. R. Weiss, "Lineamenti per una storia degli studi antiquari in Italia", in *Rinascimento*, IX [1958], p. 172) or denied (cf. Cocke, "Masaccio and the Spinario", p. 22), not least because of their unreliability from an archaeological point of view. Disagreeing with Heckscher, Cocke (pp. 22-3) maintains that the columns were lower than those depicted in Marcanova's *Antiquitates*, and the fragments therefore much more visible. In support of this thesis, one might recall that Giovanni Rucellai described the remains of the "giant" as being "*on a piece* of a column". A very useful account of the ancient sculptures in front of the Lateran is P. Fehl, "The placement of the equestrian statue of Marcus Aurelius in the Middle Ages", in *Journal of the Warburg and Courtauld Institutes*, 37 (1974), pp. 362-7.

31. *A Catalogue of the Ancient Sculptures Preserved in the Municipal Collections of Rome. The Sculptures of the Palazzo dei Conservatori*, H. Stuart Jones (ed.), Oxford 1926, pp. 173-5 (with bibliography). Faint traces of gilt still remain on the hand (p. 174). On the presence of the fragments in the Palazzo dei Conservatori in 1510, cf. F. Albertini, *Opusculum* ... , in *Codice topografico*, IV, p. 491. On the identification with Constantine, see K. Krast, "Das Silbermedaillon Constantins des Grossen mit dem Christusmonogramm auf dem Helm", in *Jahrbuch für Numismatik und Geldgeschichte*, 5-6 (1954-5), pp. 177-8.

32. See the narrative compiled by "Magistrum Monacum Monasterii S.S. Andreae et Gregorii de Urbe",

published as an appendix to G. Soresini, *De Scala Sancta ante Sancta Sanctorum in Laterano*, Romae 1672.

33. This plan, which subsequently became the basis for all later reconstructions, was introduced by Severano, who first published it, in the following terms: "a plan which the architect, Francesco Contini, most meticulously compiled on the basis of the site [i.e., the Lateran] and its remains; from the plan of classical Rome printed by Bufalino in the time of Julius III; from the drawings of it to be seen in S. Pietro Montorio and in the Vatican Library; and from the accounts of those who had seen some part of it" (Severano, *Memorie sacre*, I, p. 534).

34. Lauer, *Le palais*, p. 298 (the lacunae are in his text): "Item in cappella ... est lapis quadratus quattuor columnis marmoreis, sub cujus ... altitudo Domini Nostri Jesu Christi, antequam crucifigeretur, staturam corporisque magnitudinem denotat, supra quem numerati fuerunt triginta denarii a Judaeis Judae traditori, ac etiam a Judaeis super Christi vestem jactae sortes. In fine presentis Aulae sunt tres Portae antiquae, quae erant in Domo Pilati, per quas transivit Jesus Christus, dum a Judaeis traheretur."

35. *Johannes Burckhardi Liber Notarum ab anno MCCCLXXXIII usque ad annum MDVI*, E. Celani (ed.), Città di Castello 1910 (*Rerum Italicarum Scriptores* [n.s.], XXXII, I), I, p. 83 (12 September 1484): "benedictione per pontificem, ut supra, data, ascendit per basilicam predictam ad palatium lateranense et quum pervenisset ad primam aulam magnam, que aula concilii nuncupatur, positum fuit faldistorium ante gradus lapidis, super quattuor columnas positi, qui mensura Christi appellatur, ubi papa sedit, renibus ad dictum lapidem versis" (and cf. ibid., p. 66, 26 August 1484). Both passages refer to the coronation ceremony of Innocent III, not that of Alexander VI, as G. Rohault de Fleury erroneously says in *Le Latran au Moyen Age*, Paris 1877, p. 257. The "aula" mentioned in the *Tabula* of 1518 (see n. 34 above) is clearly the *Aula del Concilio*, or Council Chamber ("aula concilii"). These pieces of evidence are only apparently contradicted by a passage in A. Fulvio (*Antiquitates Urbis* ... , [Romae], 1527, cc. XXIIIr-v): "Ab altera vero Basilicae parte ubi nunc aeneus surgit equus extant iuxta Sancta Sanctorum marmorei gradus numero XXVIII, per quos Christus ad Pilatum ascendisse dicitur, ubi pensilis et flexuosa longo incessu occurrit porticus ab Eugenio IIII instaurari coepta a Nicolao V et Syxto IIII successive restituta, ubi in primo aditu iuxta basilicam S. Ioannis a sinistris mensura staturae Christi ubi lapis super quo numerati dicuntur XXX argentei quibus venundatus est a discipulo Iuda. Paulo ulterius occurrunt tres portae marmorae per quas ingressus dicitur ad Pilatum iuxta antiquam pontificum suggestum, deinde duae porphyreticae sedes ubi novus pontifex attrectatur ... ". The sixteenth-century translator renders the obscure phrase "ubi in primo aditu iuxta basilicam S. Ioannis occurrit a sinistris mensura staturae Christi" by referring the "ubi" to the "porticus" that precedes: "and in the first vestibule of the said portico (*del detto portico*) along by the church of S. Giovanni there is on the left hand the measure of the height and stature of Christ" (A. Fulvio, *L'antichità di Roma ... con le aggiuntioni et annotationi di Girolamo Ferrucci*, Venice 1588, c. 54r). "Ubi in primo aditu" actually refers to the northern façade of the Papal buildings ("ab altera vero Basilicae parte"): there indeed follow ("paulo ulterius occurrunt") the three doors known as "Pilate's doors"; situated in the Aula del Concilio, and then ("deinde") the two porphyry seats placed together in front of the San Silvestro chapel (*Johannes Burckhardi Liber...*, I, p. 83, as well as sheets 39 and 43 of Contini's plan, already referred to). Fehl (pp. 363-4, n. 10) notes the obscurity of the passage from Fulvio, without, however, clarifying its meaning. On Fulvio, see R. Weiss's general account in "Andrea Fulvio romano (*c.* 1470-1527)", in *Annali della Scuola Normale Superiore di Pisa*, class of literature, etc., s. II, XXVIII (1959), pp. 1-44.

36. Lauer, *Le palais*, p. 104; J. Mabillon, *Musei Italici, tomus secundus*, Lutetiae Parisiorum 1689, p. 564.

37. Severano, I, pp. 587-8, records the two columns "near ... the stone", without specifying their whereabouts, but clearly alluding to the Aula del Concilio.

38. On the present position of the three doors, see P. Lauer, *Le trésor du Sancta Sanctorum*, Paris 1906 fig. 1; and *Le palais*, p. 321; M. Cempenari and T. Amodei, p. 80. On the stone and on "Pilate's" columns, see Lauer, *Le palais*, p. 333; E. Josi, *Il chiostro lateranense. Cenno storico e illustrazione*, Vatican City 1970, p. 17, nos. 167-8.

39. R. Wittkower and B.A.R. Carter, "The Perspective of Piero della Francesca's 'Flagellation'", in *Journal of the Warburg and Courtauld Institutes*, 16 (1953), pp. 292-302.

40. Ibid., p. 296.

41. Rohault de Fleury gives an identical measurement (*Le latran*, plate 51).

42. On the column in the church of Santo Stefano in Bologna, which was also held to be equal to Christ in height (it was about 173 cm high), see G. Uzielli, *L'orazione della misura di Cristo*, Florence 1901 (extracted from *Archivio storico italiano*), p. 6. The manuscript evidence is discussed in the following note.

43. Ibid., pp. 7ff. The prayer-book begins: "Most holy prayers to be said daily with all devotion and to be hung up in the entrance of the house or in the shop or else carried about the person to ward off the plague and every adversity". In a Ricardian manuscript, on the other hand, Christ's stature is given as 1.74 m; other

instances give greater heights, up to approximately 1.80 m. (cf. G. Uzielli, *Le misure lineari medioevali e l'effigie di Cristo*, Florence 1899). According to Uzielli, the linear measures or *braccia* then current in Italy derived from the various measurements attributed to Christ's height, on a ratio of 1:3: thus the "raso" or "braccio" of Turin, equal to .599 m., corresponds (to within 6 mm.) to one-third of the height of Christ in the Holy Shroud (1.78 m.) (ibid., p. 10). The thesis, in all honesty, seems interesting rather than convincing. It is worth noting in passing that Uzielli states that the figure covered by the Holy Shroud measures 1.78 m. — the same height as the Lateran columns (to which he does not refer). On the other hand, those who believe in the authenticity of the Holy Shroud hold Christ to have been 1.83 m. tall, and (despite the evidence) claim that this is the same as the height of the Lateran columns: cf. P. Savio, *Ricerche storiche sulla Santa Sindone*, Turin 1957, pp. 172ff. On the wish to obtain a physical image of Christ, the apocryphal *Epistola di Lentulo* is interesting: the text of this fifteenth-century document (widespread also in the following century) is given in the Italian edition of Baxandall, pp. 64-5.

44. Vasari, II, p. 496.

45. Clark, *Piero*, p. 35.

46. Gilbert, "Figures", pp. 43-4.

47. Borgo, "New Questions", p. 549. Here the bearded man is identified as a Hebrew priest, and Piero is credited with the belief that the Greek priests had continued the traditions of the Old Testament in the matter of their habiliments.

48. Gouma-Peterson, "Historical Interpretation", p. 232, n. 87.

49. Among the various references to this lost fresco, it is worth noting Ghirardacci's, who tells us (*Historia*, III, I, p. 159) that Bessarion appeared "kneeling without a hat".

50. F. Sansovino, *Venetia città nobilissima et singolare*, Venice 1581, cc. 131r, 132v.

51. Vast, p. 299. Among other works, Vast refers to Bartolomeo Montagna's altarpiece and to Vincenzo Catena's *Holy Conversation*, both in the Accademia. A posthumous portrait of Bessarion has also been identified in Cosimo Rosselli's fresco of the *Crossing of the Red Sea*, in the Sistine Chapel; this has traditionally been attributed to Piero di Cosimo, but it is now generally denied that the latter had any hand in this group of frescoes (cf. M. Bacci, *Piero di Cosimo*, Milan 1966, pp. 128-9, where the discussion on this point is summarized).

52. The painting preserved in the canonical sacristy of Urbania cathedral (which I was able to see by courtesy of Don Camillo Leonardi) is something of an exception. E. Rossi (*Memorie ecclesiastiche di Urbania*, Urbania 1936, p. 104) held it to be a portrait of Bessarion, very different physiognomically from other portraits (see C.H. Clough, "Cardinal Bessarion and Greek at the Court of Urbino", in *Manuscripta*, VIII, Nov. 1964, pp. 166-7, n. 33), whereas it is actually a copy of the portrait of Taddeo Barberini in the costume of a prefect, by Maratta (cf. M. Aronberg Lavin, *Seventeenth-Century Barberini Documents and Inventories of Art*, New York 1975, fig. 5 and p. 429). Among the posthumous portraits, no reliance can be placed on the bas-relief from Ferrara reproduced in *Miscellanea Marciana di studi bessarionei* ... , Padua 1976; and that reproduced in J.-J. Boissard, *Icones quinquaginta virorum illustrium* (Frankfurt 1597, I, p. 136) is altogether imaginary. On the other hand, and even though it is a late copy, the small portrait preserved in *Ludovici Bentivoli virtutis, et nobilitatis insignia* ... , Bononiae 1690, is interesting from a physiognomical point of view (see Aula V, Tab. I, H. III. 37.2, Bologna University Library; T. De Marinis mentions another copy of this extremely rare little book in *La legatura artistica in Italia nei secoli XV a XVI*, Florence 1690, II, pp. 3-4). The text of a speech given by Bessarion in 1455, on the occasion of his bestowing on Ludovico Bentivoglio a work that he had been given by Nicholas V, is reproduced in this work, from a manuscript belonging to Bentivoglio; the little book opens with a dedication by J. de Bergomoriis. The "L" of the *incipit* ("Leto iucondoque animo ... ") is illuminated with a tiny portrait of Bessarion; this, like the other engravings that accompanied the volume (printed in Bologna), was derived from the miniatures that decorated Bentivoglio's manuscript, now lost. (The text of this same speech of Bessarion's is given in Vat. Lat. 4037, without the miniature; this, like the volume printed in Bologna, is referred to by L. Bandini, *De vita et rebus gestis Bessarionis cardinalis Nicaeni ... commentarius*, in *PL*, 161, p. XIX, n. 46). 86

53. R. Weiss, "Two Unnoticed 'Portraits' of Cardinal Bessarion", in *Italian Studies*, XXII (1967), pp. 1-5. Weiss regards the first of these two "portraits" (which is not reproduced here) as very stereotypic, whereas he believes that the second can properly be called a true portrait of Bessarion around the year 1455, when the Cardinal was a little over fifty. The anthem-books are now discussed exhaustively in an essay by G. Mariani Canova, "Una illustre serie liturgica ricostruita: i corali del Bessarione già all'Annunziata di Cesena", in *Saggi e memorie di storia dell'arte*, 11 (1978), pp. 9-20.

54. This was pointed out by L. Frati, *Dizionario bio-bibliografico ...* , Florence 1934, p. 83.

55. On the medal, see A. Armand, *Les médailleurs italiens des quinzième et seizième siècles*, Paris 1883, III, p.

158, no. 6. The diptych, reproduced in the monograph by A.A. Kyros (Athens 1947; 2 vols.) was kept in the Marciana: in 1954, however, it proved to have been lost (cf. M. Luxoro, *La biblioteca di San Marco nella sua storia*, Florence 1954, p. 21, n. 14).

56. Cf. S. Ortolani, *S. Andrea della Valle*, Rome n.d., caption to fig. 25; C. Seymour jnr., *Sculpture in Italy - 1400 to 1500*, London 1966, pp. 156, 158.

57. It is reproduced before the frontispiece in the *Miscellanea Marciana*.

58. *Miniature del Rinascimento* (Vatican City 1950, p. 55) does not recognize Bessarion as the Cardinal depicted in the miniature (which is described as "of the French school"); see, however, the earlier note by R. Rocholl, *Bessarion*, Leipzig 1904, p. 213.

59. T. De Marinis, *La biblioteca napoletana dei re d'Aragona*, II, Milan 1947, pp. 53-5, and III, plate 77. The codex was written in 1471 by Joan Marco Cinico, and illuminated by Cola Rapicano: De Marinis surmises that Cola Rapicano may have had as his collaborator Andrea Contrario himself, since the latter's pictorial talent was praised by Perotti and by del Valla.

60. De Marinis, II, pp. 28-9, and III, plate 32. The codex was illuminated by Gioacchino de Gigantibus, between 1472 and 1476. J. Ruysschaert ("Miniaturistes 'romains' à Naples", in De Marinis, *La biblioteca, Supplemento*, Verona 1969, pp. 272-3) attributes the portraits, including the one of Bessarion, to a collaborator of Gioacchino's, possibly the same miniaturist who illuminated the codex cited in the preceding note.

61. Schaffran, pp. 153-7.

62. On the disputed question of collaboration between Justus of Ghent and Pedro Berreguete, C. Gnudi's essay remains valuable ("Lo studiolo di Federico da Montefeltro nel palazzo ducale di Urbino (Giusto di Gand-Pedro Berreguete)", in *Mostra di Melozzo e del Quattrocento romagnolo*, Forlì 1938, pp. 25-9). Post (*A History of Spanish Painting*, Cambridge [Mass.] 1947, IX, I, p. 134) attributes the *Bessarion* to Justus of Ghent, referring to G. Briganti's researches. Briganti, however, drew a distinction between drawing (by Justus) and painting (by Pedro): cf. "Su Giusto di Gand", in *La critica d'arte*, XV (1938), p. 111.

63. Cf. the work by Schioppalalba (but publ. anonymously), *In perantiquam*, pp. 149-50, where the copy is attributed to Giannetino Cordeliaghi, known as Cordella, a pupil of Giovanni Bellini (whom Fogolari mistakenly identifies with Andrea Previtali: cf. Schaffran, p. 157, n. 17a). See S. Moschini Marconi, *Gallerie dell'Accademia di Venezia - opere d'arte del secondo XVI*, Rome 1962, pp. 200-1.

64. On the history of Giovio's compilation, and especially on the copies of the portraits of famous men, see L. Rovelli, *L'opera storica ed artistica di Paolo Giovio ... Il museo dei ritratti*, Como 1928, pp. 144ff. A more general account is P. Ortwin Rave, "Das Museo Giovio zu Como", in *Miscellanea Bibliothecae Hertzianae ...*, Munich 1961, pp. 275-84. The passage from Vasari forms part of his life of Piero: "And then, having been called to Rome by Pope Nicholas V, Piero carried out two stories [i.e., two narrative sequences] in the upper chambers of the palace, together with Bramantino of Milan" (VI, pp. 528-9). There follows a digression concerning Bramantino's portraits and on the copies of them made by Raphael. We have already commented on the implausibility of Piero's alleged trip to Rome under Nicholas V: meanwhile, as Milanesi long ago remarked, there is no possibility that Piero and Bramantino collaborated, because it was out of the question chronologically, since Bramantino is thought to have been at work in the Vatican half a century later, in the early sixteenth century (Vasari, VI, pp. 528-9). Moreover, it has now been denied, on stylistic grounds, that Bramantino could have painted the lost originals from which some of the portraits in the Museo Giovio (including the one of Bessarion) are probably derived: the series of fresco portraits in the Vatican actually date, it is argued, to the mid-fifteenth century (cf. W. Suida, *Bramante pittore e il Bramantino*, Milan 1953, pp. 91-3). Battisti has recently claimed that Vasari probably mis-attributed to Bramantino a series of fresco-portraits done by Piero in an adjoining room (I, p. 110).

65. According to a famous anecdote related by Pius II, the beard cost Bessarion election to the Pontificate, because some of the Cardinals maliciously interpreted it as a sign of enduring links with the Greek schismatics (*Pii secundi ... commentarii*, p. 42).

66. For a general account, see R. Weiss, "Jan Van Eyck's Albergati Portrait", in *Burlington Magazine*, XCVII (1955), p. 146.

67. In the section that follows, I make a correction, on an important point, to the first Italian edition. This fresh hypothesis has been prompted by a criticism made by Salvatore Settis (first advanced in a review that appeared in *La Stampa*, 1 June 1981, then elaborated in a private letter of 7 July 1981). To Settis I am entirely grateful. Any errors of interpretation that remain are, of course, my own responsibility.

68. A. Coccia, "Vita e opere del Bassarione", in *Il cardinal Bessarione nel V centenario della morte (1472-1972)*, Rome 1974, p. 25 (kindly pointed out to me by Dr C. Bianca).

69. R. Loenertz, "Pour la biographie", pp. 117-18.

70. *Compendio delle sette età di Arezzo descritto da Don Alessandro Certini Castellano*, dated 1650 (BCCF, ls

369, unnumbered documents; cf. also Aliotti, *Epistolae et opuscula*, I, p. 27, n. b) in which, under the heading "Insigniti di dignità ecclesiastiche", one finds the following biography: "Gio. Francesco Bacci (*recte*, Giovanni di Francesco) clerk to the Camera, nuncio to Caesar, most celebrated jurisconsult, very dear to the House of the Medici, who laboured tirelessly on behalf of the Holy Church. Anno 1445". I have not succeeded in finding an explanation for this date.

71. The importance of this particular has been opportunely brought to attention by Battisti (*Piero*, I, p. 325), who sees in it (quite certainly wrongly) a Ducal insignia. On the manner of notifying Cardinals appointed *in absentia*, see G. Moroni, *Dizionario di erudizione storico-ecclesiastica*, vol. 48, Venezia 1848, pp. 151-2 (*sv.* "nunzio apostolico"); vol. 23, Venezia 1844, p. 222 (*sv.* "fascia"). The custom of sending absent Cardinals the beret or little red cap at the time of their appointment was only established in 1464 by Pope Paul II; it was not until even later (1591) that the habit was extended, by Gregory XIV, to include Cardinals belonging to monastic orders (as was the case, in fact, with Bessarion); see A. de Saussay, *Panoplia clericalis . . .* , Lutetiae Parisiorum 1649, p. 593; G. Moroni, *Dizionario*, vol. 5, Venice 1840, p. 171 (see "Berrettino o zucchetto cardinalizio").

72. The correlation between the development of linear perspective and the rise of modern historical consciousness is a theme addressed by Panofsky on a number of occasions. Cf. also C. Ginzburg, "Da A. Warburg a E.H. Gombrich", pp. 1023, 1046-7.

73. On Francesco del Borgo, in the past wrongly considered a relative of Piero's, see the researches of Ch. L. Frommel, some of whose results were presented at a conference held recently in the Biblioteca Hertziana at Rome.

74. J. Babelon, "Jean Paléologue et Ponce Pilate", in *Gazette des Beaux-Arts*, s. VI, IV (1930), pp. 365-75 (on p. 367, through an oversight, Bessarion is said to have died shortly after the patrons of Florence). It should be noted, all the same, that the examples mentioned by Babelon all post-date the *Flagellation*, so testifying to the success enjoyed by Piero's decision (whether the first of its kind, we do not know) to portray John VIII as Pilate. See also Gouma-Peterson, "Historical Interpretation", p. 219.

75. J. Gill, *Personalities of the Council of Florence*, Oxford 1964, pp. 102-24, and more specifically the same author's *The Council of Florence*, pp. 402-3, where Gill insists that the Emperor's hesitancy was a decisive factor in the failure of the Council of Florence. Cf. also ibid., pp. 349, 369.

76. On the complex position of the patrons during this period, see now S. Settis' rich study "Artisti e committenti fra Quattro e Cinquecento", in *Intellettuali e potere*, C. Vivanti (ed.), Torino 1981 (*Storia d'Italia Einaudi, Annali*, 4), pp. 701-61.

77. F. Babinger, *Maometto il Conquistatore*, Turin 1970, p. 174.

78. F. Cerasoli, "Il viaggio di Pio II da Roma a Mantova . . . " in *Il Buonarotti*, s. III, IV (1890), pp. 213-18.

79. *Pii Secundi . . . Commentarii*, Romae 1584, p. 68. The six cardinals were Calendrini, Borgia, Estouteville, Taillebour, Colonna and Barbo; cf. also G. Voigt, *Enea Silvio de' Piccolomini*, Berlin 1863, pp. 30-1.

80. C. Ghirardacci, *Historia di Bologna*, A. Sorbelli (ed.), Bologna 1933, III, I, pp. 169-70.

81. Pius II, *Orationes politicae et ecclesiasticae*, G.D. Mansi (ed.), Lucae 1755, I, p. 268: translated the passage is as follows: "O noble Greece, are you now brought to your demise and death? How many once famous and powerful cities are now extinguished? Where today shall we find Thebes, Athens, Mycenae, Larissa, Lacedemon, Corinth, and those other memorable strongholds whose walls, and even whose ruins, now exist no longer? No-one can so much as show us where they stood. We have often sought after Greece in Greece itself, when in truth it was only Constantinople, among so many corpses of cities, which has survived."

82. "Let us break their bands asunder, and cast away their cords from us" (Authorised Version). Battisti has already drawn attention to the relevance of Psalm 2 to the theme of the Crusade (I, p. 320: in line with his own interpretation, he also detects in them a possible exaltation of dynastic power).

83. "Many a time have they afflicted me from my youth, may Israel now say: Many a time have they afflicted me from my youth: yet they have not prevailed against me . . . The Lord is righteous: he hath cut asunder the cords of the wicked. Let them all be confounded and turned back that hate Zion. Let them be as the grass upon the housetops, which withereth afore it groweth up . . ." (Authorised Version: the psalm is 129 in AV, whereas in the *Bibbia Concordata* [Milan 1968] it is 128). Cf. L. Mohler, "Bessarions Instruktion für die Kreuzzugspredikt in Venedig (1463)", *Römische Quartalschrift*, III-IV (1927), pp. 347-9.

84. (Translation: "Bread, wine, meat, cheese, wool, silkworms, linen, flax, crimson tinctures, wheat, tiny raisins used to dye stuffs . . . Grain costs one ducat for two bushels of the best Marquesan . . . ") Cf. Mohler, "Kardinal Bessarion", III, pp. 490-3. During the same few days, Pius II sent a letter in the same vein from Ferrara to Giacomo della Marca: cf. L. Wadding, *Annales Minorum*, Romae 1735, XIII, pp. 117-18.

85. Gouma-Peterson, "Historical Interpretation", p. 231.

86. See the letter sent from Arezzo to Piero di Cosimo de Medici on 25 November 1455 (ASF, *MAP*, V,

632). At the same time, Bacci sent another, to Cosimo (now lost). The letter in ASF gratefully acknowledges "of what great benefit your letters were to me in respect of the illustrious Signor Count of Urbino". Similar sentiments are found in ASF, *MAP*, VII, 3 (dated 18 February 1456, to Piero di Cosimo de Medici).

87. ASF, *MAP*, XXIV, 371.

88. Mercati, "Per la cronologia", p. 48, n. 1.

89. Gouma-Peterson, "Historical Interpretation", pp. 230-1.

90. Many interpreters, however, have seen all three of the foreground figures as listening to a speech.

91. The date of Buonconte's death is undisputed; not so that of his birth. According to F. Ugolini (*Storia dei conti e duchi d'Urbino*, I, Florence 1859, pp. 370ff.), Buonconte was fourteen when he went to the court of Alfonso of Aragon at Naples; this would mean that he was born in 1443. It is probably on this basis that Aronberg Lavin states that the sources indicate that Buonconte and Bernardino Ubaldini, who accompanied him to Naples, were "in their early teens" ("Triumph", p. 338). G. Franceschini, on the other hand, claims that when Pier Candido Decembrio was a guest of Federico at Urbino in 1449, Buonconte was nine years old, from which it would follow that he was born in 1440 (*Figure del Rinascimento urbinate*, Urbino 1959, pp. 115-16). Such a difference is not altogether negligible; even if, as would seem likely, the young man in Piero's painting is a somewhat idealized portrait, it is relevant to know whether Buonconte died at fifteen or at eighteen (in support of the latter view, see also G. Franceschini, "La morte di Gentile Brancaleone [1457] e di Buonconte da Montefeltro [1458]", in *Archivio storico lombardo*, s. VIII, II [1937], pp. 489-500). Now, our only evidence for deciding on Buonconte's age at the time of his death is the letter in which Biondo Flavio tells Galeazzo Sforza of that event. In it, Biondo recalls an incident that took place during his visit to Urbino with Bessarion, when Buonconte, then aged twelve ("annum agens tertium decimum"), demonstrated his knowledge of Latin (cf. Biondo Flavio, *Scritti inediti e rari*, B. Nogara (ed.), Rome 1927, pp. 175-6). Since the visit of Bessarion and Biondo to the court of Urbino took place in 1443 (cf. L. Michelini Tocci, "Ottaviano Ubaldini della Carda e una inedita testimonanzia sull battaglia di Varna [1444]", in *Mélanges Eugène Tisserant*, Vatican City 1964, VII, p. 103), we may conclude that Buonconte died when he was aged seventeen, and was born in 1441. For the place of his death, see *Cronaca di ser Guerriero da Gubbio ...*, G. Mazzatini (ed.), Città di Castello 1902 (*Rerum Italicarum Scriptores*, n.s., vol. XXI, Pt. IV), p. 68.

92. Biondo Flavio, pp. 175-6. In a letter written to Federico while the latter was away from Urbino, Buonconte speaks of "Philetius vero praeceptor meus amatissimus" (Ugolini, II, p. 519). It is not clear when Filetico became attached to the court at Urbino — no later than 1454, according to R. Sabbadini (*Epistolario di Guarino Veronese*, Venice 1919, III, pp. 474-5), who, however, misinterprets Biondo's letter to Galeazzo of 1458, claiming that the anecdote it relates concerning the thirteen — (actually, twelve-) year-old Buonconte would have taken place "a little earlier" (in fact, it occurred five years previously). Doubt has already been cast on Sabbadini's conjecture by C. Dionisotti, in "'Lavinia venit litora.' Polemica virgiliana di M. Filetico", in *Italia medioevale e umanistica*, I (1958), p. 296, n. 3.

93. For Perotti's note, itself a reply to a letter from Buonconte, see Mercati, "Per la cronologia", pp. 150-1.

94. Bessarion's letter, already remarked by Mohler, is published, as amended by L. Labowski, in Clough, *Cardinal Bessarion*, pp. 161-2.

95. Urb. lat. 373, cc. 120r-v (the ode, which opens the second book of Porcellio's *Epigrammi*, is entitled: "Ad Boncontem divino ingenio adolescentulum Federici prin. filium"), with emendations based on Urb. lat. 708, cc 55r-v, where there is the variant reading "Dirigit in girum nunc quoque victor eques". Translation: "In the beauty of his face and figure, and in the wonderful nobility of his intelligence, the boy is truly the offspring of Jove. He expresses himself alike in Latin and in Greek, and sweet is the melody that flows from his honeyed mouth. Just as Aecides, instructed by Chiron, was fleet of sword, eye, hand and foot, so is this child, who would vanquish even the Phrygian Paris should he vie with him in archery. Now he presses the hard spurs to the flanks of the foaming steed; now, like the son Tyndaris, he guides him in the course. He is famed for his singing, his dancing, his gymnastics, his skill at ball, and his playing of the lyre ... " The same verses are quoted by G. Zannoni, "Porcellio Pandoni ed: Montefeltro", in *Rendiconti della R. Accademia dei Lincei (cl. di scienze morali ecc.)*, o.s. IV (1895), p. 119.

96. Ugolini, I, p. 371.

97. *Cronaca*, p. 67 (the passage is from the first version).

98. Biondo Flavio, pp. 175-6.

99. *Federico da Montefeltro duca di Urbino. Cronaca di Giovanni Santi*, H. Holtzinger (ed.), Stuttgart 1893, pp. 52-3; *Cronaca di ser Guerriero da Gubbio*, pp. 66-7; Urb. lat. 373, cc. 125v-126r ("Sepulchrum Boncontis Montefel."). For more verses on Buonconte, see ibid., cc. 124r-v ("Bonconti adolescentulo omni virtum (!) generum predisertissimo"). On Porcellio, see, in addition to G. Zannoni ("Porcellio Pandoni"), U. Frittelli,

Giannantonio de' Pandoni detto il 'Porcellio', Florence 1900.

100. Franceschini, "La morte", p. 499.

101. His likeness is not preserved on any of the coinage of the period (cf. R. Reposati, *Della zecca di Gubbio e delle geste de' conti e duchi d'Urbino*, 2 vols., Bologna 1772; on p. 265 of vol. I, thanks to a misinterpretation of B. Baldi's *Vita e fatti di Federigo di Montefeltro* (of which see the Rome 1824 edn, vol. II, p. 48), it is said that Buonconte died when he was fourteen); nor do we have any medals portraying him (there is no record of his name in G.F. Hill, *Corpus of Italian Medals of the Renaissance before Cellini*, 2 vols, London 1930).

102. Cf. Battisti, I, p. 357. Aronberg Lavin ("Triumph", p. 339, n. 100) remarks that the youth is much paler than the two people between whom he stands, and compares this pallor to the pallor of the scourged Christ.

103. The history of this iconographic *motif* might be taken as a starting-point and developed in more depth. See P. Fehl's interesting but rather cursory remarks: "The Hidden Genre: a Study of the *Concert Champêtre* in the Louvre", *Journal of Aesthetics and Art Criticism*, XVI (1957), pp. 153–68.

104. Battisti, I, p. 507, n. 406.

105. See ch. 3, n. 22.

106. The chronology of the Misericordia altarpiece is obscure, though the work on it, which was to have been completed, according to the contract, in three years (cf. Battista, II, p. 10), clearly dragged on for very much longer. Commissioned in 1445, it was still unfinished in 1455, at which point the Confraternity confronted Piero with a sort of ultimatum, asking him to complete the work within forty days (cf. Beck, "Una data"). It has been noted by Battisti — counter to Gilbert's supposition that this request relates to a different commission, not otherwise documented — that in 1458 Piero was probably still defaulting on some contract entered into while he was a minor: hence his signature is validated by that of his father when, on the eve of his departure for Rome, he empowers his brother Marco to act on his behalf. This hypothesis seems confirmed by the sum paid by the Confraternity of the Misericordia of San Sepolcro to Marco in January 1462 "in part payment for the picture painted by his brother Maestro Piero" (Battisti, II, p. 11). Unless we accept Gilbert's elaborate hypothesis, this "picture" can only have been the polyptych commissioned in 1445, now clearly finished ("painted"). How long it had been complete we do not know (Battisti offers no good reason for his claim that "we can consider the *terminus ante quem* of 1462 as post-dating the work's completion by some while": cf. ibid). At all events, this chronology, based on documentary evidence, is not inconsistent with Piero's having intervened to alter the portrait of Giovanni Bacci in 1459. It should be noted that Longhi's proposed chronology, based on stylistic factors, assimilates the later sections of the altarpiece — that is, the figures of the worshippers — directly to the Uffizi diptych (*Piero*, p. 207).

107. See R. Longhi, "Piero dei Franceschi e le origini della pittura veneziana", in *Scritti giovanili (1912–1922)*, I, Florence 1961, p. 87, which demonstrates the connection between Piero and Antonello da Messina by comparing the latter's *San Sebastian*, now at Dresden, with the scourged Christ and the blond youth in the *Flagellation*, and which also compares the latter to the Arezzo *Prophet* ("the identity is complete"). See also the same author's *Piero*, p. 47.

108. Vasari, II, pp. 498–9. E.H. Gombrich drew attention to this passage in an article in the *Burlington Magazine*, 94 (1952), p. 178.

109. On the basis of this formal analogy, and others, Gilbert ("Change", pp. 31–2) argues that the Urbino picture is close in time to this phase of the Arezzo cycle; but he dates both around 1463.

110. H.L. Roberts, "St Augustine in 'St Jerome's Study': Carpaccio's painting and its Legendary Source", in *Art Bulletin*, XLI (1959), pp. 283–97; E.E. Lowinsky, "Epilogue: The Music in 'St Jerome's Study'", ibid., pp. 298–301. See further J. and P. Courcelle, *Iconographie de Saint Augustin. Les cycles du XVI siècle*, Paris 1969, p. 104, n. 2 and plates LXIV, CIX; and the same authors' volumes devoted to the fourteenth and fifteenth-century cycles (Paris 1965, 1972) for other representations of St Augustine's vision. Also, see G. Perocco, "La scuola di San Giorgio degli Schiavoni", in *Venezia e l'Europa. Atti del XVIII congresso internazionale di storia dell'arte*, Venice 1956, pp. 221–3; and *Carpaccio nella Scuola di S. Giorgio degli Schiavoni*, Venice 1964, p. 134; Z. Wazbinski, "Portrait d'un amateur d'art de la Renaissance", in *Arte veneta*, XXII (1968), pp. 21, 28, n. 5 (which refers to an oral communication with V. Branca).

111. It was my daughter Lisa, then aged twelve, who made me aware of the existence of an analogy between the two paintings.

112. *Tutta la pittura del Carpaccio*, G. Perocco (ed.), Milan 1960, pp. 12–13; L. Pacioli, *Summa de arithmetica* ..., Venice 1523 (first edn 1494), dedication; Euclid, *Opera*, Venetiis 1509, cc. 31r–v (where there is a list of those present at the introductory lecture). For a swift biographical sketch of Pacioli, see G. Masotti Biggiog-gero's appendix to the *De divina proportione*, Milan 1956.

113. Perocco, *Tutta la pittura*, p. 59 (in connection with the date, now illegible, on the *St. George Slaying the*

Dragon). Perocco suggests 1507 as the date of the cycle's completion; J. Lauts, 1508 (*Carpaccio*, London 1962, p. 31).

114. Perocco, *Tutta la pittura*, p. 15. Longhi has emphasized Carpaccio's indebtedness (by way of Antonello) to Piero: see "Il Carpaccio e i due 'Tornei' della National Gallery", in *Ricerche sulla pittura veneta*, Florence 1978, p. 82; for the link with Antonello, see "Per un catalogo del Carpaccio", in *'Me pinxit' e quesiti caravaggeschi*, Florence 1968, pp. 78-9.

115. *Vittore Carpaccio — Catalogo della mostra*, P. Zampetti (ed.), Venice 1963, p. 300, no. 10. V. Goloubeff, who first published the two drawings, hypothesized that they were in this sequence ("Due disegni del Carpaccio", in *Rassegna d'arte*, VII, 1907, pp. 140-1). Golouboff observed that the figure in the first drawing more resembles an astrologer or an alchemist. Lauts (p. 273) takes the two Moscow drawings, and a drawing similar in style — of a young, beardless scholar seen in profile — kept in the British Museum, to be three of a projected series of portraits of philosophers; he is therefore inclined to rule out any connection between these drawings and the *Vision*. The opposite opinion is maintained by D. von Hadeln, *Venezianische Zeichnungen des Quattrocento*, Berlin 1925, p. 57.

116. M. Muraro, *Carpaccio*, Florence 1966, p. 104, n. 10.

117. Cf. Pacioli, *Summa*, dedication.

We have traced a complex set of iconographic references to Church unity and the Crusades in the *Baptism* and the *Flagellation*, and in the second and more integrated part of the Arezzo cycle. All of these relate in one way or another to the cultural, political and religious interests of Giovanni Bacci or of those, who for various reasons were connected with him. Negative proof of this is given by the fact that such themes disappear from Piero's paintings after the completion of the Arezzo cycle[1], when Bacci ceased to play the role of patron.

It may now be asked whether this influence was a matter of iconography alone. Once finished with the Arezzo frescoes, it is certainly true that Piero (then aged barely forty-five) engaged upon a very different and less demanding stylistic course. It hardly seems right to speak of a regression (though some have done so) when we look at work such as the Uffizi diptych, the Senigallia *Madonna* (now at Urbino), or the Brera altarpiece. It is equally impossible to assess what it meant to Piero to end his relationship with Giovanni Bacci and his circle. It would be absurd, certainly, to challenge the fanciful image of the artist shut away amidst his wholly formal researches by overemphasizing the influence a patron may have exercised over purely stylistic options[2].

All that is permitted is the cautious hypothesis that Piero's exceptional mastery of perspective would have helped to attract the attention of a cultural circle interested in every type of technological innovation. Let us recall in this connection a fact that may be pertinent: Tortelli inserted under the heading "Horologium" in his *De Orthographia* a long list, drawn up by Lorenzo Valla, of inventions undiscovered in classical times. The list includes some connected with art, such as the *manicordo* and the *niello*. Bessarion himself, moreover, wrote a letter shortly after 1440 advising Constantine Palaeologus, the Moorish despot, to avail himself of the advances made by Western technology[3].

Giovanni Bacci's dependent situation as a client of the Medici does, on the other hand, help to explain, paradoxically, why Piero received no Florentine commissions. That did, indisputably, owe something to reasons of taste[4]. It is equally certain, however, that Bacci was able to recommend his protégé to Sigismondo Malatesta or Federico da Montefeltro thanks to the intercession of the Medici, but not to put forward his name to the Medici themselves. Bacci, in his letters to his patrons, recalled in tones half-gratified and half-nostalgic the protection he had formerly enjoyed, and the experiences he had gathered as he travelled from court to court; he gave advice on the situation in Arezzo, urging Piero di Cosimo to appoint a sheriff "who might go searching and speaking about the country and make some show of terror" to put down "the insolence and boldness" of the peasants towards "merchants, craftsmen and gentle folk"[5]. He asked Lorenzo for a post that would allow him to get away from Arezzo, reminding him discreetly that Federico da Montefeltro "is used to keep and to give every emolument to his friends and to his men."[6] The Medici, however, remained deaf to his pleas. In vain, Bacci returned to the charge: "I stay here where I have never been content, and so pray Your Majesty to deign to take me away from this hell, for my heart could know and feel no other hell than to dwell in this city which is set in a worse place than any other I have ever seen."[7]

This plea, one of so many, dates from 29 April 1476. Giovanni Bacci's last surviving letter was written in December of the same year. We do not know when he died:

shortly afterwards, perhaps. He wished to be buried in Rome, in the church of Santa Maria Nova, where another clerk to the Camera Apostolica also from Arezzo, had been buried before him[8]. His mausoleum, destroyed during the alterations made to the church in the second half of the seventeenth century, no doubt bore some nostalgic record of his brief career in the Papal administration, which had been so rudely broken off, thirty years earlier, when he fell out with the Cardinal Camerlengo, Ludovico Trevisano.

Notes

1. De Tolnay remarks on this, but in general fashion, and in a context that minimizes the importance of the point: "Allusions to the history of the Eastern and Western Churches make up no more than secondary episodes in his painting. They disappear following the Arezzo cycle. The important point is that his ability to form a complete and solid universe was due to the quality of his Faith ... " ("Conceptions réligieuses", p. 239: trans. from the French. The essay is dedicated to Jacques Maritain.).

2. This thesis is put forward in Clark's monograph. Longhi uses much less forthright language, speaking of a lack of "further real progress ... following the first great poetic invention at Arezzo"; elsewhere, he notes that part of Piero's later work, starting with the Roman frescoes, has been lost (*Piero*, pp. 57, 91). We have argued above that this chronology cannot be maintained.

3. A. Keller, "A Renaissance Humanist looks at 'New' Inventions: the Article 'Horologium' in Giovanni Tortelli's *De Orthographia*", in *Technology and Culture*, 11 (1970), pp. 345-65, which should be read in the light of O. Besomi, "Dai 'Gesta Ferdinandi'"; A.G. Keller, "A Byzantine Admirer of 'Western' Progress: Cardinal Bessarion", in *Cambridge Historical Journal*, II (1965), pp. 343-48.

4. Longhi, *Piero*, p. 98.

5. ASF, *MAP*, XVII, 328 (the letter is addressed to Piero di Cosimo de Medici).

6. ASF, *MAP*, XXIX, 144 (the letter is dated 6 March 1473).

7. ASF, *MAP*, XXXIII, 312 (the letter is addressed to Lorenzo de Medici).

8. "Monsignor Giovanni di Francesco Bacci, clerk to the Reverend Camera Apostolica, lived for many years, as ... can be seen from his tomb in the church of San Francesco in the Campo Vaccino at Rome": so wrote Gamurrini (*Istoria*, III, p. 328). The church in question was actually Santa Francesca Romana, formerly known as Santa Maria Nova. Not long after Gamurrini wrote these words (in 1673) the restoration of the church, which radically altered its appearance, must have taken place; in course of this, many of the funeral monuments within it were destroyed, among them those of Gentile Fabriano (cf. P. Lugano, OSB, *S. Maria Nova [S. Francesca Romana]*, Rome, n.d., p. 5) and of one "Flodericus de Aretio", clerk to the Camera Apostolica, who died in 1403 (cf. V. Forcella, *Iscrizioni delle chiese e d'altri edificii di Roma dal secolo XI fino ai giorni nostri*, Rome 1873, II, p. 6). Forcella does not mention Giovanni Bacci's funeral monument among those to be found, or formerly to be found, in Santa Maria Nova (cf. ibid., pp. 3-16, 527-8). I have examined in vain ms. Vallicelliano G. 28, *Antiquae Inscriptiones Ecclesiarum Romanae Urbis collectae a Carolo de Secua* (recte, *Serva*) *Antonio Bosio et Ioanne Severano* (on Santa Maria, cc. 33-4). Nor have I been able to trace Giovanni Bacci's will: neither in the State Archives at Florence, nor in the collection of legal instruments from Santa Maria Nova kept in the Rome State Archives (ASR, *Congregazioni religiose soppresse, Olivetani, S. Maria Nova*, no. 5), nor in the documents published by O. Montenovesi ("Roma agli inizi del secolo XV e il Monastero di Santa Maria al Foro", extr. from *Rivista storica benedettina*, 1926), which in any case refer to a period earlier than that with which we are concerned. I was unfortunately unable to gain access to the archives of the Fraternity of the Arezzo Laicty, which are currently being put in order.

Index

11/12

Please renew or return items by the date shown on your receipt

www.hertfordshire.gov.uk/libraries

Renewals and enquiries: 0300 123 4049

Textphone for hearing or 01992 555506
speech impaired users:

L32b/12.19

Hertfordshire